1-14-10

If It Takes All Summer

If It Takes All Summer

Martin Luther King, the KKK, and States' Rights in St. Augustine, 1964

Dan R. Warren

THE UNIVERSITY OF ALABAMA PRESS
Tuscaloosa

Typeface: ACaslon

∞

The paper on which this book is printed meets the minimum requirements of
American National Standard for Information Sciences-Permanence of Paper for
Printed Library Materials, ANSI Z39.48-1984.

Library of Congress Cataloging-in-Publication Data

Warren, Dan R., 1925–
If it takes all summer : Martin Luther King, the KKK, and states' rights in
St. Augustine, 1964 / Dan R. Warren.
    p.   cm.
Includes bibliographical references and index.
ISBN-13: 978-0-8173-1599-3 (cloth : alk. paper)
ISBN-10: 0-8173-1599-3 (cloth : alk. paper) 1. Saint Augustine (Fla.)—Race
relations—History—20th century. 2. King, Martin Luther, Jr., 1929–1968.
3. African Americans—Civil rights—Florida—Saint Augustine—History—20th
century. 4. Civil rights movements—Florida—Saint Augustine—History—20th
century. 5. Ku Klux Klan (1915–)—Florida—Saint Augustine—History—
20th century. 6. Saint Augustine (Fla.)—Politics and government—20th century.
7. State rights—History—20th century. 8. Warren, Dan R., 1925– 9. Lawyers—
Florida—Daytona Beach—Biography. I. Title.
F319.S2W365 2008
323.1196′073—dc22

                                                        2007029482

To my children, Christine, Danny, Raymond, Joe, Ruthie, and Adam

Contents

Foreword

For the first time in the history of the civil rights movement, a political insider reveals an eyewitness account of the relationship between money, law, and a white power structure that virtually shut blacks out of the social and economic life of the nation's oldest city. A southerner by birth, Dan Warren was the state attorney for Florida's Seventh Judicial Circuit. He provides a graphic account of racist attitudes of those in power, which created a vacuum in the political leadership of the community that was quickly filled by the KKK. The void created a dangerous challenge to Martin Luther King's peaceful demonstrations.

The 1964 demonstrations in St. Augustine came at an important stage of the civil rights movement. Earlier that year the Senate had begun debating passage of the Civil Rights Act. Nineteen of the South's most powerful senators began a filibuster against passage of the act. If successful, the filibuster threatened the entire civil rights movement. Warren's innovative use of the grand jury to start a dialogue between the black community and moderates in the white community was an act of moral and political courage. In an effort to find a political solution to the racial crisis, he met privately with King, the governor of Florida, and others. Using contemporary newspaper accounts, interview transcripts, and his personal recollections, he gives the reader an absorbing account of the behind-the-scenes struggle to overcome the determined efforts of the political leaders of the community to defeat King's efforts.

Warren gives a close-up and personal account of how the Ku Klux

Klan, the nation's oldest terrorist organization, gained virtual control of St. Augustine through lack of political and religious leadership. The unbridled Klan violence came close to defeating the efforts of Martin Luther King in St. Augustine. Warren's account of the legal crackdown against the Ku Klux Klan is fascinating.

In a dramatic showdown between state and federal control, Dan Warren is confronted with his constitutional and moral duty to protect the rights of the demonstrators. His confrontation with the governor's efforts to control the demonstrations through a stale, states' rights fiction of nullification and the resulting constitutional showdown in federal court in Jacksonville are riveting and absorbing.

Recounting a critical moment in the history of the civil rights movement, the book is not only engaging but also an important addition to the historical record of the movement.

Morris Dees

Acknowledgments

This book began as an autobiography written primarily for my children. The project was started in 1999; however, when I reached the St. Augustine racial crisis of 1963–64, the more I wrote, the more I realized that this part of my life was a book, not a chapter. Encouraged by my loving wife, Stasia, whose patience and support gave me the freedom to devote full time to the venture, I began in 2001 to write of my experiences in St. Augustine. This story could not have been written without her encouragement and understanding. I am also indebted to the staff at the University of Alabama Press and especially the critical peer reviews as the project progressed. The staff's encouragement through four revisions gently led me to the conclusion that I should write about the subject I knew best—the St. Augustine racial crisis—and leave a comprehensive discussion of states' rights for another book.

I also owe much thanks to Tippen Davidson, the owner and publisher of the *Daytona Beach News-Journal* who, regrettably, passed away shortly before the book was published. He made available the newspaper's archives and gave permission to use some of the photographs that appear in this book. I am also deeply indebted to my childhood friend David L. Swain, former editor of the *Japan Christian Quarterly,* who spent days with me editing early versions of the book and made important contributions to its style and content. Kay Semion, associate editor of the *Daytona Beach News-Journal,* reviewed early drafts of the manuscript and gave freely of her time and advice. I am also indebted to Charles Tingley, director of the St. Augustine Historical Society, for access to their files and to the Public Library of Volusia Country, Florida; to Gwendolyn Duncan, president of the Fortieth Anniversary to Commemorate the Civil Rights Demonstrations in St. Augustine; David Nolan, historian; and Melvin Thomas, who generously agreed to allow the use of photos taken by civil rights demonstrators in St. Augustine. I am especially grateful to Dr. Robert Hayling, whose perseverance against all odds was an inspiration to me. My thanks also to Anne R. Gibbons, copy editor, whose skills crystallized the message and bridged the inconsistencies of the manuscript into a coherent story.

Finally, to the memory of two of my sons, Robert DeBruce Warren II and David Calloway Warren, whose short lives were always in my thoughts, urging me on to complete the project.

If It Takes All Summer

Introduction

In the summer of 1964, as the elected state attorney for Florida's Seventh Judicial Circuit, a huge circuit that included St. Augustine, I watched as the "nation's oldest city" became the final battleground in the long struggle for passage of a meaningful civil rights bill. Die-hard segregationists, who believed that the War between the States had been fought but not lost, opposed any concession to equality for black citizens. They were quickly joined in the fight by the Klan, the nation's oldest homegrown terrorist organization.

The Lost Cause myth—which proclaims that southerners fought the Civil War not to maintain the "peculiar institution" but to preserve the sanctity of states' rights and emphasizes battlefield glory instead of Confederate defeat—was very much alive in St. Augustine. In the previous summer, the flames of hatred and prejudice that lay smoldering in the ashes of a burned-out system of customs and beliefs suddenly burst forth and became a raging fire.

St. Augustine is the oldest continuously settled city in the United States. In 1564 Admiral Pedro Menendez de Aviles of Spain seized Ft. Caroline, located near the mouth of the St. Johns River, from the French. A year later he founded a city some thirty-five miles to the south, which he named St. Augustine.[1] On March 11, 1963, Vice President Lyndon Johnson was the speaker at a dinner held in St. Augustine to organize the new Quadricentennial Commission, established by Congress to plan the elaborate celebration in 1965 for the four hundredth anniversary of the city's founding. There was one flaw in plans for the dinner: it failed to include blacks.

The deliberate exclusion of a major segment of the city's citizens doomed the celebration from the start. The committee's carefully laid plans to encourage a flood of tourists, and their dollars, to attend the event would collapse in chaos. Martin Luther King Jr. and legions of his devoted followers would come as uninvited guests steeled with the determination to end segregation in the business community, the city, and the county. It would also bring the Ku Klux Klan to the nation's oldest city. The Klan would be more welcome than King.

On May 5, 1964, after a hard-fought campaign for reelection to the office of state attorney, I was drawn into the escalating crisis and faced my own moral and legal dilemma. In telling the story from my vantage point as the top law enforcement official in the circuit, I have tried to be as true to events as possible. In retelling the events that occurred in St. Augustine in 1963 and 1964, I have relied not only on my memory but also on eyewitness testimony of others who experienced these same events, and on a scrapbook of newspaper accounts of the day that my wife, Mary, kept. I had also prepared a thirty-nine-page outline of a book that I hoped to write one day and dictated two hours of my thoughts onto a cassette tape. I have cross-referenced the stories about the St. Augustine crisis published in the *Daytona Beach News-Journal* with those of the *St. Augustine Record*, as well as other newspaper accounts from around the state. I have also drawn liberally from the archives of the St. Augustine Historical Society.

The founders of this nation knew they were speaking to future generations when the Declaration of Independence was adopted. Slavery was an important economic force in the new nation for both the North and South, but the founding fathers knew the issue of slavery could destroy the noble experiment in self-government. Yet they could not muster the will of the nation to address the issue. For Thomas Jefferson, the problem of slavery was a blot on the nation's character as ominous as the dangers faced by the republic during the American Revolution. This thought, which he described as a "firebell in the night," filled him with foreboding. As Jefferson observed, "We have the wolf by the ears, and we can neither hold him, nor safely let him go. Justice is in one scale and self-preservation in the other."[2]

The troubling question of why so many southern leaders clung to segregation for so long after the Civil War and even after the passage of the Thirteenth, Fourteenth, and Fifteenth Amendments to the Constitution was still unanswered when the civil rights crisis first broke over St. Augustine in 1963. These amendments were passed to ensure full citizenship to the newly freed slaves, but despite their passage, little changed in the South. On the blood-soaked battleground of Gettysburg, President Lincoln confidently predicted that the nation would experience a "new birth of freedom."[3] But it would be another hundred years before the collective will of the people would finally be heard clearly enough in Congress to force passage of the Civil Rights Act of 1964.

In February 1965, shortly after the crisis had subsided, I wrote an account of my impressions in preparation for a speech I had been invited to give at Boston University. Oddly, the speech was widely publicized through the courtesy of the Citizens' Council, which paid for a full-page advertisement in the *St. Augustine Record* that contained most of the speech. The Council stated it was published to advise citizens of St. Johns County what their state attorney was saying about them in Boston. Meanwhile, I had already forwarded a copy of the speech to Mabel Chesley, an associate editor for the *Daytona Beach News-Journal.* I intended for the speech to be published on the same day I delivered it in Boston. As I spoke to the students and faculty of Boston University's College of Law and School of Theology, I wanted the citizens of St. Johns County to know exactly what I was saying.

In preparing my remarks I made a chronological list of the critical events and an outline for an account I hoped one day to write about the racial crisis. Later, I was interviewed by David Garrow, author of *Bearing the Cross: Martin Luther King, Jr., and the Southern Leadership Conference,* and by David R. Colburn, author of *Racial Change and Community Crisis: St. Augustine, Florida, 1877–1980.* It is from these various sources that I have framed the setting for my story, confident that this account accurately portrays the events as they occurred and provides a context for my emotions and thoughts at the time.

When quoting or paraphrasing from contemporary accounts, I use the racial terms of the day because they reflect the general attitude toward race that prevailed in St. Augustine at the time. In all other contexts, I use "black" and white" to denote race. In keeping with generally accepted practices of scholarly publishing, I have omitted courtesy titles except when they elucidate a person's profession (e.g., Judge Mathis, Sheriff Davis) or when a woman is referred to in the sources by her husband's name (e.g., Mrs. L. B. Mosley). Some of the people involved in the St. Augustine events were personal acquaintances of mine, and in those instances I have referred to them by first name (e.g., George [George Allen]).

More than forty years have passed since those tumultuous days and nights when the nation's attention was focused on the struggles in St. Augustine. The overt racism of many in the South, determined to maintain segregation at any cost, has disappeared only to mutate into newer, less obvious forms of discrimination. The new manifestations of discriminatory practices that swept the South in response to the Civil Rights Act of 1964 challenge a new generation of Americans to seek a solution to lingering racial antagonism.

In 1967, I resigned as state attorney, gave up my quest to run for Congress, and reentered private practice. During the ensuing years I devoted all my energies to defending those charged with crimes and providing for a growing family that eventually numbered seven children. St. Augustine always remained in my mind, and as the years passed, I became convinced that racism was not dead; it was very much alive in our legal and social institutions. To me, repressive and hypocritical laws designed to fight the nation's so-called war on drugs are directly related to new forms of racism, which are evident in the disparity in the sentences given black offenders. Racism is also apparent in racial profiling by law enforcement.

History was my major at Guilford College and has always been my first love. Nonetheless, I make no pretense of being a historian, only a witness. The views expressed in this book are the ones I held at the time, buttressed, I hope, by the wisdom that comes with age. Here is a personal account of the struggle for equality that occurred in St. Augustine and a southern lawyer's view of how that struggle gave meaning to the promises of equality made more than two centuries ago.

I   Protest and Reaction

In 1964 St. Augustine became a battleground in America's unfinished Civil War. That war had been fought to preserve the Union and bring a measure of equality to millions who had been held in slavery. At the end of that great struggle, it was the fervent hope of the nation that passage of the Thirteenth, Fourteenth, and Fifteenth Amendments would end the nightmare of slavery. It was not to be. Instead, slavery was replaced with a degrading form of second-class citizenship: segregation.

St. Augustine is the oldest continuously occupied city in the nation, and 1965 would mark the four hundredth year of its founding. In March 1963 city fathers planned an elaborate dinner to dedicate the first phase of restoring the old section of St. Augustine, called the Avero restoration area. The vice president of the United States, Lyndon Johnson, had been invited to deliver the welcoming address. But no blacks were among the local luminaries and prominent citizens invited to attend the momentous occasion. This exclusion of a large portion of the community set off a series of events that ultimately brought Martin Luther King Jr. and the Southern Christian Leadership Conference (SCLC) to St. Augustine.

Congress had passed a resolution in 1962 authorizing the establishment of a Quadricentennial Commission to celebrate the four hundredth anniversary of the founding of St. Augustine. The resolution called for the appointment of two members of the commission from the House, two from the Senate, and one from the Department of the Interior; the remaining members were to be appointed by the president. The House appointed Florida representatives D. R. Matthews and William C. Cramer; the Senate, Florida senators George Smathers and Spessard Holland. Conrad Wirth, director of the National Park Service, was the Interior appointee. In March 1963 President John F. Kennedy appointed the remaining members: Henry Ford II from Detroit; J. Peter Grace, from New York City; Joseph P. Hurley, from St. Augustine; Herbert E. Wolfe from St. Augustine; Edward Litchfield from Pittsburgh; and Charles Clark from Washington D.C.[1] However, Congress failed to provide funds for the commission's work.

In May 1963 Senators Holland and Smathers introduced a bill authorizing a federal appropriation of $350,000 dollars to help finance the city's four hundredth anniversary celebration.[2] Despite the use of state and federal funds, no one from the black community was invited to attend nor was any black appointed to the commission. Incensed over the promoters' insensitivity in ignoring one-quarter of the city's population, civil rights activists conducted a series of protests that ignited the final battle in the efforts to achieve passage of a meaningful Civil Rights Act.

At the time, the events taking place in St. Augustine had little significance for me. But for civil rights activists in St. Augustine, such as Fannie Fulwood and Elizabeth Hawthorne, president and secretary, respectively, of the local chapter of the National Association for the Advancement of Colored People (NAACP), the exclusion of blacks from this historical celebration was an "undemocratic" act unworthy of financial support from the federal government. During Vice President Lyndon Johnson's March 12 visit to St. Augustine, his chief of staff had agreed to intercede with local officials and to set up a meeting between members of the local chapter of the NAACP and the city commissioners of St. Augustine to air their complaints. That promise was not kept.

On May 7, 1963, they sent a heartfelt letter to President Kennedy. "Since St. Augustine is the nation's oldest city we feel democracy should work here," they wrote. Calling the president's attention to the fact that "St. Augustine still maintains segregated public facilities, public schools" and that "Negroes are employed as laborers or in manual jobs by the city and county, let us prove to the Communists and the entire world that America's oldest city can truly be a showcase of democracy." They also reminded the president of promises made by George Reedy, the vice president's chief of staff, to intercede with local officials, complaining that "the city commission failed to keep its promise for a meeting with a Delegation of Negro Citizens the day after Mr. Johnson's visit." In closing they pleaded, "our organization will await your advice and assistance in correcting these conditions."[3]

Their plea was in vain. The president did not respond. The city, however, was "shocked" that two local leaders of the NAACP would ask that federal funds be withheld from a national celebration to honor the nation's oldest city. The mayor, James E. Lindley, released their letter to the press as he and other members of the city commission left for Washington to attend the first working session of the all-white Quadricentennial Commission. He did not respond to the NAACP's request that two black members be added to the commission.

The NAACP had an active branch in St. Augustine. Two of its members, Robert B. Hayling, a local dentist, and Goldie Eubanks, a minister, were outspoken critics of the racist policies of the city. Hayling, an adviser to the Youth Council of the NAACP, had recruited members from the local black college and from the community to demonstrate against the failure of the county and city to fully desegregate its public facilities.[4] Hayling and Eubanks strongly resented the city's segregation policies and deeply felt the snub to the black community of not being included in plans for the quadricentennial celebrations. Both were fearless, in Hayling's case, perhaps even to the point of recklessness.

They represented a more militant approach to the civil rights movement than the moderate stance usually taken by the NAACP, and not even a direct appeal from NAACP president Roy Wilkins not to "disrupt the proceedings" could deter Hayling from taking direct action.[5] Along with other local NAACP members, he and Eubanks responded to the snub by threatening to organize a picket during the dinner. To emphasize their determination, they urged the president of the local chapter of the NAACP, Fannie Fulwood, to send a telegram to Vice President Johnson to alert him to the fact that the dinner was a segregated affair and members of the black community were not welcome. This had the desired effect, especially when the vice president learned that city officials were seeking federal funds for the celebration.

When the vice president announced he would not attend the dinner if blacks were not included, the committee reluctantly agreed to invite twelve, although those invited were required to sit at segregated tables.[6] This public snub and the failure of city commissioners to meet with members of the NAACP increased the growing racial tensions in the city. City officials finally agreed to hear their grievances and set a meeting time in May. When members of the NAACP arrived, they found only the city manager on hand to meet them, with a tape recorder so they could air their complaints to the city commissioners. They did so, pouring out their recorded complaints as if the commissioners were personally present. Commissioners finally met with the committee on Sunday, June 16, 1963, but some members were abrasive and accused the demonstrators of being led by "Communists" or the "Kennedys" who, they said, were behind the civil rights drive.[7]

This further fueled Hayling's outrage and he heatedly promised to fight the practice of segregation in St. Augustine until "my last dime is gone."[8] It was not an idle threat. Ultimately segregation would be eliminated from the city's businesses, but the price Hayling paid was high. He gave up his practice in St. Augustine and in 1965 moved to Cocoa Beach. Hayling was one of a new breed of young black civil rights activists who were tired of waiting for long-overdue equality. Hayling had the courage and determination to commit all his financial resources to end segregation in the city, even at the expense of losing his practice.

In 1960, recently discharged from the air force as a lieutenant, Hayling had purchased the active and profitable practice of Rudolph Gordon, the only black dentist in St. Augustine. It was said that Gordon had as many white patients as blacks, and he was a well-respected member of the community. Hayling initially retained most of Gordon's white patients. But that changed when he took the lead in efforts to end segregation in the city. After the death of Medgar Evers, field secretary for the NAACP in Mississippi, Hayling issued a statement saying that "passive resistance is no good in the face of violence. I and others of the NAACP have armed ourselves and we will shoot first and ask questions later."[9] His practice began to suffer as the white power structure turned its fury on him and others in the community who advocated any means necessary to end segregation in the city.

The threat to use force also fueled a white backlash, igniting the Klan, whose members soon surfaced and engulfed the city in nightly acts of violence. The John Birch Society was also active in the city, primarily through the influence of Hardgrave Norris, a physician and prominent member of the community. He was a close ally of Joseph Shelley, another physician, who in 1963 had been elected to the city commission and was soon to become mayor.

The militant stance taken by Hayling and his allies made them an immediate target of the radical elements in the white community. Some people claimed that the Communists were behind the movement and that Hayling had been sent into the community to cause trouble. Many argued that his presence had created the problem, arguing that he was responsible for upsetting the allegedly harmonious relations that existed before he arrived. They pointed to the community's acceptance of Gordon as proof that Hayling was the problem. Rumors that the Communists were involved in the movement were soon accepted by many in the community as the truth, and sufficient reason for those in power to ignore demands for change.[10]

Though most whites in the community were hostile toward Hayling, his support from a number of young blacks in the community began to grow. As the united voice of the white community hardened against him, and the hostility intensified, so did the determination of his enthusiastic followers to bring an immediate end to segregation. Hayling's grit and determination attracted many students from the local high school and from Florida Memorial College.

Florida Memorial was a small Baptist college located on the outskirts of the city. Students from the college began to gravitate to Hayling and Eubanks, providing the nucleus of civil rights activists in St. Augustine. The college, however, was drowning in a sea of red ink. Its president, Royal W. Puryear, was desperately trying to keep the small school from going under and needed the financial support of the local white power structure to keep it afloat. In an effort to maintain his relationship with city leaders, he initially forbade students from participating in the growing demonstrations. But most students ignored the prohibition, and despite Puryear's efforts to stay clear of the growing racial unrest, local financial support for the college, meager as it was, virtually disappeared. The board of trustees, in a desperate attempt to save the school, voted to move the college to Miami. Bitter over this sequence of events, Puryear decided to join the protest movement. As it grew, he became more vocal, and expressed pride in his students for their courage and bravery. He, too, would eventually have to leave the city.

At this time, I was the state attorney for Florida's Seventh Judicial Circuit. Originally appointed to the post by Governor Farris Bryant in the summer of 1962, I had successfully run for election in September 1962 to serve out the unexpired term of the former state attorney, W. W. (Billy) Judge, who had resigned. I was up for reelection in 1964 and spent much of my time in St. Augustine either campaigning or trying felony cases. The circuit was vast, encompassing Volusia, Flagler, Putnam, and St. Johns counties. Daytona Beach, where I lived, was the largest city in Volusia County; St. Augustine was the largest in St. Johns County.

The circuit stretches for 150 miles along Florida's northeast coast, from just north of Cape Kennedy to just south of Jacksonville. The St. Johns River meanders along the western borders of the circuit, except for Putnam County located west of the river. At that time, Florida's population was spread along the coast, with a vast wilderness of pine and low-lying hammock land blanketing the interior. Small cities, such as Deland in Volusia, Bunnell in Flagler, Palatka in Putnam, and Hastings in St. Johns, were small dots of population in this vast track of wilderness. I traveled the circuit from my home in Daytona Beach, trying criminal cases, attending to grand juries, and investigating felony crimes in all four counties.

Demonstrations in St. Augustine began in earnest during late July 1963. On July 26, a group of young people were arrested for delivering copies of an editorial published in the *Daytona Beach News-Journal* to the homes of influential St. Augustine citizens. The editorial was critical of city officials in St. Augustine for the highhanded manner in which they had handled the growing unrest in the city, especially the acts of St. Johns County judge Charles Mathis Jr.[11] Copies of the editorial hand-delivered during the evening meal did not aid in the digestion of indignant residents.

To combat growing demonstrations, local law enforcement officials began making arrests, primarily for criminal trespass. This broad criminal statute gave owners of business establishments the right to order "undesirables" from their premises. Failure to leave constituted the crime of "trespass after warning."[12] Four young demonstrators, arrested for distributing the editorial critical of Judge Mathis, were convicted in city court for breach of the peace by "unlawfully" distributing handbills. Each was to pay a fine of one hundred dollars or serve thirty days in jail.

Mathis disqualified himself from hearing these charges because his name was mentioned in the editorial, but he did order two juveniles taken into custody on other charges and held for juvenile detention hearings. He also ordered that they be taken from their parents until they promised to obey "all regulations in the future, including those against picketing." On August 1, 1963, nine more demonstrators were convicted in Judge Marvin Greer's justice of the peace court for sit-ins at two local drugstores. They also had to pay one hundred dollars or serve thirty days in jail.[13] This triple legal assault against demonstrations in the city was an unusual move by judicial officials and the convictions quickly filled the limited capacity of the small county jail.

The pattern in St. Augustine of ignoring the mounting racial crisis was in stark contrast with other cities in Florida, where biracial talks were taking place and the barriers of segregation were falling. On September 14, 1962, nine months before the demonstrations started in St. Augustine, the Florida Advisory Committee to the U.S. Commission on Civil Rights held its first public meeting in Daytona Beach. The committee's function was to collect the opinions of leading citizens on voting rights, employment, and the administration of justice. The first meeting of the committee was set to discuss job opportunities for blacks. Community leaders, including all elected county and city commissioners, were invited to attend. Though many failed to appear at the meeting, claiming conflicts in their schedules or previous commitments, Herbert Davidson, editor of the Daytona Beach paper, encouraged community leaders to sit down and discuss the many problems facing the community.

In an editorial supporting the goals of the committee, the *Daytona Beach News-Journal* deplored the "limited job opportunities for blacks" and asserted that the answer to the problem was better educational opportunities. "It is time that moderates of both races get together to tell the political power structure to begin honest reform, and time for the business communities to ignore the 'Bull' Connors who use political power to maintain the status quo. It can't be maintained any more than our own nation could have remained as colonies of a foreign power."[14]

Herbert Davidson attempted for many years, through his newspaper, to create an atmosphere of tolerance and goodwill between the races. Through editorials and in-depth news stories, he continually called attention to the inequitable policies in education and job opportunities that existed in the community, deploring the waste of human resources as a result of these policies. In the early 1950s, community leaders in Daytona Beach such as J. Saxton Lloyd, owner of Lloyd Buick Cadillac, who was also a member of the board of trustees of Bethune-Cookman College; Mary McLeod Bethune, president emeritus of Bethune-Cookman College; Richard V. Moore, president of Bethune-Cookman College; and many others responded to his plea. They were the early pioneers for racial equality in Daytona Beach, and along with others they paved the way for a peaceful and orderly end to segregation.

Rogers P. Fair, the black chaplain of Bethune-Cookman College, together with members of the Greater Daytona Beach Ministerial Association, also provided leadership. Shortly after the Supreme Court's decision in *Brown v. Board of Education*, Fair was appointed president of the integrated Halifax Area Ministerial Association, which was comprised of individuals from five separate municipalities: Daytona Beach, Holly Hill, Ormond Beach, South Daytona, and Port Orange. In 1957 he preached at the first integrated religious service during the annual Easter sunrise service held each year at the Band Shell on the beach. Early in the 1960s Leon Hurwitz, rabbi of Temple Israel, established the first Ecumenical Council of Ministers in the Greater Halifax Area to deal with the problems of integration. Most churches in the community followed his lead.[15]

On June 1, 1963, nearly a hundred representatives of various religious and fraternal organizations met at the Daytona Beach YWCA and issued an "urgent appeal to the power structure of the community." They called on those in power to "recognize that the community is not satisfied with segregation in facilities licensed to service the public and in employment" and "to make the necessary changes" that were sure to take place, one way or the other. Their joint resolution called attention to the fact "that segregation practices jeopardize the economic and human relations climate of the community." The committee also urged the "community [to] start work immediately to solve these problems in order to avoid the alternative of disruption occasioned by demonstrations by local groups and/or by the influx of outside pressure groups."[16] Twenty leading merchants in the city banded together and desegregated their eating establishments without any difficulty.

A council of concerned citizens also established the Halifax Area Council on Human Relations. Chaired by Mrs. L. B. Mosley, wife of Lilburn Mosley, distinguished minister of the Tourist Church (later known as the Seabreeze United Church of Christ), the group began a campaign to enlist other churches in an effort to change people's attitudes toward blacks. She encouraged other organizations to attend and an impressive cross section of community leaders responded, including representatives of Bethune-Cookman College, B'nai Brith, the YMCA, the Halifax Area Ministerial Association, the Volusia County Mental Health Association, and United Church Women, as well as Leon Hurwitz, and Marshall Taxay, rabbis of Temple Israel and Temple Beth El, respectively.[17] This united effort by a large number of religious institutions opened lines of communication between public officials and business groups. The effort to foster better race relations sent a message to public officials that they were determined to end segregation. Soon public officials in other areas in the county began to take notice and acted to systematically achieve desegregation.

At a meeting of the National Baptist Deacons Convention in Daytona Beach on June 24, 1963, its presiding officer, Hugh Morris of Montclair, N.J., addressed the growing unrest in the black community throughout the country. He told the more than four hundred delegates at Mt. Bethel Baptist Church that "there is the emergence of a new Negro, one with courage and determination, whose patience has become exhausted, and he has decided that 100 years is long enough to wait for freedom, and he will wait no longer."[18]

In neighboring counties the process of eliminating racial barriers was preceding in an orderly manner as community leaders established biracial committees and took other steps to eliminate the segregationist practices that prevailed throughout the state. Those in power listened to and acted on complaints from the black community. This was an essential first step to avoid the unrest taking place in St. Augustine. But community leaders in St. Augustine neither listened nor acted.

On July 9, 1963, Orlando's mayor, Bob Carr, announced that fifty-six area motels, hotels, and restaurants had been desegregated. He gave credit for this accomplishment to the Advisory Committee on Interracial Relations. Formed in June, the committee represented a cross section of the city's population, including bankers, chamber of commerce members, an editor of the *Orlando Sentinel*, politicians, ministers, a physician, civic workers, and retirees from both races.[19]

On July 10, William Hathaway, mayor of New Smyrna Beach, met with William Truly Jr., chairman of the Youth Organization for Racial Equality, a local ad hoc committee of black activists, and representatives of the Community Improvement Association to discuss desegregation of city facilities. In this meeting the mayor suggested a biracial committee was needed to deal with problems associated with desegregation. The mayor sent letters to all civic clubs asking for nominations to the committee. All across central Florida communities were beginning the delicate process of dismantling segregated public facilities.[20]

On July 11, the Titusville City Council approved two resolutions calling for the immediate desegregation of all recreational facilities and of removal of signs on municipal property restricting use by race. On July 12, city officials in St. Petersburg adopted a resolution desegregating all city-owned and -operated public facilities, including the public beaches at St. Petersburg. In Jacksonville, Mayor Hayden Burns agreed to a biracial committee after a group of blacks asked for the appointment of a committee to study the problems of segregation, and in neighboring Gainesville a biracial committee recommended local motels be integrated immediately.[21]

In Daytona Beach, Stanley Nass, a young city commissioner, met with black leaders in an attempt to address the problems that would be encountered with the integration of city facilities, and on July 12, 1963, all city-owned and -operated public facilities were desegregated. On July 30, four Daytona Beach city commissioners publicly took a stand against segregation. Mayor Owen Eubanks announced that negotiations had been going on for several weeks with members of the Volusia County Restaurant Association to work out a desegregation plan. The beaches had been desegregated for a number of years, but blacks continued to complain of being harassed by whites, especially during the summer months when many visitors from other southern states visited Daytona Beach. The commissioners assured blacks who complained that the laws would be strictly enforced and that harassment would not be tolerated. J. H. Adams Jr., chairman of the Representative Committee of Negro Organizations, on August 6, 1963, commended the city commissioners for their efforts to resolve the area's continuing integration problems.[22]

During this period, while surrounding communities were peacefully and effectively addressing the myriad difficulties of desegregation, the situation in St. Augustine continued to deteriorate. On August 16, 1963, the Florida Advisory Committee to the U.S. Commission on Civil Rights held an all-day meeting in St. Augustine to study the growing racial unrest. Community leaders boycotted the meeting, but Frank Howatt, a local white attorney who had represented three blacks in recent court cases, testified that "the situation would improve if biracial talks are held." Royal Puryear, president of Florida Memorial College, testified that he had been called "Uncle Tom by my own people, but now I want to say that nothing is more pleasing to me than to see men and women, boys and girls born in this town expressing a desire for freedom." He added that "Mississippi, where I came from, was a pretty bad place but you could get people to sit down and talk." Sadly, he noted, he was "embarrassed to live in [St. Augustine]." He told of his school's opportunity to receive a challenge grant of twenty thousand dollars if he could obtain matching funds from the community. From the 556 letters he wrote to local residents, he had received only three gifts. The trustees of the college, he said, had voted to move the college out of St. Augustine.[23]

The background section of the 1963 *Report of the Florida Advisory Committee to the U.S. Commission on Civil Rights* took the state to task for being "too timid" in its support of civil rights. The committee, headed by Tallahassee banker George Lewis II, charged that the "white establishment" in the state excluded blacks from power and as a result "qualified Negro leaders must live outside the white establishment, continually denied his right to contribute to community advancement. His advice is never sought in community planning, except in token instances when he may be granted a seat on an urban renewal board or membership in a relatively powerless human relations committee or organization. Even then, he suffers from the taboos—for those integrated groups are not free to meet at any hotel, motel or civic center."[24]

The report condemned the situation in St. Augustine, finding that "civil rights conditions in St. Augustine are considerably worse than in most if not all other cities in the state." The report also found that "Negroes are excluded entirely from the white power structure" and suggested that a biracial committee was needed to defuse the situation. It also recommended that federal contracts for Fairchild Stratos Corporation, the largest employer in St. Augustine, be suspended "until it ends discrimination practices and the intimidation of Negro workers." It further recommended that the federal government "withhold funds from the state of Florida until the minor Negro children taken from their families for civil rights activities were released from custody of the state."[25]

At the end of the hearings, the committee called St. Augustine "a segregated super-bomb aimed at the heart of Florida's economy and political integrity" and noted that "the fuse is short." Mabel Norris Chesley, an editorial writer for the *Daytona Beach News-Journal*, was a member of the committee, as was Tobias Simon, a civil rights lawyer from Miami. Even these dire warnings failed to move city officials in St. Augustine.[26]

On May 29, 1963, an election was held in St. Augustine to choose a new city commission. Joseph Shelley was the top vote-getter in a field of six candidates. On June 3, at its organizational meeting, the commissioners selected Shelley as the new mayor of St. Augustine. He and his followers would bring a new attitude of defiance to the growing dissatisfaction of the black population. Responding to the criticism, Mayor Shelley replied, "I don't feel that it is the business of the city commission to tell private businesses how to run their business." He added, "We have no biracial committee here because it could do nothing we have not already done."[27]

Lewis L. Mitchell, an Episcopal priest in Daytona Beach and the executive director of the Florida Council on Human Relations, was in St. Augustine during August. He compared the efforts made by city officials with those he had observed in Birmingham, Alabama. Mitchell said he had seen some of the worst racial disturbances there, and, after observing conditions in St. Augustine, predicted that unless city officials found some way to come together with the demonstrators more hostility and bitterness would surely be the result. No city official he talked to in St. Augustine was willing to engage in biracial talks.

Shelley, an implacable southern conservative, denied the charges and rejected the findings, adding that "the population of St. Augustine was 76.7% white and 23.3% Negro and that 20% of city government jobs were held by Negroes. There is no discrimination there." The mayor failed to point out that blacks occupied only the low-paying, menial jobs in the city. None were in a position of authority.[28]

Shelley's remarks set the tone for other public figures, even though such adamancy would have a negative effect on business. The mayor's attitude toward race relations became the city's official response, and despite the growing body of evidence that racial tensions were mounting—not from outside sources but from within the community itself—local leaders would not soften their stance. Shelley would play an important role in how city officials responded to the demands of the local chapter of the NAACP and later to those of Martin Luther King Jr. and the Southern Christian Leadership Conference. This intractable attitude would ultimately have disastrous results.

Robert Welch founded the John Birch Society in 1958. His controversial right-wing views, published as a "private letter" in the *Politician,* included the statement that "my firm belief that Dwight Eisenhower is a dedicated, conscious agent of the Communist conspiracy is based on an accumulation of detailed evidence so extensive and so palpable that it seems to me to put this conviction beyond any reasonable doubt."[29]

Hardgrove Norris, a prominent St. Augustine physician who established a chapter of the John Birch Society in St. Augustine in 1963, would play an important role in the coming conflict as a friend and supporter of the mayor. The John Birch Society, David R. Colburn wrote in *Racial Change and Community Crisis,* "acted as a brake against racial moderation." Senator Verle Pope, highly respected in St. Augustine, and by many others in the state, said, "There was a very active group, who might be said to be of a John Birch variety, who were prominent and very strong.

They were the leaders in the Kiwanis Club. They were on the vestries in the churches. Wherever you turned it was the same small group of people who were in power in the various organizations."[30]

My former assistant in St. Augustine, Hamilton Upchurch, said that Birch sympathizers made a conciliatory position on the race question untenable. "Every job had a name and a face," he said. "If you proposed anything even . . . at a cocktail party that was in any way conciliatory . . . you were ostracized by the extreme right wing."[31] The consequences of dissent were obvious to anyone who might have been tempted to buck the official party line taken by the mayor that there was no discrimination in St. Augustine.

An insightful view into Hardgrove Norris's thinking can be found in an article titled "St. Augustine: Rape of the Ancient City" written after the conflict subsided. The article, which was reprinted in *American Opinion*, a magazine edited by the founder of the John Birch Society, was widely distributed in St. Augustine in 1964. Norris wrote, "At no time [during the crisis] did the peace of St. Augustine become threatened." Only after the federal court in Jacksonville (under Judge Simpson) "turned the demonstrations loose by interdicting the right of the city to impose and enforce the ban on night time demonstrations" and when "the Governor of the State of Florida intervened directly in the internal administration of law enforcement in our community," did disruptions occur. This "unbelievable ban," he asserted, was responsible for the ensuing violence.[32]

Norris's view that the city had the right of "interdiction" not only against the actions of the federal government but also those of the state of Florida tells a great deal about the repressive policies adopted by the power structure of St. Augustine to deal with the growing racial crises. The idea of "interdiction" in the internal affairs of the state by the federal government had its genesis in the Carolina doctrine, a theory first devised by John C. Calhoun in 1828. Never officially adopted, it began the long and deadly process of threats by southern states to secede from the Union under the unintended ancillary theory of nullification. Now, according to Norris, the doctrine of "interdiction" had found fertile ground in the charter of the city of St. Augustine.[33]

Strangely, this theory would also find a champion in the governor who,

Norris charged, had interdicted the state of Florida into "the internal administration of law enforcement in our community." Norris's views fit snugly with those of the mayor's, and in a strange way, with those of Governor Bryant. In the final analysis, in dealing with the upcoming crisis, the governor and city officials would use the theory of "interdiction" and "nullification" in the attempt to defeat civil rights in St. Augustine under the doctrine of states' rights. They would refight the Civil War, one more time.

On May 20, 1963, the U.S. Supreme Court rendered a quartet of important decisions that would have a decisive impact on future demonstrations in St. Augustine. The Court overruled convictions for sit-ins that occurred in 1960–61 in four southern states. However, the Court left unanswered the question of whether private businesses had a right to exclude individuals based on race. Justice Harlan was the only dissenting Justice. His dissent presaged an ominous warning that this issue would fuel the coming turmoil soon to engulf St. Augustine. He wrote in *Peterson v. Greenville* that "an individual's right to restrict the use of his property, however unregenerate a particular exercise of that right may be thought, lies beyond the reach of the Fourteenth Amendment. . . . Freedom of the individual to choose his associates or his neighbors, to use and dispose of his property as he sees fit, to be irrational, arbitrary, capricious, even unjust in his personal relations are things all entitled to a large measure of protection from government interference."[34] This dissenting opinion fit the ideology of Mayor Shelley and other city leaders as they confronted the growing demonstrations.

The mayor was from neighboring Palatka, in Putnam County. Forty-eight years old when he was elected, he was from a prominent Roman Catholic family, with important connections to the political establishment in St. Augustine. His brother, Walter, was a well-known lawyer in Daytona Beach. Shelley had graduated from the University of Florida and Temple University Medical School. A senior medical student at Temple when the Japanese bombed Pearl Harbor, he was a second lieutenant in the army infantry reserves. Upon being called up, he was transferred to the Medical Advisory Corps, where he served eleven months in combat in Europe. After the war, he returned to Palatka where he worked with a local doctor, Allen Guranious. There, he met Vernon Lockwood, a surgeon from St. Augustine, and was invited to come to St. Augustine and set up a practice. He trained with two other surgeons, Hardgrove Norris and Raymond Cafarc, and his acceptance in this elite group of physicians assured his success in the tight group that controlled city politics.[35] His entry into politics as a candidate for the city commission was a natural progression in the tightly controlled political life of the city.

Norris's views, which were closely allied with the John Birch Society, resonated with those of Shelley and others who controlled the city. This offers a revealing insight into the thinking of those who controlled St. Augustine. The Society was careful not to be tagged with a racist agenda. Their battle cry was that the federal government was trying to disregard states' rights.[36] These views sat well with St. Augustine's power structure, and Norris would collaborate with the mayor, St. Johns County sheriff L. O. Davis, and others in an attempt to defeat the civil rights movement in St. Augustine. Official recalcitrance combined with the growing resentment of the younger activists resulted in more demonstrations and more arrests.

The mayor's attitude toward the black community, especially his view that there was no need for a biracial committee, coincided with those of the governor, Farris Bryant, who refused to even meet with members of the Florida Advisory Committee. The governor's argument that the commission "is another intrusion in the state's affairs by the federal government" was a rather stale states' rights argument used by southern politicians to maintain their control over the internal affairs of the state, including the practice of racial segregation. These opinions found strong support among those who controlled St. Augustine.[37]

In an editorial, the *News-Journal* sounded a warning: "It is time that the civil rights issue is removed from community streets and resolved in the halls of Congress. The Constitution, ever since the passage of the civil rights amendments, requests this in a thrice repeated phrase": 'Congress shall have the power, by appropriate legislation, to enforce the provisions of [these] articles.'" The editorial continued, "At long last, a President has presented a full program of implementation of the rights of all American citizens to equality."[38]

The feeling in the black community of isolation, neglect, humiliation and fear began to take its toll. City officials' refusal to recognize the contributions made by blacks throughout St. Augustine's history or include blacks in the celebration of that history was at the heart of the matter. As the summer of 1963 wore on, the heat and humidity became yet another obstacle for the demonstrators, especially as most demonstrations initially took place during the day. To escape the heat, activists began scheduling nighttime demonstrations. But the night provided protection for the Klan's hit-and-run tactics. Soon Klan members from surrounding counties would engulf the city, carrying out acts of terrorism against the demonstrators and anyone who appeared to agree with their goal of racial equality.

During the long hot days of August and September, temperatures often reached a hundred degrees or more and humidity rose to 80 or 90 percent. Afternoon showers, common during these months, offered little relief. As the temperature rose, so did the tempers of those who controlled the city. The demonstrations further inflamed the testy tempers of those in the community determined to maintain segregation.

At noon on Labor Day, 1963, a group of some 150 people gathered in St. Augustine's city park, where slaves had been sold before the Civil War, to listen to pro–civil rights speeches. The park is in the heart of the old city, across the street from the Roman Catholic cathedral that was also home of Joseph Hurley, bishop of St. Augustine and a member of the Quadricentennial Commission. People often gathered in the park to rest under the shade of huge live oak trees that afforded some relief from the summer heat, especially when cool breezes blew in from the river a scant three hundred feet to the east. Most gathered to talk or play checkers or just relax. On this occasion a peaceful, quiet, and orderly group of blacks and whites had assembled. Because it was Labor Day, the gathering was unusually festive.

Without warning the platform was suddenly cordoned off; police officers and deputy sheriffs began making arrests. A deputy drove up in a bus that had been parked close by and with other officers arrested twenty-seven individuals—but only those who had taken part in previous demonstrations or were NAACP leaders. They were charged under a city ordinance prohibiting public meetings without a city permit.

Hayling and Earl Johnson, an attorney from Jacksonville, challenged the arrests, arguing that the gathering was not a public meeting but a spontaneous association of citizens, peaceful and lawful. They also argued that the ordinance was an unconstitutional violation of the right of free speech and assembly. These arguments fell on deaf ears as city court judge Richard Weinberg found those charged guilty. He did comment, during the course of the bench trial, that the argument advanced by Earl Johnson was "well taken." After the arrest, permits were sought, but city officials declined to issue one.[39]

Hayling was not going to be intimidated by the Klan or the city. On the night of September 18, 1963, he and three other men decided to take a ride. The Klan was holding a meeting on a vacant lot about two miles south of the city. The gathering had been well advertised and handbills had been distributed urging whites to attend.

Whether Hayling deliberately set out to find the meeting or simply happened upon it is not clear. But in any case, he and three other men confronted the Klansmen. The four men were severely beaten. Officials from the NAACP sent telegrams to the Justice Department and to Governor Bryant calling for an investigation, but to no avail. Reflecting on the matter later, Hayling remarked, "We were just curious to see what was going on, but I guess we shouldn't have been."[40] That night Hayling called me to report the incident and ask that the state attorney's office intervene.

At that time, Florida state attorneys had jurisdiction only over felony cases. Misdemeanor cases were handled by the county prosecutor. My office did not have funds for investigating crimes. Without either jurisdiction or money, I had to rely on the St. Johns County sheriff, L. O. Davis, to investigate the incident. Of the four sheriffs in the circuit, the St. Johns County sheriff had the reputation of being the one most lax in enforcing the law. Davis was an affable, likable individual whose easygoing approach to law enforcement was tolerated by most voters in the county. In fact, his approach was the source of much of his popularity. His live-and-let-live philosophy sat well with many.

I was not eager to become involved in the developing crisis. I had my hands full simply trying felony cases all over the large and busy circuit. Crime was on the upswing throughout the region, and the Seventh Circuit with a heavy influx of tourists was no exception. I was relieved the county prosecutor would be handling the more than two hundred cases then pending in the misdemeanor courts of St. John's County.

I was concerned however about the growing racial problems and began legal research on First Amendment and due process rights. The main issue was the constitutional right of peaceful assembly, the right to petition the government for redress of grievances, and due process under the First and Fourteenth Amendments. This research would later become valuable when the violence escalated and I became personally involved in the crisis.

After talking with Hayling, I did call Sheriff Davis and requested information about the incident. He reported that a number of individuals had been arrested and deputies on the scene intervened in the fight before serious injuries occurred. The sheriff told me he had no idea why Hayling and the others had decided to go to the rally, but all the individuals involved in the fight had been arrested on misdemeanor charges. Their cases were pending in the local justice of the peace court. I merely asked the sheriff to keep me informed.

On September 27, 1963, Hayling, Clyde Jenkins, James Houser, James Jackson, and Patricia Neeley filed a petition in the U.S. District Court in Jacksonville, Florida, seeking an order preventing officials of St. Augustine from interfering with their peaceful demonstrations for racial equality. They also "asked for restraining orders prohibiting Mayor Joseph Shelley, City Commissioners, the City Manager, Police Chief Virgil Stuart, and Sheriff L. O. Davis from interfering with their public meetings, freedom of speech, or the distribution of leaflets and other peaceful protests against segregation in St. Augustine."[41]

On October 16, 1963, Hayling was convicted of assault on two men at the Klan rally; he had to pay one hundred dollars or serve sixty days in jail. He immediately appealed.[42] On November 29, James Houser, a codefendant who was with Hayling at the time of the incident, was cleared when the Klansmen he was accused of assaulting failed to appear and Judge Grier dismissed the charges. At Hayling's trial, Clarence Wilson and Lawrence Bessent, both Klansmen who allegedly witnessed the altercation, testified that when the four men drove down a side road near the speaker's platform, they tried to persuade Hayling and the others to leave; instead they were attacked by the men. Wilson and Bessent had been charged for engaging in the free-for-all but were later acquitted. After his conviction, Hayling again called, complaining bitterly of the injustice in St. Augustine's judicial system. At that time, there was little I could do but listen to his complaints.

On October 24, 1963, an event occurred that did involve my office. And, ready or not, we would be fully engaged for the remainder of the year and into the next. On that Friday night, William Kinard, a white twenty-five-year-old fisherman from St. Augustine was shot and killed in the Lincolnville section of St. Augustine. As they passed the home of Goldie Eubanks, a number of shots were fired, allegedly from Eubanks's house. One shot hit Kinard in the head, killing him instantly. The driver of the car was a son of Holstead Manucy, the local Klan leader and president of the Ancient City Gun Club. With him were three friends, Dixon Stanford, James Edward Scaff, and Kinard. Stanford and Scaff were in the backseat; Kinard, with Manucy driving, was in the front. A loaded shotgun, held by Kinard between his legs with the barrel pointed toward the floorboard, discharged, blasting a hole in the vehicle. Apparently, when he was hit, he had his finger on the trigger and pulled it by reflex, causing the gun to discharge. Over the past few weeks there had been other incidents in this mostly black section of St. Augustine, usually instances of young marauding whites allegedly harassing blacks, especially during the night.

Sheriff Davis called to inform me of the shooting and ask that I come to St. Augustine immediately to discuss the case. The fight between Hayling and the Klan plus the fatal shooting of Kinard allowed me to call for the impanelment of a grand jury to investigate the incidents and possibly use the grand jury to calm the growing violence in St. Johns County. I had been contemplating such a move for some time. A grand jury has the jurisdiction not only to investigate crime, any crime, but also to investigate and make comments on any incident that affects public health, safety, and welfare. The grand jury would soon become the only avenue open to address the growing racial problems in St. Johns county because lines of communication between the demonstrators and city officials were closed.

On Sunday evening, October 26, the night Kinard's wake was held at

Gus Craig's Funeral Home, I drove to St. Augustine with my son Dan, then nine. I conferred with the sheriff and talked with some of the witnesses who were at the wake. I questioned the others who had been in the car at the time of the shooting about why they were riding in the area at night with a loaded shotgun. Each replied it was dove season and they usually carried loaded guns in their cars, but it did not escape my attention that you don't hunt doves at night from a car in a residential area. The shotgun was primed and loaded, with Kinard's finger on the trigger, ready to be discharged at any moment. There was no doubt in my mind that these four had been looking for trouble. Unfortunately, when they found it, the result was Kinard's death.

There were a large number of Klansmen at the wake, and I could detect the undercurrent of unrest that permeated the gathering. I knew trouble was in the offing and it would not be long in coming. The Klan was active in other areas of the circuit, especially in Volusia County. Jason Kersey, a grand dragon of the Klan and a man I knew, lived in the farming community of Samsula in Volusia County, where he and other Klan members held weekly meetings in a barn on his property. A huge cross on top of the barn was lit each Thursday evening to announce that the Klan was meeting. I knew other members of the Klan as well and was aware that this terrorist organization could easily be roused to violence against those they hated and despised. They were even capable of murder.

On the night of October 28, a few hours after Kinard's funeral, a series of violent acts occurred. A home occupied by a black just outside St. Augustine was riddled with gunshot. Buckshot and .22-caliber bullets were fired into two black nightclubs, a food market, and two residences. A hand grenade, fortunately a dud, was thrown near one of the nightspots. The funeral had brought out the Klan in force, with more than two hundred people in attendance according to Sheriff Davis. Many were ardent Klansmen. The sheriff attended the funeral with Klan leader Connie Lynch, a racist fundamentalist preacher from California. As usual, Lynch made the most of the tragic event with one of his trademark fiery tirades designed to stir the emotions of people who needed little encouragement to seek revenge.

Lynch had made his appearance in St. Augustine in the fall of 1963 at one of the Klan's night meetings just outside the city. He was there, he said, to support the segregationists, and he soon joined forces with Holstead Manucy and his Ancient City Gun Club with its many Klan members. There was no doubt of Lynch's hatred for blacks and especially his hatred for Martin Luther King Jr. In June 1963, at a Klan meeting, a poster was displayed portraying King's head mounted on the body of a raccoon with a caption "Martin Luther Coon, and All His Little Coons, Are Going to Go Down, Like Good Tar Went Up." The reference to blacks being burned up "like good tar" sent a clear message that the Klan would resort to violence. Later, in a gathering in the city park, Lynch was quoted as saying "Martin Lucifer Coon—that nigger says it's going to be a hot summer, I will tell him that 140 million white people know how to make it a hotter summer." As author David Colburn noted, Lynch, "misquoting the Bible as was his fashion, implored his white audience to 'remember the words of Jesus Christ, who said, "You can't love two masters." You love one . . . and you HATE the other. . . . Now it may be some niggers are gonna get killed in the process,' he ranted, 'but when war's on, that's what happens.'"[43]

On October 30 I requested a grand jury be impaneled to investigate Kinard's shooting and the escalating violence that was sweeping the city. As a grand jury has the power to investigate any matter affecting the health, safety, and welfare of a community, I requested Judge Howell Melton to specifically include this power when instructing the jury on their duties. The city was on edge from the violence resulting from the murder of Kinard. City officials canceled the traditional Halloween trick or treat and asked parents to keep their children home. Although some visible changes in the city's segregationist stance occurred—traditional White and Colored signs were taken down from public restrooms and drinking fountains—a number of drugstores and lunch counters refused to integrate their places of business. Some owners signed warrants against blacks who refused to leave during sit-ins.

The effects of the violence were reaching Tallahassee, the state's capital. The governor began to take notice, but not action, other than to assign investigators from his office and from the Florida Sheriff's Bureau to St. Augustine. He also ordered the Florida Highway Patrol to crack down on traffic violations.

In preparation for the meeting with the grand jury, I subpoenaed a number of the county's leading citizens to appear and testify before the jury. Among them was President Puryear of the Florida Memorial College. I drove out to the college before his scheduled appearance and discussed the growing racial problems with him. He expressed his bitterness over the sad turn of events that had affected the college and his concern about Hayling's adversarial approach in confronting racial issues in the community. These tactics, he believed, had created financial problems for the college. With equal force he criticized local businessmen who had failed to come to the college's support, even after he prohibited students from taking part in demonstrations.

There was intense disagreement between the teachers at the college and the civil rights demonstrators as to the most effective way to achieve their mutual goals. Hayling had strong support among the younger members of the community, and it was this dedicated cadre of young people who were carrying the main burden of the demonstrations.

It was a bitter time for Puryear. He had devoted his professional life to the task of educating young blacks and dreamed of building a college that would prepare his students to participate in a society that had separated them from the mainstream of American life. These dreams had been shattered by the business community's withdrawal of financial support.

We spoke of the stark difference between the attitude of the business communities in St. Augustine and those in Daytona Beach, which also had a black college. He of course knew the history of Bethune-Cookman College, founded in Daytona Beach by Mary McLeod Bethune, and of the strong financial support the college received from the local business community. Puryear bemoaned the fact that in 1963 he had been able to obtain gifts from the St. Augustine business community totaling less than five hundred dollars. He spoke of the opportunity to receive considerable matching funds, which had been lost because he could not persuade the community to match the conditional grants. Those funds could have kept the college afloat.

On Tuesday, November 5, the grand jury returned indictments charging Richard Eubanks and Chester Hamilton with second-degree murder. Goldie Eubanks Sr. was also indicted as an accessory after the fact.[44] In an interim presentment, the grand jury, comprising sixteen whites and two blacks, found the Ku Klux Klan was exploiting the racial unrest, with violence and confusion as the result. After returning indictments, the grand jury recessed, and at my suggestion voted to reconvene in December to continue its inquiry into the racial unrest in the city. My decision to use the power of the grand jury in an attempt to resolve the difficulties was not popular with city officials, but the grand jury was the highest body of integrity in the county, and this fact muted the criticism.

On November 8, the NAACP, meeting in Winter Haven, Florida, adopted a resolution pledging full support to the three men charged in the slaying of Kinard. The resolution accused St. Augustine police with brutal treatment of blacks and the St. Johns County Sheriff's Department of giving "the go-ahead signal to violent elements of the area, including the Ku Klux Klan." The NAACP noted that it "does not believe in violence as a course for achievement of our rights, yet we can't overlook the fact that resistance to the ending of racial segregation is fostered by the elected officials of that city."[45] The NAACP was having some influence in solving racial unrest in other sections of Florida, but not in St. Augustine.

On November 14 federal judge William McRae, who had been assigned the petition of Hayling and others to enjoin the mayor and city officials against interfering with peaceful demonstrations, denied the petition. In the order he ruled that the petitioners did not come into court with "clean hands," referring to the statement made by Hayling he would "shoot first and ask questions later."[46] In the twelve-page decision, the judge was critical of Hayling. "The court," he wrote, "is of the opinion that the Plaintiff[s] did not come into court with clean hands. Their leadership and particularly Robert B. Hayling have displayed a lack of restraint, common sense and good judgment, and an irresponsibility which have done a disservice to the advancement of the best interests of all the plaintiffs and others in St. Augustine who are similarly situated. Problems which might well have been solved by intelligent action have been handled with deliberate provocation and apparent intent to incite disorder and confusion."[47]

This jurisdictional matter was fatal to granting injunctive relief in federal courts. In order to obtain the relief requested in the petition, it was necessary that the petitioners come into court with "clean hands," that is, without fault in the controversy. The suit was dismissed with prejudice. It could not be filed again. City Attorney Robert Andreu was elated at the outcome: "It is the finest type of order we could obtain. The ruling is a one hundred percent victory for the city."[48]

The court ruling accelerated the deteriorating relationship between the NAACP and Hayling. This relationship had been souring for some time, and shortly after the federal court denied Hayling's petition, he and Eubanks resigned from the NAACP. Without support from this powerful civil rights organization, the St. Augustine movement began to lose cohesion, but the enthusiasm of the young people was not dimmed.

In addition to the NAACP and the SCLC, the Congress of Racial Equality (CORE), John Lewis's Student Nonviolent Coordinating Committee (SNCC), and the Nation of Islam, with its dynamic spokesman Malcolm X, were among the leading forces of the civil rights movement. But there was a growing absence of agreement over the form the movement should take, including questions about King's nonviolent tactics. The temperament of more volatile leaders such as Hayling, the young militants he represented, and some of the older veterans of the movement was beginning to come to the fore. The growing dispute between various civil rights organizations over the best way to aid those in the Senate who favored passage of the sweeping civil rights bill and how best to achieve their mutual goals would soon surface in St. Augustine.

The NAACP's policy was to effect change through politics, to demonstrate around the conference table—so long as those with whom they were negotiating showed good faith and if progress was being made. This position was challenged by leaders of the SCLC. They believed negotiating with most southern leaders was counterproductive. Martin Luther King believed the only way to force southern leaders to make changes in racial practices was to force a crisis through civil disobedience and peaceful demonstrations that would dramatically affect the economy of the community. King and his supporters were confident that this would bring about the necessary changes to the social structure and force politicians to make concessions to protect their business interests. Therefore, they believed, the key to success lay in peaceful protest, not negotiations. Others in the movement thought change could only be brought about through revolution. It was against this background that demonstrations had occurred across Florida, including the state's capital, Tallahassee, and the more populous city of Jacksonville. Civil rights activists now turned their attention to St. Augustine and its quadricentennial celebration.

As the civil rights bill slowly worked its way through Congress, anti-segregation protests taking place throughout the state were growing in intensity. Florida governor Farris Bryant issued a statement in which he acknowledged that blacks had the right to demonstrate for civil rights and assured those protesters that the state would not interfere "unless there is trouble."[49] He would, however, use his power to try to control the demonstrations and to challenge the efforts of federal courts to interfere with his right to control the domestic affairs of the state.

The breach between the NAACP and the leaders of the civil rights movement in St. Augustine offered King a way to help galvanize the conscience of the nation and overcome the stranglehold that many populist leaders of the South held over the political systems of the region, especially the members of the Senate whose opposition to the pending civil rights bill threatened its passage.

The year 1964 was a critical one for the civil rights movement. King and the SCLC hoped to loosen the bond between private business and segregation in the South by appealing to the nation's conscience. King set out not only to change the unjust laws and customs of the South that segregated the races but also to change the moral character of those who had allowed segregation to become entrenched in the social fabric of the region. What King attempted to do was wrest power from a class that had ruled the South since George Washington's time. His tactics were based in part on the strength of his own religious convictions—and in part on the role religious institutions played among his southern brothers in Christ. He trusted church members to do the right thing.

This trust was misplaced. The appeal to the collective conscience of most southerners fell on deaf ears. Prominent American theologian Reinhold Niebuhr pointed this out in his book *Moral Man and Immoral Society*. Generally, he argued, religious institutions could not be counted on to respect moral rules, particularly when it came to a matter involving the self-interests of the institution and its members.[50]

The tragic assassination of President John F. Kennedy brought profound and unexpected changes to the civil rights movement. Lyndon Johnson, the new president, embraced the cause and made the civil rights bill, then pending in the House Rules Committee, the centerpiece of his domestic policy. President Johnson knew that the only way to change the mores of the South was through the rule of law. The death of President Kennedy would also open the door of the White House to Martin Luther King Jr.

On December 3, 1963, King met with the new president and told him that antidiscrimination demonstrations would resume in various areas around the country by the middle of December. He informed the president that the moratorium on demonstrations, which leaders of several civil rights groups had called following the assassination of President John F. Kennedy, was only temporary.[51]

King found not only a sympathetic audience in the new president but also a strong advocate for the civil rights bill that had been introduced earlier that year by the Kennedy administration. During that administration, King had failed to convince a rather lukewarm president of the necessity to issue a "second emancipation proclamation." The movement would find in the new president someone who had a vision of equality for the nation's minorities as focused as their own. The day King met with the president was the third meeting Johnson had held with black leaders in recent days.

In St. Augustine, the grand jury that had recessed on November 5, 1963, reconvened on December 17 to consider the recent racial disturbances and try to find a solution. It subpoenaed members of the clergy, representatives of tourist accommodations, the head of the chamber of commerce, bank officials, the president of the local black college, the superintendent of public education, schoolteachers, farmers, and merchants from both races. Individuals directly involved in racial disturbances were excluded in an effort "to obtain, insofar as was possible, the true feeling of a cross section of the community." "Every effort was made," the grand jury noted, "through the required oath of secrecy, to encourage each individual who testified before the Grand Jury, to do so fully, without fear of his testimony being revealed."[52]

The grand jury found that the recent racial unrest had resulted from a breakdown of communication between the two races. Into this explosive situation, two militant elements exploited the "explosive and controversial" issue. The Klan, the grand jury wrote, did not represent the majority view of the white citizens in St. Augustine, and "two individuals used extremely bad judgment in attempting to present their problem" to city officials. It did not name the two individuals but it was obvious to all in St. Augustine that the grand jury members were referring to Robert B. Hayling and Goldie Eubanks.

After making certain findings of fact, a majority of the grand jury members agreed that the present state of hate and racial unrest could have been avoided; it also deplored the tragedy of losing the "Negro College that has resided in this community since 1917." The jury expressed its collective feelings as to what the community needed to do: "The Grand Jury feels that there are many sincere and dedicated individuals, representing both races living in St. Johns county, and when given the chance to sit down and discuss these differences that they will be able to resolve the same, insofar as is humanly possible."[53] The highest moral civil authority in the county had spoken. The community's leaders did not respond.

St. Augustine was about to reap a whirlwind of violence through the inaction of city and county officials.

2 Where Does St. Augustine Stand?

St. Augustine in 1964 was a small coastal city located on the east coast of Florida about forty miles south of Jacksonville. As in Daytona Beach and other cities along Florida's east coast, it was separated from the mainland by the Intracoastal Waterway. Bracketed by the San Sebastian and Matanzas rivers, the harbor at St. Augustine had been the gateway to the New World when Spain held Florida.

To the west, vast stretches of virgin forest extended to the St. Johns River, the western boundary of St. Johns County. Punctuated here and there by potato farms, the area provided excellent hunting and fishing. This isolated area also offered ideal hiding places to make the fiery 110-proof moonshine still available in much of rural Florida. At Twelve-Mile Swamp, bisected by Nine-Mile Road, was a section of forest maintained by the Ancient City Hunt Club. Most of the land was owned by three or four individuals and by paper companies.

When the city was founded by the Spanish, it was the gateway to Florida's wilderness interior, guarded by the well-fortified Castillo de San Marcos, which dominated the inlet. For centuries the most important fort in Florida, it had become the central tourist attraction of the modern city. The heart of the old city centered on this imposing structure, maintained by the National Park Service.

In the nineteenth century the Florida East Coast Railway had its terminus in this famous city, which was also home to the railroad's founder, Henry Flagler. During this golden age, the city was a winter playground for the wealthy. John D. Rockefeller and other northern millionaires often visited, prompting the erection of beautiful churches and grand hotels. Graceful homes surrounded by huge water oaks shaded the city's streets. It was a genteel, elegant city, but it concealed a rigid racial divide between its large black population and the more affluent white community.

Flagler had built the Ponce de Leon Hotel just west of the park in the center of St. Augustine. The old slave market was located in the park, and it was this symbolic spot that the Klan claimed as its own in 1964. Here, the Klan gathered on most nights during the height of the racial strife to harass the demonstrators that marched by the park to the older section of the city. Flagler had also built the Alcazar and Cordova hotels adjacent to the Ponce de Leon, where wealthy visitors once congregated to escape the northern winters. Later the wealthy would move farther south as Flagler extended his railway down the east coast, but St. Augustine remained a reminder of the wealth and grandeur of the past.

Stately homes in the affluent white neighborhood were scattered throughout the inner city, in close proximity to Lincolnville, where most of the blacks resided. That community would become a part of the conflict soon to engulf St. Augustine. Lincolnville was not a ghetto like those found in many southern cities because St. Augustine was not a typical southern city. Its population was a rich mixture of the old and new worlds. Minorcans were a distinct and powerful ethnic minority. Their descendants had migrated to St. Augustine from Minorca, one of Spain's Balearic Islands in the western Mediterranean. They were well established in the city and fiercely maintained their independence and cultural heritage. Despite their small numbers, the tight solidarity of this group made for a powerful political force. Later, Greeks would also migrate to the city. They came primarily from New Smyrna Beach, a settlement south of St. Augustine in Volusia County. Though they too maintained their ties to the old country, they exerted little influence in the city.

Although small, the Roman Catholic population exerted a political power much greater than their numbers suggested, due in large part to the influence of the Catholic church. The diocesan cathedral was located in the center of the city, just to the north of the park. The church's influence was augmented by the fact that Mayor Shelley was a Roman Catholic.

The most important political group was comprised of Anglo-Saxons and Scotch Irish, descendants of settlers who had arrived when the city was controlled by England in the eighteenth century. This powerful group combined with the Catholics to control the politics of the city and the county. The small clusters of Greeks and still fewer Jews mixed well with the larger groups, and the slow pace of life gave everyone except blacks a feeling of security. Blacks had been an indispensable part of the community since its first days. Spain had established a free colony of blacks in St. Augustine in 1739, although it was eventually absorbed into the greater community.

Blacks worked as manual laborers and as servants in the tourist trade, primarily in restaurants and as drivers of the horse-drawn carriages. Many black women served as maids in the households of the more affluent whites but few shared in the economic opportunities of the larger community. In the twentieth century the presence of a black college provided a core of educated professionals, but the white business community failed to support the college in any appreciable degree or to engage the talents and skills of its graduates.

St. Augustine had few industries. The most important, after tourism, was the aircraft maintenance and repair facility located at the local airport. There, obsolete aircraft from the naval air base at Cecil Field in nearby Jacksonville were repaired, refurbished, and sent to Central and South America or to National Guard units in the United States. The tidal estuaries and the many coves and bays of the numerous waterways surrounding the city were ideal breeding grounds for shrimp and redfish. Sturdy boats made in local shipyards in St. Augustine were sold up and down the coast for use in the harvesting of shrimp, to meet a growing demand for seafood in the many restaurants and fish markets in the city.

The city's ambivalent attitude toward blacks is best illustrated by the success of Gene Johnson, a local black. He and his large family lived at Matanzas inlet, just south of St. Augustine and operated one of the area's busiest and best-known fish houses, serving some of the most delicious fish, chowder, oysters, and shrimp to be found on the eastern seaboard. His rustic restaurant, with its dirt floors and rundown atmosphere, recreated the ambiance of an old Florida cracker house and attracted tourists and local people from miles around. A gregarious giant of a man,

Johnson steamed oysters over a roaring outdoor fire by placing sections of corrugated tin roofing over the fire and piling a bushel or two of oysters on top of the hot tin. These were covered with burlap bags soaked with river water, and the steamed bivalves were served to his happy customers. He challenged those brave enough to eat one of his fiery pickled Minorca peppers to do so without crying. Few could.

The community might accept local dentist Rudolph Gordon and restauranteur Gene Johnson, but it would not tolerate attempts to abolish segregation. And few in St. Augustine paid any heed to the violence the Klan would bring to the city. The Klan, many argued, also had legal rights.

In St. Augustine the Klan found a favorable climate in which to practice its hate, especially in the sheriff's office. The sheriff, L. O. Davis, was a friend of Holstead Manucy, the local leader of the Klan and head of the Ancient City Gun Club, which boasted many Klan members. The name Manucy was carved in a city monument honoring the small band of immigrants who came to América from the Spanish island of Minorca. They first landed in New Smyrna Beach, some seventy-five miles to the south, then settled in St. Augustine. Born in St. Augustine in 1919, Holstead Manucy was a Roman Catholic. In explaining this apparent contradiction in the Klan's message of hatred of Catholics, Jews, Communists, and blacks, Manucy was quoted as saying "a Catholic ain't supposed to be a member of the Klan. But it's caused me no trouble. Definitely not!"[1]

Early on in the demonstrations an article appeared in the *Daytona Beach News-Journal* highlighting the problem in question: "Where does St. Augustine stand?" the headline asked. "The lines of resistance are tightening, and there is no communication between the races. The Police Chief, Virgil Stuart, like the Sheriff, is an ardent segregationist. So are the commissioners. A state official in the city, who refused to be quoted on his views of the clash, refuses to take leadership, saying he can't afford, politically, to get involved."[2] The reference to the sheriff and the police chief, as well as the city commissioners, as ardent segregationists went to the heart of the problem in St. Augustine. The grand jury's report on December 15, 1963, had urged "sincere and dedicated" individuals to sit down and discuss their differences. No one in St. Augustine would dare

"sit down" with Hayling or Martin Luther King. The resulting racial conflict was the inevitable result.

L. O. Davis had not supported my candidacy in the 1962 special election, but after the election we had become friends, especially when I successfully prosecuted three murder cases in St. Augustine. For the moment,
I was riding a wave of popularity and had his support in the upcoming
election.

Davis, a native of St. Augustine, had first been elected sheriff in 1949.
He was descended from a family whose members were involved in politics, business, sports, and education in the city. A Populist, he had served
in the U.S. Army during World War II, and for a while he had been a special agent for the Florida East Coast Railway. He had also been a member
of the St. Augustine Police Department and was a volunteer coach for
St. Johns Academy and the Excelsior High School. Very popular among
a vast number of voters in St. Johns County, his supporters had included
many in the black community, until the racial crisis began. He advertised
his campaign with bumper stickers that said, "Vote for L. O." Nothing
more, just "Vote for L. O."

The governor once called me to complain of reports he had received
from the commander of the naval air station in Jacksonville. "Dan," the
governor said, "I've had complaints from the commander that some of
his sailors have come down with a social disease that they say came from
their encounters with prostitutes in St. Johns County. You have to do
something about this situation." I protested: How could I rely on the sheriff to conduct an investigation, he obviously knows about the operation,
and I had no funds to conduct an investigation. With only a part-time
investigator, I said, there was little I could do about the situation unless I
had help from the state. He replied that with or without help, I had to do
something about it.

I wrote a letter to the sheriff advising him of the governor's concerns
and asking him to conduct an investigation and report back to me. A
few weeks later I received his reply. It went something like this: "Dear
Mr. Warren: I have conducted a full and complete investigation into the
rumor that prostitution is being conducted at a truck stop called 'Across
the Border.' For the last two weeks I have had two uniformed officers

in marked patrolled cars observing the area and they advise that they can detect no activity of prostitution." I forwarded the reply to the governor with the notation, "You see what I mean?" Later the governor provided us with the investigative forces necessary to conduct a raid and we closed down the operation. On most days, except during the demonstrations, L. O. could be found fishing in his small boat under the Bridge of Lions and later in the evening at the American Legion, drinking with his buddies.

St. Augustine's chief of police was Virgil Stuart. He began his career in law enforcement with the department in 1934. Promoted to the rank of captain in 1936, he was named chief in 1958. A staunch supporter of the John Birch Society, he firmly believed the civil rights movement was Communist inspired. During the coming crisis, L. O. Davis overshadowed him. Law enforcement officers in St. Johns County and the city of St. Augustine were poorly trained and this lack of training caused many of the problems we initially encountered with crowd control. The refusal of the sheriff and the police chief to negotiate with any civil rights organization would create a void that would be filled by the nation's oldest terrorist's organization, the Klan.

The Florida Advisory Committee to the U.S. Commission on Civil Rights issued a report calling for the Justice Department to investigate the Ku Klux Klan in St. Augustine. "The recent beating of Negro leaders by the Ku Klux Klansmen should serve as a warning that the atmosphere in St. Augustine is attracting lawless hoodlum elements which thrive on violence and bloodshed. . . . The Justice Department should assure that Klan members are subject to all of the limitations that attach to membership in an organization that has been officially designated as subversive." The KKK had long been on the attorney general's list of subversive organizations, it noted. This report was apparently ignored by the Justice Department. The Klan's violence would be felt in brutal confrontations with the peaceful demonstrators.[3]

The KKK was active in St. Johns County before the appearance of SCLC members in St. Augustine. After their arrival, the Klan, promoting its doctrine of fear, hate, and prejudice, began holding night meetings just outside the city. The ritual burning of the cross, with hooded

Klansmen chanting their words of hate, sent a chilling message to community leaders: the Klan would lead the fight to keep St. Augustine segregated. The message went unheeded and the city's leaders refused to moderate their inflexible determination to resist any change in the city's social structure. Those who trumpeted the Klan's threat were told they had just as much right to demonstrate as did the NAACP, the SCLC, Hayling, and the local demonstrators.

The Klan was not alone in fostering hate and fear. There were splinter groups under the umbrella of bigotry. They joined forces during the demonstrations in 1963 and 1964 and brought the worst elements of all the hate groups into the community to represent the perverse ideology of the Klan: hatred of blacks and minorities.

The Klan has always thrived during times of social change especially in the South, but their influence had declined after the Depression. However, even in decline, their ability to whip up racial hatred remained strong among many southern whites. Their rallying cry—"a return to fundamental principles"—appealed to many southerners who opposed federalism and cherished a long-held belief in states' rights. Some, though not all, praised Adolph Hitler and denounced the "Communism of FDR and the Jews" and the various "isms" of labor organizers. Since its modern-day reappearance, one persistent theme had emerged in the ideology of the Klan: to resist any change in the segregated social structure.[4]

The real power within the Klan in St. Augustine was centered in three men. One was J. B. Stoner, a lawyer from Atlanta. He believed that segregation was essential to the security of the white race. The fact that he was an attorney gave the local Klan a thin aura of legitimacy. An extreme racist and anti-Semite, Stoner would become the premarch speaker who in 1964 led the assembled Klansmen in the rituals of hate that permeated their meetings in the old slave quarters, the geographical heart of old St. Augustine. Stoner's speeches were always peppered with the N-word. He used it liberally to arouse the passions of the hundreds of white hoodlums who gathered in the park eager to cause trouble. He aroused the crowd using his words of hate like a choirmaster directing the faithful. Stoner and his associate Connie Lynch were masters at fomenting hate, much as Hitler had roused his followers in Germany, urging them to lash out at the Jews and other minorities. Stoner and Lynch mobilized the gathered Klansmen in much the same fashion, but few in St. Augustine could see the similarity of the appeals.

Stoner was born in 1924. His father died when he was five, and a few years later he contracted polio, leaving him with a pronounced limp. When he was sixteen, his mother died. In 1942, exempt from military service, he joined a Chattanooga unit of the KKK and was soon elevated to kleagle by Imperial Wizard James Colescott. According to a biographical sketch in *The Ku Klux Klan: An Encyclopedia,* Stoner's obsession with anti-Semitism became the center of his life. In 1944 Stoner sent a petition to Congress, urging passage of a resolution that "Jews are the children of the Devil." In 1945 he organized the Stoner Anti-Jewish Party, advocating legislation that would "make being a Jew punishable by death." He continued to be active in the Klan until 1950, when Sam Roper's Associated Klans of America expelled him from the organization. Moving to Atlanta, Stoner teamed with Edward Fields to organize the Christian Anti-Jewish Party. In 1958 he became active in the National States' Rights Party (NSRP), a pseudo-Nazi group that adopted the SS symbol of Hitler's storm troopers.[5]

In 1959 Stoner declared himself "arch leader" and imperial wizard of the new Christian Knights of the Ku Klux Klan, based in Louisville, Kentucky. In 1963 Stoner lectured a group of NSRP members in Birmingham, Alabama, on how to construct time bombs. In September of that year, Stoner returned to Birmingham in time for the church bombing that killed four black children, but he was never linked to the killings. On September 23, 1963, he was one of eight NSRP members indicted for violent interference with school desegregation in Birmingham. He came to St. Augustine in 1964 and teamed up with Connie Lynch, a leader of the United Florida KKK.

Lynch was born in 1913. In David R. Colburn's book *Racial Change and Community Crisis,* he is described as "one of ten children of an indigent cotton farmer from Clarksville, Texas, who sympathized with the plight of the poor—but only poor whites." An accomplished speaker in the tradition of southern street evangelists, Lynch could influence and inflame a crowd like no other racist of his time, including Stoner.[6]

I witnessed Lynch in action on numerous occasions, but I will never forget the night I first watched one of his hate meetings. The air was filled with shouts and screams of frenzied Klansmen who closely resembled crowds at Nazi rallies in 1930s Germany. Wearing a vest made from a Confederate battle flag, Lynch predicted that there was going to be a race war throughout the nation and when the smoke cleared there weren't going to be anything but white faces. I left the area wondering how such an event could be happening in America just two short decades after the defeat of fascism in World War II.

The last of this trio of radical, racist demagogues was Holstead Manucy. A potbellied-pig farmer and convicted moonshiner he was the self-proclaimed president of the fifteen hundred–member Ancient City Gun Club, some of whom were closely allied with the Klan. He and his followers would join with Lynch and Stoner to fight the civil rights movement in St. Augustine. It is ironic that the failure of leadership in St. Augustine allowed their voices to be the ones the world would hear. As the racial drama unfolded, I would come to know all of them.

According to Manucy, the Ancient City Gun Club was a civic organization. Among the members were two U.S. deputy marshals and other well-known members of St. Augustine's power elite. Membership in the "civic club" was not a formal undertaking; to join you only had to give Manucy a check labeled a donation. This was the only membership requirement. No records were kept. The only paper trail of membership was the canceled check. According to Manucy, the organization was an uncharted, unincorporated, and voluntary association. There is no question that some of its members were ardent Klansmen.[7]

The gun club performed a rather peculiar but valuable service for some of the wealthy landowners in St. Johns County, especially those who owned large tracts of land west of St. Augustine. This vast forested area stretched to the St. Johns River, some thirty miles to the west. The slash pine that grew profusely in the fertile sandy loam was a valuable commodity. Most of the land was planted in a species of fast-growing pine that was used to supply pulpwood for neighboring paper plants. Cellulose fiber extracted from the pulp was used in products such as paper towels and napkins. The huge Hudson paper plant in Palatka, west of St. Augustine, relied upon these trees for the vital pulp they used in manufacturing their paper products. Most trees were harvested by pulpwood cutters, mainly black crews, who performed this dangerous, dirty, backbreaking work.

These "independent contractors," called "pulpwood niggers" by those who used them, were, in truth, indentured laborers. The fiction of an independent contractor was used as a legal device to avoid the costs of liability and workers' compensation insurance that would be required if they were employees of the landowners or paper companies. The workers were totally dependent on the middleman, who contracted for their labor, bought the cut logs, and stored them in wood yards (usually also owned by the middleman) until the timber could be sold to the paper mills. Many of the middlemen also owned the equipment used by the cutters, such as the chain saws and trucks needed to harvest the logs and haul the cut timber to the storage yards.

Fire and poaching on this vast unfenced stretch of forest were a constant problem for the owners. To protect their lands, owners granted leases, often without charge, to hunting clubs whose members hunted over and looked after the land. The Ancient City Gun Club controlled much of the land through such leases. Any fee charged for the use of the land was nominal, usually just sufficient to pay for liability insurance that covered the landowner against injury to the hunters.

One of my assistants, Sunny Weinstein of St. Augustine, owned a number of acres in this area and allowed the Ancient City Hunt Club to use his land for exclusive hunting rights. I asked him about the practice. He said it served multiple purposes: the Hunt Club looked after the land, keeping poachers out and others from burning it down. It also served another purpose; it was a safe place to manufacture the much sought after "white lightning" still being made in this undeveloped section of Florida's interior.

Holstead Manucy was a dedicated moonshiner, and with his club policing the land, he could engage in this practice without interference from law enforcement. He was in fact an unsworn deputy sheriff in the St. Johns County sheriff's department, and the club served as an unofficial law enforcement agency, providing services just like those performed by official agencies. Manucy encountered little interference from the sheriff, particularly when it came to moonshine.

After I become state attorney, a farmer living just west of St. Augustine called and asked me to come by and see him. When I arrived, he complained of a still located near his farm. When I asked how he knew this, he said that when moonshiners make "a run of 'shine" the distinctive odor of fermenting alcohol can easily be detected, especially in the evening. He suspected that Holstead was involved. When I brought the matter to the sheriff's attention he assured me he would investigate. The next day the farmer called and said someone had strewn tacks in his driveway. He suspected the sheriff had told Manucy that he had filed a complaint.

In 1963 Manucy had recently been released from the federal penitentiary after serving a prison term for illegal whiskey manufacture. In the looming racial crisis, the hunt club became an ally and surrogate for the Klan's violence. Against the backdrop of hatred and violence that permeated the city, I was perplexed by Mayor Shelley's adamant refusal to act on the complaints of the demonstrators and especially his refusal to heed the grand jury's call for the creation of a biracial committee. This would have allowed the parties to sit down and discuss ways and means to eliminate segregation from the city, as other cities around the state had done. I was also concerned by the mayor's claim that there was no race problem in St. Augustine. Even leaders who wanted to take a more moderate view, such as state senator Verle Pope, the "lion of St. Johns County," were caught in this culture of complicity. The mayor's inflexible posture virtually ensured the civil rights crisis would escalate.

Governor Farris Bryant, while acknowledging the right to demonstrate peacefully, refused to intervene or to cooperate with the U.S. Commission on Civil Rights in its efforts to avoid the racial crisis, claiming it represented a federal intrusion into state affairs. The committee urged the governor to take action in St. Augustine, expressing concern about the state's image "in view of the quadricentennial celebration" and noting that it was "inconceivable [that] we should put before the world such an example."[8] Bryant, like many southern governors, hoped time would solve the problem. A states' righter, Governor Bryant firmly believed that the federal government had no right to intervene in the internal affairs of the state. Because states possessed the right to control purely local affairs under the Tenth Amendment, and given the limits the Supreme Court had placed on the power of the federal government to interfere with local affairs, the doctrine of states' rights became an insurmountable barrier to abolishing segregation, especially in St. Augustine.

Governor Bryant's intransigent attitude toward states' rights was supported on the editorial page of the local newspaper, the *St. Augustine Record.* The publisher, A. H. Tebault Sr., was a staunch states' righter. An editorial published on October 3, 1962, titled, "Governors Ignore State Rights," pointed out that during the recent Southern Governor's Conference in Hollywood, Florida, which had ended the day before, the governors failed to even mention the federal invasion of the campus of the University of Mississippi. "Only the Governor of Alabama has been heard in the Southland on Governor Barnett's behalf. . . . Southern Governors should stand out as champions of States Rights. If they fail in this duty, then centralized federal government will continue to grasp for power."[9] The editorial was referring to the recent contempt citation against the Mississippi governor Ross Barnett in the James Meredith case and his defiant refusal to admit Meredith to the University of Mississippi. President Kennedy had nationalized the National Guard when, in the all-night riot that erupted, three bystanders were killed and 160 U.S. marshals wounded.

During the 1963 civil rights crisis in Mississippi, front-page headlines in the *St. Augustine Record* proclaimed, "Mississippi Governor Again Defies Order of Federal Government" and "Mississippians Express Anger at Government." There was little question where the newspaper stood on states' rights and integration. The senior Tebault, owner of the newspaper, died on April 11, 1963, but his son A. H. Tebault Jr. would take his place with a fervor for states' rights equal to that of his father. The mayor, newspaper editor, and local church dignitaries reflected the conservative, unyielding attitude of the community's business and political leaders.

The *St. Augustine Record* was a powerful voice in the community. Once, when I organized a raid using the constable to break up the world series of cockfighting (an illegal gambling operation conducted openly in St. Augustine) without consulting the sheriff, the editors of the local newspaper pontificated in a front-page story that there should be more trust between the state attorney's office and the sheriff's department. In a reply to the editor, I said that the sheriff certainly knew of the gambling operation: He had personally welcomed the gamblers to cockfights in St. Augustine and had even taken up a collection for the poor from the assembled gamblers before the event began.

In 1964 a new era began for the civil rights movement, one that would eventually break the stranglehold southern "barons" had held over civil rights legislation since Reconstruction. President Lyndon Johnson made passage of the Civil Rights Act the centerpiece of his domestic policy. If passed, the law would mark the beginning of the end of segregation in interstate commerce, which had prevailed in the South since Reconstruction ended in 1877, and would grant basic civil rights to the nation's black population, which now numbered 17 million.

As the new year opened the Speaker of the House of Representatives, John W. McCormack, announced that an effort would be launched on the following Monday to try and have the civil rights bill voted out of the House Rules Committee and bring it up for a vote on the floor of the House. It was successful, and on February 10, 1964, the House passed the Civil Rights Act of 1964 by a vote of 290 to 130.

The U.S. Senate had been debating its version of the bill for eleven weeks. During this time senators had managed to agree on only one issue: the bill needed to be amended. A total of seventy amendments had been proposed by Senate Republican leader Everett M. Dirksen. The fight centered on the right to jury trials for defendants charged with criminal contempt under the act. Southern senators were also fighting for the right of states to have the sole power to act if existing state law covered the same subject matter as contained in the Senate bill. This position reflected the attitude of most southerners that the federal government had no right to interfere with states on such local matters, a right that had been preserved under the Tenth Amendment. If changes to the bill were not made, passage of the bill was in doubt. Nineteen southern senators threatened to filibuster the bill if their demands were not met.

In St. Augustine, passage of the bill by the Senate was a major issue, and leaders in the community knew they could count on Florida's Democratic senators, Spessard Holland and George Smathers, to filibuster. Senator Hubert H. Humphrey, floor manager for the civil rights bill, could count on only sixty-two senators to vote for cloture. He needed sixty-seven.

Senator Ervin, from North Carolina, sounded the alarm among southern senators. The bill, he said, "offers the most monstrous blueprint for government tyranny ever presented to Congress."[10] Senator Holland said the proposed bill was as unenforceable, as the Eighteenth Amendment, which had introduced prohibition, had been. He also noted there was evidence of a growing opposition to the bill in the northern states.

The threat of a filibuster in the Senate had a good chance for success. Since the end of Reconstruction southern leaders had effectively blocked any effort by Congress to pass legislation that would end segregation; however, the nation's collective perception of segregation's evils had begun to change, primarily through the influence of the relatively new broadcasting medium, television.

Images of police officers using cattle prods, fire hoses, nightsticks, and attack dogs to break up demonstrations shocked and appalled many Americans and certainly influenced how the rest of the world viewed our country. Segregation was increasingly seen not only as unjust but also as immoral, and the move to eliminate it from society was slowly gathering force. Nightly broadcasts of real-time images of brutal law enforcement methods awakened the conscience of most Americans. The moral perception of the nation slowly changed. Martin Luther King was a past master at using this new tool to achieve his goals.

Hayling's resignation from the NAACP in 1963 and the rejection of his petition for an injunction set the stage for the dramatic entrance of King and the Southern Christian Leadership Conference into the city in 1964. As the New Year began, the civil rights movement in St. Augustine faltered. The criticism of the tactics used by Hayling and Eubanks by federal judge William McRae, coupled with the indictment of Eubanks in the death of William Kinard and the adverse report of the St. Johns County grand jury, left the movement in near collapse.

The only bright spot was the unrequited ardor and enthusiasm of the young people to the movement. They were steadfast in their determination to confront the inequalities that existed in St. Augustine and intent on bringing racial equality to blacks. However, they badly needed new leadership to guide them through the legal obstacles that the political elite of St. Augustine had placed in their path. Arrests of demonstrators were escalating, and financial resources for the movement were exhausted. Though their devotion to Hayling had not diminished nor had their enthusiasm for the cause, Hayling's assertion that he would "shoot first and ask questions later," referred to in Judge McRae's order, and his breach with the NAACP left the small band of demonstrators with a cause but no leader.

The movement in St. Augustine was left without a national voice. After the grand jury report on December 17, 1963, there was a lull in the demonstrations. Then, on March 20, 1964, Hayling, Goldie Eubanks, Henry Twine, and others drove to Orlando, where the SCLC was holding its annual meeting, to meet with Martin Luther King's aides. Leaders of St. Augustine's civil rights efforts had begun to fear that the movement would cease to exist without help.[11] Hayling called on the SCLC for that help. The SCLC agreed to take up the cause.

Hayling's appeal to the SCLC heightened the conflict between him and the power structure in St. Augustine. And it gave some credence to complaints that the civil rights movement was controlled by outside agitators exploiting otherwise peaceful race relations. It also hardened the resolve of the white community to resist changes in local race relations.

If King and other SCLC leaders had learned any lesson from their protests throughout the South, it was the value of the press. Television, with its shocking images of racial violence beamed nightly into most American homes, was a powerful tool that, used wisely, could influence not only national but also international opinion.

King and the SCLC leadership would move into St. Augustine's maelstrom of hate, prejudice, and fear in the spring of 1964. As they did, the world was watching as Congress debated a long overdue civil rights bill that would change the South and the nation forever. King would find a city seething with resentment. The moral issues he sought to set forth would be smothered by the hate and prejudice stirred up by the Klan and by lack of leadership from the political and religious leaders of the city. There was little doubt where the majority of the people in St. Augustine stood on this conflict.

3   Birth of a Social Conscience

The seeds of a social conscience were sown in my psyche from birth, planted there by my mother. "Danny Boy," she would say, "hold your head high. You are just as good as anyone, no better but just as good. Don't you ever let anyone put you down." Her deep religious beliefs made it a mortal sin to act superior to another human being, and this idea was drummed into my soul. It formed the solid foundation of a belief system I could use to put these thoughts into action.

As life's experiences accumulated, an awareness of the unequal social conditions that surrounded my life slowly began to emerge. I would struggle to understand the nature and reasons for the social and economic forces that enveloped my southern roots, but not until I reached the age of reason would I fully understand the importance of my mother's precepts. As I began to make my own decisions, the ideals and beliefs she planted in my mind would shape my conscience. I sometimes made the wrong decision, but I was never in doubt about what was right. As I grew to maturity in Greensboro, North Carolina, I had to deal with the inequities and prejudices of a class system that permeated every aspect of our lives. I would not challenge the racist aspects of the system until I encountered the influence of the Quakers at Guilford College.

I was born on October 10, 1925, in my grandmother's house in Concord, North Carolina. Our family was living in Greensboro at the time, but the Calloway girls, of whom my mother was one, usually returned to their mother's home to give birth to their children. It was a tradition in the family that older members of this large and gregarious group would be available to help with the birth and care of family children. Neither I nor my brothers nor my sister was born in a hospital. Even though my grandmother died in 1929, when I was only four, my earliest memories are of being in her home surrounded by the warmth and love of my many cousins, uncles, and aunts. Those were carefree happy years; none of us were aware of the economic turmoil and hardship that the coming Depression would bring to our lives.

Greensboro, economically and culturally, was a much different place to grow up in than Concord. In 1925, as now, Greensboro had a larger population than Concord. It was the center of a thriving economy until the Depression came in 1929. Cosmopolitan and wealthy, it had a rigid class system controlled by a small, close-knit group of successful industrialists, lawyers, businessmen, and churchmen. These individuals, generous in financial support of worthy causes that interested them, kept a tight rein on the social order that separated the rich from the poor, both black and white.

During the desperate conditions of the Depression, our family, like millions of others, was caught in a struggle to survive. This experience had a significant impact on my thinking, especially as I tried to understand the larger issues that brought about the Depression. My father laid down the law early in our lives: none of his children would ever work in a cotton mill. Although the mills provided most of the city's economic vitality, he would not even allow us to wear the overalls produced by "sweat labor." His constant refrain was that we must go to college before starting to work. It was an ironclad rule in our family that education came first, a job second. My father knew the riches, intellectual and economic, that education brings and that through it lies the main avenue for escape from the social and economic strictures of a closed society. I had no idea how this could be accomplished, since our financial condition was rather precarious, but I never doubted that it would happen, because my father ruled it would.

The Warrens were of modest financial means but proud. A Scots Presbyterian, my father's mother named him after the Scottish king Robert De Bruce. He worked at the local post office as a mail carrier. He was a gentle man who loved his family and his country and contrary to the prevailing view of the day, seldom used the rod to enforce discipline. A nod, a scowl, or a cough was sufficient signal of his displeasure, and all his children tried hard to gain his approval. He taught us the nobility of duty and the importance of citizens serving their country. True service was to be accomplished without reward or complaint. Duty had its own reward, he often said.

My father gave to all of us in the family a sense of pride in being an American and a sense of the patriotic duty needed to protect and defend the principles on which it was founded. When the "Star-Spangled Banner" was played, whether in public or at home, we had to stand at attention and place our hand over our heart. If outdoors, our head had to be bare, and in either place, we had to stand at attention until the last refrain. Duty, my dad taught us, was a moral obligation compelled by the privilege of living in this country; it must be freely given, without expectation of money or fame.

The principal industry in Greensboro was the manufacture of cloth. The Cone Manufacturing Company was then the world's largest producer of denim. The mill was a power unto itself, akin to the feudalism of medieval Europe. Smaller plants, called "jobbers," were scattered throughout the city. These plants would purchase raw cloth from the large mills and turn it into overalls and jeans. The three main textile plants of the Cone complex were surrounded by mill villages, all owned by the Cones. Most of the workers' personal needs were met by company stores, also owned by the Cones. The Proximity plant, where denim was dyed to give it the distinctive blue color popular with workers, was located about half a mile from our home. The plant was separated from our neighborhood by a large tract of wooded land and the main north-south line of the Southern Railway. The plant whistle sounded promptly at 6:30 each morning, calling workers to their jobs. When the last whistle was blown at 7:00 a.m., all employees were expected to be at their assigned station.

Social status in a strict class system distinguished the relative worth of an individual, enforced by an equally strict system of mores. These customs controlled your life from birth to death and were often more binding than formalized legal codes. When I was growing up in Greensboro, we learned a saying: "If you were not born into it or married into it, you didn't get into it." Perhaps it was the effect this closed society had on my life, and my mother's constant reminders to hold my head high, that caused me to oppose segregation, which held another class of citizens in an even tighter grip of repression.

Once, during the early days of the Depression, Greensboro experienced a resurgence of the Klan. The fathers of some of my friends were members, and I was teased and taunted by a few boys in the neighborhood because my father was not a member. I knew nothing of the Klan and asked my father why he wasn't a member. Whenever my father wanted to impress an essential truth, he would invite me to sit down and give me his undivided attention. He did so this time. "Dan, I want to tell you something, and I want you to remember it for the rest of your life. Anyone who goes around with a sheet over his head, scaring women and children, is nothing but a coward. I will have nothing to do with the Klan and neither will you." Of course, conveying that information to the boys in the neighborhood meant a bloody nose or two, but the point had been made and I did remember that lesson for the rest of my life. In 1964 I would profit from it when I encountered the Klan in St. Augustine.

Greensboro, like other cities in the South, was completely segregated. In our neighborhood, and in most of our daily activities, we seldom came into contact with a black, although the black community made up almost 25 percent of the population. Leaders of the community pointed with pride to the separate but allegedly equal facilities of the schools and other public facilities, referring to the "impressive physical features" and "spacious landscaped grounds surrounding them."[1] As in most of the South, blacks were all but invisible. At our church, First Presbyterian, there was one black member, a maid for one of the wealthier members of the congregation, who sat alone in the balcony. Once, during a service, she was given special recognition for having been with the family for thirty years. As she sat in the balcony of that huge church, she seemed more of a curiosity than a member.

In Ethel Stephens Arnett's history of Greensboro, published by the University of North Carolina Press in 1955, only five entries, plus five photographs, describe the contributions of blacks to the growth of Greensboro. There are many references to the financial contributions of the city's wealthier citizens, those who helped in making construction of the hospital and school possible. Their contributions were indeed impressive, but the emphasis in the book was on how well segregation was working, and it kept alive the myth of the quality education that blacks were supposedly receiving under the separate but equal doctrine of a segregated society. In 1954 the Supreme Court rendered its *Brown v. Board of Education* decision. Overturning the separate but equal doctrine rendered in *Plessy v. Ferguson,* the court quoted from studies conducted by Kenneth and Mamie Clark and in the now-famous footnote 11 recounted the devastating psychological effects segregation had on young children. In a unanimous decision they wrote that "to separate black children in grade and high school from others of similar age and qualifications solely because of their race generates a feeling of inferiority as to their status in the community that may affect their hearts and minds in a way unlikely ever to be undone."[2]

Churches in Greensboro played an important role in enforcing mores regarded as essential to the survival of the community. These often constituted a force greater than the rule of law, especially in the churches where status and customs reinforced precepts of Christian conduct peculiar to certain denominations. Class churches in the South, as Liston Pope explains in his book *Millhands and Preachers,* are "especially designed for the working class."[3] This was the most significant factor in the social differences among churches in the South, especially those that promoted standards of conduct drawn from literal interpretations of the Bible, and to be faithfully followed by its members. "Class churches" not only made it possible for religion and segregation to coexist, but also permitted religion to play a role in southern society beyond bringing the "good news" to the faithful.

Religion in Greensboro, as in most of the South, reinforced and maintained political and economic mores. Religion and the class culture it supported played an important role in allowing the prevailing prejudices toward blacks to flourish. Inbred bias in many denominations was indispensable in placating and controlling whites as well, especially under the harsh economic conditions of the time.

The power to condemn someone's soul to hell, especially in a culture that held to a belief of the fundamental necessity to be "saved," can be a strong deterrent to change and especially to control "ungodly" civil unrest. The idea that Jesus Christ paid the price for all a person's sins eliminates the need for a "religious fifth amendment"; such an atonement frees one of the sin of segregation and allows believers to escape the pangs of a guilty conscience. It also allows them to escape responsibility for dealing with the second-class status and inequitable treatment of blacks in a segregated society.

I was made aware of religion's social and political power during the Depression. Conditions in textile plants in Greensboro, as unions sought to improve the horrible working conditions of mill workers and to compel mill owners to pay a living wage, sparked a series of strikes beginning in 1929. Starting in Gastonia, strikes eventually reached my hometown in 1934. Mill villages, owned and operated by the mills, were designed to keep workers tied to the looms with little chance to escape the monotonous drudgery and dangers of making cloth. Such villages, as Liston Pope explains, "were an effective instrument of control over labor, and also assured a permanent labor supply."[4]

White Christian churches were among the most powerful institutions in the South. Whenever the economic stability of a community was threatened or social conformity was challenged, most of these churches remained silent. In Greensboro, they were seemingly indifferent to the terrible conditions that prevailed in the mills. During the 1934–38 labor strikes in Greensboro, labor leaders regarded churches as some of their worst enemies. Ministers preached against involvement in the strikes, thereby implicitly demanding that parishioners ignore the labor and wage disputes between the mill owners and their employees. Preachers often denounced unions and strike organizers as having been possessed by "godless Communism" and as "outside agitators."

It was not unusual for ministers to remind their members of the many benefits the mills brought to the community and simply gloss over the appalling working conditions at most mills. Despite those conditions, child labor violations, and low wages for textile workers, no church in our neighborhood made any public statement condemning these practices. When, in 1927, a group of forty-one southern churchmen signed "An Appeal to Industrial Leaders of the South" to make changes in wage and working conditions, they were denounced as meddling theorists who had no firsthand knowledge of the conditions they were deploring.[5] Those who attempted to change the Jim Crow practices that existed in the South received the same treatment.

When labor unions called for a strike at Cone Mill in the 1930s, North Carolina's governor called out the National Guard and deployed troops on the roofs of the fortresslike mills, with machine guns mounted on the parapets. Outside workers were brought in, and the strike was broken in short order. I recall seeing grown men, gaunt from hunger and suffering from lung diseases due to the dust and lint that filled the air in the mills, loitering at the baseball diamond across from the Proximity plant of the Cone Complex, idling away time while on strike for a penny-per-hour raise.

The power to maintain law and order was reserved to the states, and the federal government could interfere only if a state could not maintain the peace. No governor would ever admit that he could not maintain law and order within his state, and no governor ever called for federal assistance to maintain order, relying instead on the state-controlled National Guard. Calling out the state's Guard was a powerful tool when civil disturbances threatened the social order, and the governor of North Carolina used this option when labor unrest threatened the industrial powers that fueled the state economy.

The only way for most poor whites to escape the life of a mill worker was to die. For me, the way out came when Japan bombed Pearl Harbor in 1941. When America went to war, my two older brothers immediately joined the U.S. Army Air Corps and became fighter pilots. I was only sixteen when the Japanese bombed Pearl Harbor, but I was determined to get into the war as quickly as I could, with dreams of becoming a fighter pilot like my brothers. The air corps then had a program, QAC, which stood for "qualified air cadet," to lure high school seniors into the air force before they were drafted into the army. This option was available to high school students who had reached age seventeen and a half. The only difficulty was that parental consent was necessary to join at that age. Dad was agreeable, but my mother was reluctant. In one of the few times I ever lied to her, I told her the air force would allow me to finish high school. She finally consented since I would be eligible for the draft when I became eighteen.

I enlisted and was sent to Camp Croft, South Carolina, to be sworn in. Shortly thereafter I reported to Pope Field at Ft. Bragg, North Carolina. I quickly washed out as a cadet and wound up in Italy as a nose gunner on a B-24, a heavy bomber, where I flew bombing missions into Germany, Austria, Czechoslovakia, Hungary, Italy, and Yugoslavia. It was on these missions that I came to understand the full meaning of inequality.

On our first mission, our group of planes assembled over Bari, a port city on the Adriatic in southern Italy, and headed out for the long run to a target in Austria. We had to pass close to Aviano in northern Italy where the Germans had one of their main fighter bases. I was one scared teenage nose gunner as we approached the mainland. Then I saw our fighter escort, a canopy of P-51s with flame-red tail markings. The relief I felt at the sight of those protective fighters gave me a deep sense of comradeship with the pilots. I thought of my two brothers and felt a personal kinship for whoever was flying the planes that gave us protection from German fighters. Later I would find that those who flew the "Red Tails" were black pilots from the 99th fighter group. They were later to become famous as the Tuskegee Airmen who, according to some sources, never lost a bomber to enemy fighters on any mission for which they provided cover. The 99th had been formed by the air corps in 1942 at the urging of First Lady Eleanor Roosevelt.

Many other groups provided fighter cover for the 15th Air Force. The 325th Fighter Group flew P-51s with a checkerboard red and white tail design, similar to but not as distinctive as that of the Red Tails. P-38s also provided cover as did P-47s. But it wasn't just the red tails that set the 99th apart from the other bomber escorts. Because all the pilots of the 99th were black, they were segregated from their own comrades in arms. At the time I gave little thought to segregation in the air corps, but after I started college I would take notice.

Shortly after graduating from law school I become friends with Charles Bailey, one of the original Tuskegee airmen; he had flown 132 missions in Africa and Italy. Charles lived in Deland, Florida, where I went to law school. After I graduated in 1952, I sought him out and we formed a friendship that lasted until his death in 2002. I attended his funeral, at which the air force gave him a full military burial, with a missing-man formation flyover, taps, and the final rifle volley. As they lowered his casket into its final resting place, I wondered why it had taken so long to acknowledge the worth of this brave man.

When the war was over, I returned to high school to obtain my diploma, and in 1946 I enrolled at Guilford College, just outside Greensboro, determined to become an attorney. Guilford was the oldest coeducational college in the South. Chartered in 1834 by the Society of Friends, or Quakers, the college attracted teachers dedicated to the principles of equality. Through the quiet grace and inspiration of their beliefs, Quakers attempted to inspire in each student a deep feeling of trust and respect. It was at Guilford that I began to understand the injustice of segregation. The school both preached and practiced equality for all individuals. The faculty members believed that every person had intrinsic worth—just as my mother had taught me.

David Stafford, Marjorie Mendenhall Applewhite, and Ernestine Milner had the most impact on my social conscience while I was at Guilford. These three would influence my thinking on the social issues of the day and inspire in me a deep respect for the worth of each individual. Quakers speak of the inner light, an apprehension of God, that each individual had within his being. Looking within one's own soul, without creeds or ecclesiastical forms, they patiently wait for the inner light of God to be revealed. Being a Presbyterian, steeped in the idea of predestination, I found the concept that each individual had a personal insight into God's will a revolutionary idea.

One of the most interesting courses I took at Guilford was in sociology; it was taught by David Stafford. We explored the effects that segregation had on public education and on the ability of blacks to successfully compete in private enterprise. The domino effect of unequal education was reflected in almost every aspect of their lives, even in the government services they received. In a project to test how ingrained the practice of segregation was, we joined with students and professors at North Carolina Agricultural and Technical State University (NCA&T) and Bennett College, two black schools in Greensboro. Our goal was to integrate the social services of Guilford County. The county department of public welfare was headed by a superintendent under the direction of a board of directors. At that time the chair of the board was the head of the history department of the University of North Carolina for Women at Greensboro, a white institution, known locally as WCUNC and now called University of North Carolina at Greensboro.

My counterpart was a young college professor who was head of the history department at NCA&T, a school founded in 1891 as a land grant institution for blacks. Located on twenty-five acres east of the city center, it enrolled approximately twenty-five hundred students and in 1947 was the largest college for blacks in the state. We drove to the WCUNC campus to meet with the chairman of the board and made our case for integrating the social services based upon fairness and economy. The chairman said it would not work. When I pressed for a reason, he said the board met once a month for a dinner meeting and there was no eating place in Greensboro that would serve blacks and whites together. If that was the reason, I replied, the answer to the problem was simple: eliminate the dinner meeting. He was rather astonished that I could entertain such an idea and brushed it off with a disdainful look of annoyance. When the meeting was over, he asked that I remain, after rather curtly dismissing my counterpart. He knew my father and asked: "Does your father know what you are doing?" "No," I replied, then added, "but if he did, he would advise me to do what my conscience dictated."

We left, defeated by the insensitivity and illogic of a social order that placed the importance of dinner over the goal of achieving equality. The experience reinforced my opinion that segregation was not only immoral but also totally without reason. It added a new layer to my social conscience, one that would harden into a determination that someday, somehow, I would be in a position to make a difference in changing this racist system.

An opportunity came in 1952 when I was fresh out of law school. My wife, Mary, and I were so broke we didn't have enough money to return to North Carolina so I could take the North Carolina bar examination. So we decided I should open a law office in Daytona Beach. With only $200 to our name, we leased office space at the First Atlantic Bank Building on Seabreeze Boulevard, using $120 of the money for the first and last months' rent, and I began the practice of law. But with few local contacts the outlook was not bright. Even so, we had youthful optimism and a firm belief that we could overcome any obstacle. We reasoned the best way for me to become known throughout the city was to run for public office. A city election was coming up, and we lived in a district that had a large black population. Conditions in this district were deplorable: no sewers, unpaved streets, and squalor that would rival many third world countries. I decided to challenge the entrenched and politically powerful incumbent commissioner, Combs Young, a successful businessman from an old Daytona Beach family. A deacon in the First Baptist Church, one of the largest churches in the city, he would be a formidable opponent. With the naive enthusiasm of youth, I walked into the office of the local newspaper, the *News-Journal,* and sought out the editor. I had met the publisher, Julius Davidson, but I did not know his son and editor, Herbert Davidson. A stern, aloof man, he graciously heard me out as I explained to him why I had decided to seek the office. I outlined my political philosophy and gave my assessment of the challenges the city faced.

The city of Daytona Beach had a rather sordid past. For twenty years it had been ruled by a powerful machine that supported a number of corrupt elected officials. A city commissioner of the city had once been convicted of accepting a ten-thousand-dollar bribe to vote for the mayor and had been removed from office by the governor. Convicted, he was then pardoned by the governor, with the understanding he would never again seek public office. After the war, he broke the promise and was once again holding elective office. A former mayor, Ed Armstrong, afraid that he was about to be removed from office by Governor David Sholtz, resigned and had the city commission appoint his wife, Irene, as mayor. The governor, shortly before his term expired, issued an order removing from office not only Irene Armstrong but also two city commissioners. The mayor, with her husband at her side, refused to accept Sholtz's order. Fully armed, they barricaded the doors of city hall and began clearing out records as fast as city garbage trucks could haul them away. The governor ordered the National Guard to physically remove her, but his term ended before this happened. The incoming governor's order to rescind the ouster was upheld by the Florida Supreme Court. The court ruled that Governor Schultz did not have the power of removal, thus leaving Irene Armstrong as mayor. As a result of this sort of corruption, Daytona Beach was in a state of near bankruptcy. City growth had been stifled, and gambling openly flourished. It was said among local wags that politicians from Cook County, Illinois, came to Volusia County to study corruption.

In 1948 a group of concerned businessmen who had had enough of the mismanagement and corruption formed an association to confront the problem. The group managed to move a state circuit judge from another county in the circuit and have elisors (persons appointed by a court to return a jury or serve a writ when the sheriff or coroners are disqualified) appointed to serve the processes of the court. This effectively bypassed the sheriff, and the reformers were successful in closing the numerous gambling houses. The group then decided to consolidate their reforms by supporting candidates who pledged to make the changes necessary to bring sound, honest business practices to city affairs. In 1950, Hart Long and Jack Tamm had been elected on the reform ticket, but the civic league was having trouble finding candidates for the 1952 city elections.

When the city's charter was amended, reference was made to its corrupt history. When the city sought to finance necessary improvements through bonds, the past problems were always referred to in the bond prospectus. Unfortunately, this otherwise admirable candor added a percentage point or two to the bond's interest rate. The city was so broke from past excesses that it had almost no revenue for essential services. I did not realize that Davidson was one of the community leaders determined to change the city's political leadership and was leading the campaign to elect reform candidates. The flash point in the election was over the form of government that would control the city—either an elected mayor or a professional city manager. The former had fostered the graft and corruption in the first place. I favored a strong city manager, one who would reform the city from a political piggy bank to an effective system of responsible government designed to serve the public.

Davidson called in one of his top reporters, Anne Hicks, to interview me. The next day, the newspaper headline read, "Warren to Oppose Young." The article noted that I was young and had never held public office. It also pointed out that I had said that if a candidate who believed in the same principles of government I did and had more experience came forward, I would withdraw. No one did.

The story listed my birthplace as Concord, North Carolina. The next day, my phone rang. The caller was Mary McLeod Bethune, president emeritus of Bethune-Cookman College. She had read the article and, noting that I was from Concord, said she knew the area well, having attended Scotia Seminary in that town. She was interested in my campaign and invited me to her home to meet with a group of black leaders who had also formed a civic league and were equally determined to change conditions in Daytona Beach. The result of the meeting was her personal endorsement and the group's substantial financial support in the upcoming election. I won the election in a runoff. A deep friendship with Bethune ensued, one that endured until her death in 1955.

After *Brown v. Board of Education*, my wife, Mary, then a schoolteacher was the first to volunteer to teach in one of the schools that was being integrated. In 1956 Mary and I cochaired a committee in Volusia County formed to support Farris Bryant for governor. Bryant, LeRoy Collins, and three others were in the race. Mary was pregnant with our sixth child, David; nevertheless, she campaigned vigorously for Bryant, standing on street corners holding campaign signs, attending rallies, and using the almost boundless energy she had for causes she espoused. This dedication caught Bryant's attention. When he kicked off his campaign in nearby Ocala, Mary and I were among the few from Volusia County to attend. The governor would not forget the sight of Mary, pregnant, standing in the heat of the day, holding one of his campaign signs. He lost the election to Governor Collins, but won when he ran again in 1960.

Bryant had been elected with the help of Ed Ball, the most politically influential man in the state as well as one of the wealthiest. Recalling his defeat at the hands of Collins in 1956, Bryant told me prior to the 1960 election that this time the outcome would be different. He had found out, he said, how to become governor. He would court the business community with Ed Ball's help and campaign on a platform to maintain the status quo in race relations.

Farris Bryant was a rather mild segregationist. But if it came to a showdown, he planned to use the doctrine of interposition as grounds for challenging the federal government's power to compel the state to integrate public facilities. This was the tactic he had used when he was in the Florida legislature. His pledge to maintain the status quo in race relations resonated well with most white Floridians, and the strategy apparently worked. It is interesting to recall, as David R. Colburn noted, that one of Bryant's first acts as governor was to "reappoint [Governor] Collins's statewide biracial advisory committee," but when the chairman resigned, Bryant stated that he had "chosen a new chairman, but refused to name him," and the committee was subsequently dissolved.[6]

Bryant was from Ocala, in the center of the most conservative part of the state. First elected to the Florida House of Representatives in 1946, he served five terms, becoming Speaker in 1953. Tom Cobb, my political mentor and attorney friend from Daytona Beach, served in the House with Bryant and had introduced me to him when he ran unsuccessfully for governor in 1956. Cobb encouraged me to become involved in Bryant's campaign. Bryant, a Democrat, refused to endorse Kennedy for president during the 1960 election. Florida voted for Nixon.

Bryant was not a demagogue, as were many southern politicians. In his inauguration he promised to maintain segregation without violence, anarchy, or closing of schools. When the Freedom Riders came through the state during his term, he shrewdly persuaded restaurants and bus depots to serve them. He was a progressive businessman and brought about many positive changes, including the roads so necessary to a tourist economy. He courted Disney during the 1960s and expanded the state road system serving Cape Canaveral, soon to be an important part of the race to land a man on the moon. He also doubled the number of schools in the state university system. In general, he was a good governor, though bound to the racist traditions of the past. His shortsighted view on race would cast a shadow over his otherwise progressive accomplishments.

Until Florida's constitution was amended in 1972, assistant state attorneys were appointed by the governor rather than by the elected state attorneys. These positions were pursued assiduously by young attorneys eager to make their reputation through service in the state attorney's office, which could lead to higher office. In 1961 an appointment became available in the state attorney's office for the Seventh Judicial Circuit. William "Billy" Judge, the state attorney, was a man I admired very much, and I wanted to learn the art of trial advocacy from a master, which he was.

Joe Scarlet, a friend of mine and a former classmate at Stetson Law School, who lived in neighboring Deland where the county court was located, also sought the appointment. From a prominent family on the west side of the county, Joe had clerked for Glenn Terrell, former chief justice of the Florida supreme court, and had his support at the time. The wishes of a Florida supreme court justice are seldom ignored, but in this case they were. I received the appointment from the governor. As he later told me, he had been leaning toward appointing Joe, but "I remembered Mary, pregnant, on a hot summer afternoon, holding one of my signs. I could not forget that scene, and I couldn't turn my back on you. So I gave you the appointment."

To become an assistant to Billy Judge was a dream come true. The foremost criminal lawyer in the state at the time, he had been appointed by Governor Collins to fill out the term of Pat Sams, the longtime state attorney for the circuit who had retired in 1955. However, my tutelage under Judge would be short. I had been an assistant for only nine months when Billy resigned. I had no idea of his plans. The day he resigned he called and said, "Congratulations, Dan, you're the new state attorney." I was flabbergasted. "You have to be kidding," I managed to reply. He wasn't. I was appointed that day by Governor Bryant to fill his unexpired term.

Suddenly, at thirty-six, I was the most powerful political officeholder in the large Seventh Judicial Circuit. In a political move to oust me from the very tenuous hold I had on the office, Rodney Thursby, the influential sheriff of Volusia County and a political enemy, urged that a special election be called to fill the unexpired term. The state attorney general, a close friend of Thursby, in a controversial ruling, found that a special election had to be held to fill the unexpired term. This turn of events would throw me into an election against J. Robert Durden, a popular Daytona Beach city judge and a favorite hometown boy. A glider pilot during the invasion of Normandy, he had won a Distinguished Flying Cross and Purple Heart. He would be difficult to beat. The governor set the election for an early date to give me a better chance to win, which I did—by only 346 votes. It was a hard-fought election, but with the support of the *Daytona Beach News-Journal* and the governor's endorsement, I managed to pull it off.

The Seventh Judicial Circuit covered four counties: Volusia, where I lived; Flagler, Putnam, and St. Johns. It was a sizable circuit, and I had only four assistants, one in each county. Like me, the assistants were part-time and could engage in private practice. It wasn't the dream job I had envisioned. There was no budget for the office and only one part-time investigator and one secretary for the entire circuit. Crime was on the rise in the 1960s, and trying cases around the circuit was time consuming.

Even though I was permitted to continue a private law practice, it was almost impossible to do so as I was constantly on the circuit either at a trial or preparing for one. In addition I had to handle any matter in which the state of Florida had an interest. This included bond validation proceedings and, when directed by a circuit judge, disbarment actions against attorneys; advising the circuit's four grand juries; and trying all felony cases brought by the state in the four counties. Grand juries met twice a year in each county, so that eight times a year I had to be in attendance on grand jury matters. This alone took a great deal of time.

Since being appointed state attorney in August 1962, I had spent much time in St. Augustine, and despite my inexperience, I had successfully prosecuted a number of important cases. One, the Effie Norris murder trial, called the "arsenic and old lace" case by the press, attracted nationwide attention. (The defendant was not related to local physician Hardgrove Norris.) The trial was a sensation, and the defendant was convicted of first-degree murder in the deaths of her husband and boyfriend. As I drove home late that evening, emotionally drained, I tuned in to the NBC national radio network and caught a news flash from New York: "A Florida jury has just returned a first-degree murder verdict in the Effie Norris case." It was an important milestone for me, and after the Norris conviction, my reputation as a young, green, unseasoned prosecutor changed. I was now a skillful, aggressive prosecutor and the criminal defense bar took note, as did the news media. But more importantly, I had established a friendship with Judge Howell Melton, and that would be of great help in the racial furor soon to come in St. Augustine.

Two other cases were important in helping establish my reputation as a successful prosecutor. I obtained a conviction against William D. McDaniel Sr. for the murder of his wife. A well-known businessman in the community, this was his second trial; the first had ended in a mistrial. I also successfully prosecuted Lois Vivian Lee for the hammer killing of Lester Rogers. She was arraigned on the same day that McDaniel's second trial began. These three first-degree murder cases, almost back to back, as well as other cases brought me into contact with leading businessmen of the community, including the editor of the local newspaper, A. H. Tebault Jr. My political career was prospering and I was riding a wave of popularity when the racial crisis erupted in the summer of 1964.

When I was appointed state attorney, my assistant in St. Augustine was Hamilton Upchurch, son of Frank Upchurch, the city's leading attorney. The senior Upchurch had been a candidate for governor in the 1930s and had important contacts throughout the state. Highly regarded in the legal and business community, he was a leading citizen of St. Augustine as was his son Hamilton. Unfortunately for me, Hamilton resigned shortly after my first election in the fall of 1962. I would sorely miss him. He was replaced by Sonny Weinstein, a former member of the state House of Representatives. A lawyer with a large, active law practice, Sonny did not have the backing of the political elite, but his grassroots support from the Democratic Party's rank and file made him an ideal assistant, especially during the racial troubles. Of the Jewish faith, he was a hard-working, successful lawyer and a businessman who called his own shots. Despite the fact that the community power brokers had not supported him, he commanded respect. I was lucky to have two extremely intelligent and forceful men as assistants; their experience made up for my lack thereof. Sonny quickly became one of my best friends, and I relied on him for his sound reasoning and sagacious advice.

Friends I made during the Norris trial, especially circuit judge Howell Melton and reporter George Allen, would be invaluable when the racial difficulties consumed St. Augustine in 1964. George covered the case for the *News-Journal* and became an important ally in the drama. Little did I realize it, but the looming racial crisis unfolding in St. Augustine, which would be closely followed by news media from around the world, would engulf my life throughout the summer of 1964. My life would be threatened, as would the lives of my children. In the growing conflict, I would need all the help I could muster.

4   The Point of No Return

On Friday, March 27, Mrs. Malcolm Peabody, accompanied by her friend Mrs. John Burgess, arrived in St. Augustine. They had been invited, she said, to come to St. Augustine by the Southern Christian Leadership Conference, and they had come to be arrested. The mayor was all too willing to accommodate her. He blamed the disturbances that accompanied their appearance in the city "on northern 'scalawags,' . . . who came down here with the idea of getting [put] in jail."[1]

On April 1, 1964, the headline of the *Daytona Beach News-Journal* told the story: "Mrs. Peabody Is Jailed Overnight in Sit-ins." The reality of the racial crisis brewing in St. Augustine for more than a year had been brought directly into America's living room and onto my doorstep. The image of Mary Peabody—wife of an Episcopal bishop, aristocratic mother of the governor of Massachusetts, and cousin of Eleanor Roosevelt—being led by armed deputies from a restaurant to be incarcerated in the county jail was news that shocked the nation and much of the civilized world.

She had been arrested, Tuesday, March 31, at the Ponce de Leon Motor Lodge, along with three companions, William England, a minister; Robert Hayling, a local dentist and civil rights activist; and Esther Burgess, the wife of the first black Episcopal bishop in Massachusetts. Earlier that morning Peabody had tried to attend the 10:00 a.m. Easter week communion service at Trinity Episcopal Church. The service was canceled, and when they arrived at the church a vestryman told Mrs. Peabody, "We do not want any demonstrations of any kind."[2] Undeterred, she and her companions proceeded to the Ponce de Leon Motor Lodge. When the racially mixed group was refused service, they remained at the restaurant until they were arrested.

The story attracted the attention of news organizations across the country to the growing racial crisis in St. Augustine. Soon, more than fifty media representatives from all over the world had descended on the city. They were eager to send their newspapers and television stations an account of the seventy-two-year-old Peabody's defiance of the city and state segregation laws. This act of conscience by a member of one of America's oldest and most distinguished family's fueled the flames of civil disobedience that had been smoldering for more than a year in St. Augustine.

Photographs of policemen restraining snarling police dogs while herding the genteel grandmother to a paddy wagon created a sensation throughout the United States and beyond. The jailing of Governor Endicott Peabody's mother focused attention on the segregation practices of the St. Augustine. Members of the Senate, who were at that moment debating the civil rights bill, took notice.

Tobias Simon of Miami, and John M. Pratt and William Kunstler of New York City, attorneys for the SCLC, immediately filed petitions for writs of habeas corpus in the federal district court in Jacksonville, seeking Mary Peabody's release from custody and removal of the case from state to federal court. They also sought the release of others arrested with her. In a well-coordinated effort, hearings were immediately scheduled before federal district court judge Bryan Simpson. Peabody, who elected to stay in jail two nights rather than post bond, was taken by police vehicle to the hearing in Jacksonville on April 2. Others arrested were William Sloan Coffin Jr., chaplain of Yale University; David Robinson, another chaplain from Yale; Robert Hayling, the defiant dentist and civil rights activist from St. Augustine; and a fifteen-year-old demonstrator named Annie Ruth Evans. Evans was one of a growing number of young people whose acts of courage in defying the racial customs of St. Augustine were fueling the growing protest against segregation in the city.

At the start of the hearing, the attorney representing the city made a serious mistake. He addressed Miss Evans as "Ruthie," a long-standing

and degrading practice used in most of the South to address blacks. Instantly on his feet, Tobias Simon, an expert in constitutional law, vigorously objected to the form of address. He called the court's attention to
a recent Supreme Court decision prohibiting attorneys from addressing
witnesses by their first names; Judge Simpson sustained the objection. He
instructed counsel to address the witness by her surname, prefixed by the
respectful title of "Miss." Most southerners used this mode of greeting
when addressing unmarried white women but never in addressing blacks.
Using only a person's first name clearly conveyed the idea of inferiority.

Judge Simpson refused to move the cases to federal court, ruling that
the county courts of St. Augustine must handle the cases. Judge Simpson's refusal to remove state cases pending in St. Augustine to the federal
court in Jacksonville clearly reflected deference given by federal courts
to the sovereignty of state courts in local police matters, one dating back
to Supreme Court decisions in the 1870s. Simpson did, however, order
the sheriff, L. O. Davis, to accept appearance bonds rather than the cash
bonds he had demanded. Bail bonds in state courts only required 10 percent of the face value of the bond to be paid to bondsmen. Requiring the
full cash amount of the bond was intended to deter demonstrators.[3] The
decision not to move the trials was promptly appealed to the Fifth Circuit Court of Appeals in New Orleans, where on Wednesday April 5,
1964, federal appellate court judge Elbert Tuttle ordered local prosecu-
tions postponed until the appeals court could hear the case.

To the surprise of many in the courtroom, Judge Simpson added his
personal opinion as to the merits of the case: "I hear opinions expressed
that nobody can be acquitted. I suggest that maybe not many should be.
If somebody sticks his neck in a noose and then complains that the rope
burns, there isn't much to complain about."[4] The judge would later change
his mind about the tactics used by officials in St. Augustine in the use of
city ordinances and Jim Crow laws to suppress the demonstrations and
the quality of justice available to blacks in the misdemeanor courts of
St. Johns County.

During Easter week, eighty-one demonstrators, including Mary Peabody, had been arrested, some for "refusing to move while blocking a
sidewalk." Though demonstrators picketed vital spots in St. Augustine,
such as the chamber of commerce, City Gates, the Slave Market, and the

Hotel Ponce de Leon Hotel, they did not interfere with the annual Easter parade. The parade, which always attracted large crowds, drew an estimated thirty-five thousand spectators.

Fifty-three of the demonstrators were scheduled to appear before county judge Charles Mathis the day after the hearing in Jacksonville. Since demonstrations had begun in 1963, some 238 of those arrested had had their cases stayed by order of the federal court. In the case of these 53, Judge Mathis ordered their bonds forfeited when they failed to appear in court. Simon admitted he made a mistake in failing to arrange with the court for a continuance. The defendants who failed to appear were immediately rearrested and again required to post bonds, resulting in considerable additional expense to the demonstrators. Petitions for writs of habeas corpus for these cases were immediately filed in federal court, this time with federal district court judge Albert L. Reeves, of Dunedin, Florida, who promptly ordered the defendants released on their original bonds. In a statement for the press, Simon assured Judge Mathis that the defendants would appear. He added that there had been no need to rearrest them and claimed that the rearrests constituted harassment.[5]

Lines were now drawn between officials in St. Augustine and attorneys representing the demonstrators. In the coming battle, which would be fought in the federal court in Jacksonville, the demonstrators would assert their constitutional rights to demonstrate, free from interference by state and local officials. Ferris Bryant would try to use the pre–Civil War strategy of nullification and interposition as a political tool to block federal courts from interfering with the right of the state to control civil disobedience. This would lead to a dramatic confrontation between the right of federal or state courts to control the demonstrations. At issue were the rights of free speech and peaceful assembly.

The hatred that King found in St. Augustine in 1964 was similar to the unreasoning passions that had inflamed South Carolina congressman Preston S. Brooks when he brutally cane-whipped Massachusetts senator Charles Sumner on the floor of the Senate chambers on May 22, 1856. The assault by Brooks to avenge the presumed insult to the South that Sumner made in his "crime against Kansas" speech was similar to the passions that exploded in members of the Ku Klux Klan during the summer of 1964 in St. Augustine. This unreasoning antipathy toward any effort to desegregate the races had been exploited and used by many southern politicians to protect their privileged position at the expense of blacks. And after more than a hundred years it was still working. Funds collected by St. Augustine business establishments to support the activities of the Ancient City Gun Club and its ally the Ku Klux Klan were grim evidence that the politics of prejudice were very much alive in the city.

In bringing his legion of seasoned, disciplined civil rights veterans to the nation's oldest city, Martin Luther King was seeking to demonstrate to the nation the truly evil nature of the nation's oldest problem, segregation. He also needed to demonstrate the complicity of the leaders of the city in preserving segregation. If he could not accomplish this, his claim that "St. Augustine was the most segregated city in America" would be questioned as well as his tactics of peaceful demonstrations.

For perhaps the only time in the history of the civil rights movement in the South, law enforcement officers, under an executive order of the governor, would afford protection to the demonstrators. This order would deny to Martin Luther King the most valuable tactic he had in using civil disobedience as a weapon to break the back of segregation in the South. Obstruction of this right by law enforcement would surely bring the federal courts into the battle to protect the rights of free speech and peaceful assembly. In past civil rights demonstrations in the South, King had counted on local law enforcement to interfere with these federally protected rights.

He would also force the city to come to grips with the dilemma of maintaining segregation at the same time the business community attempted to encourage tourists to come to St. Augustine to celebrate its four hundredth anniversary. King needed to keep the movement's dream alive, fueled by his controversial passive resistance demonstrations; he had to win in St. Augustine. While St. Augustine offered King the ideal place to focus the attention of the nation and much of the free world on the plight of blacks, it presented a challenge to his leadership that he had not foreseen.

In the upcoming conflict, King would be advised by Tobias Simon, one of the best constitutional lawyers of the day, possibly the best in the country. A Jew from Miami, and a Harvard-educated civil rights activist who could have made a fortune in corporate law, he chose, instead, to represent causes that would advance human rights. King could not have chosen a better advocate for the upcoming battle.[6] Violent opposition by the Klan was in sharp contrast to the peaceful marches of the SCLC. Tobias Simon knew the constitutional issues by heart. King sounded the charge when he told a cheering crowd of his followers he had come "determined to continue the struggle in St. Augustine, until the battle for justice is won. . . . We have reached the point of no return; there's no turning back now."[7]

Mary Peabody left St. Augustine on April 2, after spending two nights in jail and attending the hearing held before Judge Simpson in Jacksonville. Shortly after her arrest, she and a group of protesters asked the St. Augustine Quadricentennial Commission to withdraw support of the anniversary celebration. The letter was signed by Mary Peabody, Robert B. Hayling, Hosea Williams, C. R. Steele, William Sloane Coffin Jr., Jacques P. Bessier , and G. L. Burkholder.[8] It was an attempt to focus the nation's attention on the moral price a community must pay to continue segregation in its churches, businesses, and public accommodations.

Not everyone in Boston agreed with Peabody's act of defiance. Harold J. Ockenga, the pastor of Boston's historic Park Street Church, said that the participation of northerners in race demonstrations in the South "is doing more harm than good. . . . The whole situation is rapidly deteriorating. If we break the law by forcing the situation we are going to encourage the extremist groups. We ought to be careful what we do."[9]

The pastor of the Meriden First Baptist Church, in Meriden, N.H., thought the Communists were involved with the NAACP, and in a letter to Mrs. Bernard Segel, of Hanover, N.H., he outlined his reasoning: "That there are Communist agitators within the framework of the NAACP who are skilled in agitation is all to[o] painfully evident." Though he expressed his belief in civil rights, saying, "I believe the Negro ought to have a right as a free citizen. But not at the expense of flaunting the laws that are in existence," he also said that Mrs. Peabody acted in "an un-scriptural manner." Even the president said that civil rights demonstrations do their cause "no good when they resort to civil disobedience and threaten the health or safety of the people."[10]

In St. Augustine, a headline proclaimed: "This City Shall Survive." "Taking all things into consideration," said the editor, "we feel that St. Augustine will survive the visit of Mrs. Malcolm Peabody, the mother of the governor of Massachusetts." Expressing the view held by a majority of whites in St. Augustine, the editor continued, "St. Augustine has been selected as a 'civil rights' target, mainly to discredit the 400th anniversary in 1965. In this respect the northern press and television are cooperating to the fullest." After noting that the *Orlando Sentinel* was one of the outstanding newspapers in the state, the editor went on to quote from an editorial headlined "She Should Have Stayed In Boston." "Moving on, we find that the mother of the Massachusetts governor, a resident of Boston, came to St. Augustine to participate in civil rights demonstrations, and got herself arrested for refusing to leave a segregated restaurant when ordered to by the police. . . . On reflection, it seems Mrs. Malcolm Peabody, the Governor's mother, might have accomplished more by staying in Boston and trying to effect more harmony between the race's there." The article went on to note that in a disturbance that had occurred on St. Patrick's Day, the NAACP's float, featuring photographs of the late president, had been pelted by "beer cans, soft-drink bottles, eggs, tomatoes, ice cream, sandwiches and other debris."[11]

Citing letters that had been received from New England citizens, the editor observed that each had the same tone; he quoted from four: "This is sent," one wrote, "in hope that you will print it so the people of St. Augustine will know that a great many of us here in Massachusetts are not at all in favor of the spectacle which Mrs. Peabody is making of herself and our state." Another said, "If Mrs. Peabody is genuinely interested in furthering the cause of civil rights and racial equality, there is no more fertile field in the United States than in her home state." A writer from Stoneham, Massachusetts, said, "I am sincerely sorry and upset over the conduct of people from the state of Massachusetts, who go all over the south disobeying laws and causing race wars." The last letter was from a seventy-two-year-old Boston woman who wrote, "Boston is badly segregated and why not help the Negroes in Boston instead of traveling all the way to Florida to help them. It is hypocrisy.'"[12] The mayor of St. Augustine agreed: "People like the Peabodys live in exclusive suburbs. They don't practice what they preach. They are the true hypocrites."[13]

In an editorial that ran later in April, the *St. Augustine Record* took aim at Martin Luther King with a headline that proclaimed, "King Starts

Crusade against FBI." "The recent announcement by Martin Luther King, left-wing leader of the Southern Christian Leadership 'Conference,' . . . that the FBI and their leader J. Edgar Hoover [are] aiding the right wing in 'smearing' the Civil Rights movement is utter nonsense," it began. "There is no greater American than J. Edger Hoover," the newspaper proclaimed. A man who "has advocated that the primary goal of the Communist Party is to crush us from within," and "now, a man that advocates violence of municipal, county, state and federal law to accomplish his crusade for corrective steps in equal rights for negroes brand[s] such a man as Hoover as a 'racist.'" The editorial continued: "The FBI under the direction of Hoover has done more to eliminate the reported complaints of civil rights groups than Martin Luther King and all other civil rights leaders combined. Hoover has not found it necessary to send agents in the streets carrying signs, blocking traffic and violating the civil rights of over 90 percent of the American population."[14]

On April 5, after the Tuesday communion service was canceled, effectively blocking Mary Peabody's attempt to integrate the church, Bishop Hamilton West ordered all his churches to admit anyone who wished to attend services. On April 13, in a well-coordinated move, five blacks attended service at Trinity Episcopal Church. It had allegedly been arranged by Charles Seymour, pastor of the church. "The Negroes came in just like everyone else, and they took their seats just like everyone else. Nobody paid any attention," he said.[15]

Some members of Trinity's vestry did pay attention. They refused to follow the bishop or Reverend Seymour's lead. David R. Colburn frames the confrontation between the pastor and vestry. Meeting shortly after the service on the twelfth, members drafted a resolution to the bishop "censuring the National Council of the Episcopal Church for its position on civil rights and asking other parishes in the diocese to join with them in 'deploring the participation of Church Officials and laity in any activities, [or] demonstrations . . . which [violate] or willfully ignore the law, or which [disregard] the property rights of others, or make a mockery of the Church by using it as a tool.'"[16]

A. H. Tebault Jr., editor of the *St. Augustine Record;* Hargrove Norris, head of the John Birch Society in St. Augustine; and E. W. Trice, another conservative member of the church, made their dissatisfaction with

Reverend Seymour public knowledge. Norris called him "very weak" and willing to follow the liberal policies of the national church. As David Colburn noted, "Tebault echoed Norris's view, criticizing Seymour and the Episcopal Church, in general, for its excessive concern with the secular world."[17]

Mary Peabody left St. Augustine on April 2 but that did not end her involvement with the city. On April 13, she appeared on NBC's *Today Show;* she explained why she had gone to St. Augustine and described the hate and violence she found in the city. It was not a pretty picture she painted, and the local political leadership demanded equal time from NBC. The mayor, joined by the other commissioners, demanded that they be allowed to respond to Mrs. Peabody's allegations in order "to present the true and correct conditions that exist in St. Augustine." He said the SCLC's "spring project" was "actively engaging in violating the laws of the state and the city."[18]

After tedious negotiations with the television network, the mayor and a contingent of local officials were allowed to appear on the *Today Show* for a fourteen-minute rebuttal. The program aired on the evening of May 10. The mayor claimed that Mary Peabody's appearance "did irreparable harm to race relations in St. Augustine." He also claimed that she took the word of Robert Hayling rather than "check[ing] with him or other city leaders into the motives and grievances of the Negro leader."[19] In Mayor Shelley, the John Birch Society, the Klan, and many of St. Augustine's leading citizens, as well as the governor, Martin Luther King and his followers found adversaries who would come close to defeating their efforts at a critical moment in the civil rights movement.

During the past six months, I had spent most of my time in St. Augustine. I prosecuted four major first-degree murder cases; one, twice because of a mistrial, and now, in April 1964, I was running hard for reelection. The primary would be held in May. I had only one opponent, Joe Scarlett, a classmate from Stetson Law School. We were both Democrats and had no Republican opposition, so the election would be decided in May.

I considered St. Johns and neighboring Putnam County as essential to my reelection. In the special election that had been held in September 1962, I lost Volusia and Flagler counties but won in Putnam and

St. Johns with a margin of only 353 votes. After the election, I worked hard in the two northern counties and established important contacts among business and political leaders, especially in St. Augustine.

Hamilton Upchurch Jr. had been my assistant in St. Augustine when I first became state attorney, and through his contacts I was able to cultivate a number of important leaders in this small, tight-knit community. One of the partners in the Upchurch law firm was Howell Melton, who had been appointed circuit court judge by Governor Bryant about the same time I was appointed an assistant state attorney. I had successfully prosecuted the Effie Norris murder case before Judge Melton back in December 1963, as well as the Virginia Lee murder case that I had tried earlier in 1963. We had established a certain degree of trust during the course of the two trials and this would be important to me when my office was engaged full time in an attempt to resolve the racial conflict.

The senior Upchurch, Hamilton's father and the founder of the firm, was one of St. Augustine's leading citizens. A Presbyterian, he had been mayor of the city, a member of the Florida House of Representatives, and a state senator. He ran for governor in 1944 but was defeated by Millard Caldwell. Like most of the power structure in St. Johns County, he was a Democrat, although a conservative one. A delegate to the National Democratic Party in 1948, he had broken with the party over the race issue and helped form the Dixiecrat Party. Senator Strom Thurmond of South Carolina was nominated as its presidential candidate. Upchurch was highly respected in the community but kept a low profile, acting as an elder statesman for the community's political elite.

H. E. Wolfe, St. Augustine's most successful businessman and another of its leading citizens, was originally from Tennessee. He settled in St. Johns County in 1917 and became a farmer and a rancher. He had many business enterprises, including two banks that he founded, one in the farming community of Hastings outside St. Augustine, the other in Palatka. He served as vice president of San Marco Contracting Company, one of the state's leading road building companies and as the longtime chairman of St. Augustine's Historical Preservation Board. He also served on numerous boards, including the Florida East Coast Railway and Florida Southern College. His magnificent antebellum home on Kings Street, Markland Place, was one of St. Augustine's most beautiful residences. After his death it was donated by his daughter to Flagler College.

Charles C. Mathis, the longtime county judge of St. Johns County, used the power of his office to harass juveniles demonstrating for equality in St. Augustine. Federal judge Bryan Simpson labeled his handling of juveniles an "arbitrary and capricious act of harassment."[20] He was referring, no doubt, to the controversial order the judge entered on July 23, 1963, prohibiting picketing and participation in demonstrations by juveniles throughout St. Johns County. The "directive," issued to all "law enforcement officers and constables," ordered that "in the event any person under the age of 17 years is found to be picketing or demonstrating without an order from the juvenile court authorizing the same shall be ordered to 'cease and desist,' to immediately return to their parents or guardian and appear in the Juvenile Court the following day unless that day be a Saturday, Sunday or holiday, thence the first working day following." The directive also authorized any law enforcement officer to arrest the offender if the "child fails to immediately cease to picket." The court found that "picketing and demonstrations, by children, was detrimental to the health, morals, and well being of 'persons' subject [to] the jurisdiction of the Juvenile Court."[21] The order was certainly detrimental to their First Amendment rights.

Juveniles would play an important role in the demands by a quarter of the population for a place at the table in the celebrations scheduled to take place in 1965. And as plans for the quadricentennial got under way, reporters were flocking to St. Augustine. Mary Peabody wasn't just any "northern scalawag," she was the mother of the governor of Massachusetts and that fact could not be ignored or made to go away by her arrest.

Where the NAACP had failed in St. Augustine, the SCLC would succeed. The time was now ripe for King's dramatic entrance into the city.

5   The Fuse Is Lit

On June 11, 1964, Martin Luther King, accompanied by Ralph D. Abernathy, appeared on the steps of the Monson Motor Lodge in the heart of St. Augustine and made a bold move at a defining moment in the civil rights movement.

James Brock, the motel manager, met them at the entrance to the lodge and told the assembled group they could not enter. "We're segregated at this time," he said. King, who was accompanied by eight other civil rights activists, including William England, a white chaplain from Boston University, refused to leave.[1] After a short, polite exchange, Brock called the police. Sheriff L. O. Davis and Chief Virgil Stuart arrived on the scene and instructed the group to leave. When they refused to do so, they were arrested. King and the others declined to post bail and were locked up in the crowded St. Johns county jail. Each was charged with the misdemeanors of trespassing with malice, intent to breach the peace, and conspiracy.

What made this act of defiance particularly timely was that a filibuster of the civil rights bill had been taking place in the Senate for almost two months, a filibuster designed by nineteen southern senators to derail the bill. Passage of the civil rights bill hung in the balance and, with it, the issue of segregated private facilities catering to the general public in interstate commerce. Much of the Senate's debate on the civil rights bill centered on the equal opportunity section and the right to jury trials in all criminal cases of contempt except voting rights cases. Republican senator

Thurston B. Morton of Kentucky offered the amendments, and on June 9 the Senate voted to include trial by jury in the bill. A provision to have the federal government finance training to deal with the continuing problem of school desegregation was defeated. As the debate continued, violence was rising in St. Augustine.

By June 8, Senator Mansfield had formally filed a petition to invoke the Senate's debating limit. Thirty-eight senators signed the petition: twenty-seven Democrats and eleven Republicans. King's goal was to keep the public eye on the evils of segregation until Congress passed a civil rights bill. If the bill passed, segregation would be defeated in one fell swoop. If King lost the public's support, he could very well lose passage of the civil rights bill.

On the same Thursday morning that King and Ralph Abernathy were arrested in front of the Monson Motor Lodge, the Senate voted to invoke cloture on the filibuster that had been going on for seventy-five days. Democrats voting against cloture were Bible of Nevada, Byrd and Robertson of Virginia, Byrd of West Virginia, Eastland and Stennis of Mississippi, Elender and Long of Louisiana, Ervin and Jordan of North Carolina, Fulbright and McClellan of Arkansas, Gore and Walters of Tennessee, Hayden of Arizona, Hill and Sparkman of Alabama, Holland and Smathers of Florida, Johnson and Thurmond of South Carolina, and Russell and Talmadge of Georgia. Six Republicans also voted against: Bennett of Utah, Goldwater of Arizona, Mechem of New Mexico, Simpson of Wyoming, Tower of Texas, and Young of North Dakota.[2]

Senator Everett Dirksen of Illinois had arranged the political maneuver that finally broke the filibuster. He introduced a substitute motion, worked out by Attorney General Robert Kennedy and revised late at night, to provide for jury trials in criminal contempt cases. This had been one of the major stumbling blocks to the bill's passage. This compromise yielded the votes necessary to invoke the Senate's cloture rule.

Victory was in sight; all King had to do was to keep up the pressure. He was confident that political leaders in St. Augustine would unwittingly cooperate by defying his efforts to seek access to private businesses and accommodations that would be covered if the bill passed. One thing was sure: the nation's attention would be focused on the brutal actions of the Klan and the adamant stand elected officials of St. Augustine had taken to prevent demonstrators from protesting segregation of private businesses. In *Peterson v. Greenville* the Supreme Court failed to address the constitutionality of a state's right to arrest demonstrators and enforce trespass laws that allowed private business establishments to choose whom to serve. In that case, Justice Harlan offered a vigorous dissent, that mere enforcement of trespass laws by states in relation to arbitrary actions of private business establishments "that have chosen to exclude persons of the Negro race" is not "state action of a particular character" that violates the Fourteenth Amendment. Outlawing segregation in interstate commerce would affect almost every business establishment in the South, and across the country. This was the fuel that fed the filibuster.

The right of private business to decide who would be allowed to enter a business was dear to the hearts of most southern senators and to officeholders in St. Augustine. Passage of legislation that affected the cherished right to segregate private business was bound to inflame their collective passions. King's actions in challenging the legal premise of Justice Harlan's dissent was a bold move and hit a particularly sensitive ideological spot in the political armor of the mayor of St. Augustine. That the world would be watching had been ensured when a battery of newsmen appeared with King on the steps of the Monson Motor Lodge. St. Augustine was to become a laboratory for social justice. King's campaign for equality hung in the balance as did the passage of a meaningful civil rights bill. The specter of a racist society would also be on trial in St. Augustine. The world was watching.

Since Mary Peabody's arrest on March 31, King's entry into the conflict had been anticipated by local authorities. His threat to bring his "spring campaign" to St. Augustine to demonstrate against segregation had now become a reality. He had rented a cottage, and in anticipation of the violence that always confronted any effort to break down social barriers to desegregation, training sessions had been conducted by civil rights veterans such as Fred Shuttlesworth, C. T. Vivian, Andrew Young, and Dorothy Cotton. The training was designed to educate the young people flocking to the cause in the intricate legal and diplomatic art of self-restraint, an absolute necessity for peaceful demonstrations to be successful.

These nightly sessions were held at St. Paul's Methodist Church, where at one of the meetings Dorothy Cotton, a speaker from the Atlanta-based SCLC, had told a group of eager young people their souls were about to be tested. "March with love in your hearts," she said, love for those who would have weapons and who might set upon you. "Don't judge them by the color of their skin—don't think of them as white people, but as people with guilt in their souls."[3] The young people who responded to King's plea for help would be sorely tested but they would march unafraid into the darkness of the night with only the love in their hearts to protect them.

White Christian churches in St. Augustine were also about to be tested, for the civil rights demonstrations were a moral crusade for social and racial justice. On Sunday, May 31, several churches in the city were approached by young demonstrators seeking admission to the morning service. They were turned away. At Grace Methodist Church, a member of the church told one of the youths, "We don't know these people, we don't know you. We have no way of knowing them or understanding them. We just want to be left alone in peace."[4]

Christian churches in the South had struggled for generations over the issue of segregation. During the civil rights movement of the 1950s and 1960s, some sought to justify segregation by reference to passages found in the Bible; others sought a middle ground and attempted to avoid the issue: and some, like Charles Seymour of Trinity Episcopal, met it head on, believing that the right to worship should not be restricted by the color of a person's skin. Many who adopted that third option would be forced to resign or to leave their churches for reasons of conscience.

When the training sessions began in late May, C. T. Vivian of the SCLC was one of the people who helped prepare demonstrators for the nightly marches soon to take place. Each participant was taught the nonviolent techniques of King's movement, and each march was closely supervised by one of King's trusted lieutenants.

The training sessions began none too soon. On the evening of May 28, 1964, a group of whites roughed up Associated Press photographer James P. Kerlin and a reporter as they covered the demonstrations. Young hoodlums attacked Kerlin, taking his camera and destroying the film he had shot of the event. After law enforcement officers retrieved his camera and returned it to Kerlin, he was once again attacked and repeatedly struck in the face and back. This time his camera was dashed to the ground. Finally the sheriff and other officers rescued him and escorted him out of the area.

It was a prelude to the violence that would become a daily event. It made national news of the kind that only an attack on the news media can make and galvanized the press across the country. Soon St. Augustine was swarming with reporters and television crews from across the nation and around the world. They would remain for most of the summer.

Police Chief Stuart thought the assault on Kerlin had been "a kind of Hollywood production with cameras in action." He added, "I didn't like to have police officers participating in that kind of production."[5] Apparently Kerlin's injuries and the destruction of his camera were part of the staged event. This attitude by local law enforcement—that the demonstrations were a "kind of production"—was at the heart of the problem. Unfortunately escalating violence would now take center stage and it was real, not staged.

The *Daytona Beach News-Journal* led the way in condemning the attacks, with editorials calling for the state to end the conflict so that community leaders, in a spirit of "calm determination," could work out a solution to the city's mounting racial problem. But there were few calm minds in the hate-filled city.

On May 29, following three days of racial unrest, city officials met to consider what measures could be taken to end the increasingly disruptive demonstrations. The city manager, Charles Barrier, Police Chief Virgil Stuart, and Sheriff L. O. Davis met with Judge Charles Mathis Jr. to consider placing a ban on demonstrations. This was highly unusual, as Judge Mathis might later be called upon to pass judgment on those arrested as a result of such a ban. However, he had used his office in the past to preempt the right of juveniles to demonstrate and the meeting represented the creation of a united local front to restrict demonstrations. It also represented an effort by law enforcement and the judiciary to limit the constitutional rights of the demonstrators.

On Monday night, June 1, the city commission amended a city ordinance, making it unlawful for minors under the age of eighteen to be on city streets or in public places between 9:00 p.m. and 5:00 a.m. unless on their way to work.[6] Night demonstrations had been banned at a previous meeting, and on June 5, 1964, the city refused to issue parade permits for night marches. Parade routes were also restricted. This emergency ordinance was immediately challenged by Tobias Simon. He filed a petition on behalf of the SCLC in federal district court in Jacksonville seeking protection from the violence of the Klan and enjoining St. Augustine from interfering with peaceful demonstrations. Judge Simpson set an emergency hearing the next day.

The violence that now besieged the marchers impelled King to call a news conference and issue a warning. "The city has an opportunity to do something before demonstrations resume," he was quoted in the *News-Journal* on June 6. "When we resume demonstrations, probably early next week, it will be on a massive scale."[7] This merely hardened the resolve of St. Augustine's civic leaders, including the editor of the local newspaper. In an editorial published in the *St. Augustine Record* on Friday, June 1, the paper had printed in full an editorial written by Jack W. Gore from the *Fort Lauderdale News*.

Once again the venerable city of St. Augustine became the focal point of heated racial agitation last week, and once again the blame for this sorry situation can be put right on the backs of professional troublemakers who have come into Florida for the express purpose of stirring up strife and discord. The self-styled leader of this most recent invasion is Dr. Martin Luther King who seems to think that he and his followers don't have to observe laws which apply to others, and who, because of his propensity for stirring up trouble, always seems to attract a veritable horde of television cameramen, and newspaper photographers to record his determination to have his way regardless of who gets hurt in the process. . . . From the manner in which Rev. King and his followers are behaving one would think they have some kind of a divine immunity from observing laws all the rest of us are required to observe and respect. And from the sympathetic reaction they are receiving from federal courts, from Washington and from many newspapers and television interests, it begins to appear that we are in an era where belonging to a certain minority group conveys law breaking privileges not enjoyed by any other group of people.[8]

On Friday, June 5, the *News-Journal* urged Governor Bryant to act. It noted that so far the governor had offered no leadership in the crisis in St. Augustine, remarking that he had not even responded to known Klan activity. "The law enforcement sent into the city" the editor said, "was merely enforcement that ignores armed terrorism."[9] Apparently the governor finally got the message.

On Monday, June 8, 1964, my family and I were preparing for our annual vacation in the mountains of western North Carolina. I was in St. Augustine that day attending to some last-minute business. The 53 defendants who had been arrested in April along with Mary Peabody were to be arraigned before Judge Mathis. The hallway was packed with defendants, attorneys, and reporters. Altogether 238 people had been arrested for trespass, conspiracy, and the vague charge of being an "undesirable guest." Demonstrators awaiting trial, mostly young blacks, had been confined in an outdoor pen behind the county jail in the relentless heat of the day.

Having completed my business, I was working my way through the crowd in the courthouse when a secretary from Judge Mathis's office stopped me in the hall. She said that Governor Bryant was on the phone and wanted to speak with me. I took the call in the judge's chambers and received the news that I was to be the governor's personal representative in St. Augustine under an emergency statute passed by the legislature in 1955 to deal with racial unrest. The order clothed me with extraordinary powers that the legislature had conferred upon the governor and those acting under his authority. I had no prior indication the governor intended to take this step. "Dan," he cautioned me, "you must use this power with care. The legislature has given me almost unlimited power to deal with the existing emergency and you must be very careful and use the power only under the most extraordinary circumstances." He directed that any order I issued be cosigned by Joe Jacobs, an assistant to Jimmy Kynes, Florida's attorney general. Jacobs, a longtime friend of mine, had been assigned to St. Augustine by the attorney general. He would be easy to work with, and I welcomed his help.

The legislature kept tight control over the operation of the 1955 act by making it effective for only two years at a time. It expired on July 1 after each biannual legislative session. The act had been used only once before, by former Governor Collins when he had invoked it to help curb racial violence in Tallahassee during the desegregation of the city bus system in 1955. Under the law (chapter 14 of the general laws of the state) the governor was authorized to take all steps necessary to keep the peace and prevent violence. It granted the governor blanket authority to decide what action to take and when to take it. The act was being invoked now to deal with the critical situation in St. Augustine.

I assumed my responsibilities immediately. After King's arrest on June 11, I quickly reviewed the situation and decided it was imperative to begin a dialogue with King as soon as possible. Since no one else in authority in St. Augustine would talk with him or others in the movement leadership, I would have to do so. It was imperative that I find out what King wanted and, if it was legal and reasonable, take the necessary steps to accomplish it. I also had to make clear to King that I was not part of the problem, that, in fact, I wanted to be part of the solution and would take whatever action I could to help resolve the current difficulties.

I decided the best way to start a useful dialogue was to have the grand jury, then in recess, immediately reimpaneled and charged with the responsibility to take action. I sought out circuit judge Howell Melton, the judge assigned to St. Augustine. During the Effie Norris "arsenic and old lace" trial, Melton and I had forged a relationship of mutual trust. More importantly, I knew he had no trouble making tough decisions. When he was later confirmed as a federal judge by the U.S. Senate, it was said that in investigating his fitness to be a federal judge, the FBI could find no one who voiced a negative word about his character. His help would be important in the current crisis. Any order he issued would defuse the criticism that was sure to follow an announcement of the grand jury's actions.

The judge's chambers were on the second floor of the courthouse. I went straight to his chambers and informed him of my appointment by the governor to represent him in St. Augustine. I asked him to issue an order reimpaneling the St. Johns County grand jury. I also advised him of my intention to use the grand jury as a mediating panel to defuse the mounting violence and to have the jury appoint a biracial committee to deal with the situation. He readily agreed to my requests and drafted the necessary orders, which he signed that afternoon at 4:45.

I also asked if he would use his influence to intercede with H. E. Wolfe, his wife's uncle, to help with the appointment of a biracial committee. Wolfe was the richest and one of the most influential people in St. Augustine. A distinguished man, then in his sixties, he was the key to convincing business leaders to accept the grand jury's recommendations. If I could convince him of the need for the grand jury to appoint a biracial committee, it had a good chance for success.

The present grand jury comprised eighteen county residents, with only one black among its members. It was quite likely a majority would be hostile to the civil rights demonstrations, and I needed twelve of the eighteen members to vote for the appointment of a biracial committee. Wolfe's influence would be critical in convincing the grand jury to act over the opposition of the mayor. With his support I believed we could successfully bypass the mayor, who was blocking all attempts to deal with Martin Luther King and the SCLC.

I scheduled a session of the grand jury for 9:00 a.m. on June 12. Testimony before a grand jury is secret. Secrecy was important to protect the witnesses I intended to call from being intimidated by racist elements in the community. Grand juries are impaneled twice yearly in each of Florida's sixty-seven counties so one is always available if need arises. There was no question in my mind that someone in authority needed to start a dialogue with those seeking change, and the grand jury was the legal entity that had the highest degree of integrity in St. Johns County. The county's citizens trusted and respected it, and with Wolfe's help, I believed I could convince the grand jury to act, even over the mayor's objections. The use of a grand jury to appoint a biracial committee had never been attempted in Florida, but I saw no legal reason it could not appoint one, if a majority of jury members agreed. The Quakers had taught me there is an inward light in each person and I intended to find it in at least twelve grand jury members.

Later that day, I called Governor Bryant to advise him of the progress we were making. I also released a copy of the order signed by Judge Melton to the press, announcing that the grand jury would start taking testimony from witnesses on Friday morning, June 12. I lined up an impressive array of witnesses, with my friend Attorney General Jimmy Kynes as the first witness. A former star football player for the University of Florida, Kynes would command the respect of the grand jury. I had become acquainted with him when he was an assistant state attorney in the fifth circuit in neighboring Marion County.

It was apparent I would receive no help from Mayor Shelley. The mayor, a devout Catholic, had already expressed fixed, unyielding opinions about the demonstrations, and these views were repeatedly expressed to the press and the public. The local Roman Catholic church, like most churches in St. Augustine, had failed to take any steps to help solve the racial problems taking place, literally, at its front door. Archbishop Hurley and his priests "remained hidden behind the doors of the cathedral to avoid involving themselves in the racial crisis which occurred adjacent to and, on some occasions, on church grounds."[10] Since I could not count on the mayor or ecclesiastical leaders for assistance in solving the racial problems, I had to find it from other sources in the community. H. E. Wolfe would fill that role.

At this point in the history of the civil rights movement, at least in our area of Florida, little positive information about King had been reported to the public. He was the charismatic leader of the Southern Christian Leadership Conference, which was challenging the racial inequities that existed in much of the United States. But many people really believed that movement was controlled by Communists. King had surrounded himself with loyal aides who carried out his directions for nonviolent tactics to the letter and, at the moment, the SCLC had become the most powerful force in the civil rights movement. Depending on one's view, King was either a saint or the devil incarnate. In St. Augustine his image was not a positive one. Hayling's invitation to King to come to St. Augustine had reinforced that image. Hayling's break with the NAACP gave King the opportunity to take the lead in the civil rights movement at a most propitious moment. It was a move that would define his legacy and give to him, rightly or wrongly, major credit for passage of the Civil Rights Act.

Hayling's impetuous and often militant attempts to deal with the civic leaders in St. Augustine, coupled with his rash statements about shooting first and asking questions later, had helped solidify local opposition to the civil rights movement. This opposition applied equally to King, especially when he labeled St. Augustine "the most segregated city in America." St. Augustine was certainly a segregated city, but at that time segregation was the rule throughout the South. And despite King's observations, racial prejudice in St. Augustine was not the same as in Selma, Birmingham, or Montgomery, or even Albany, Georgia. City officials and community leaders were incensed over what they considered to be a slanderous remark against their city, and King appeared to them to be as intemperate as Hayling. That perception left little room for compromise.

In an effort to deal with King's local image, Mabel Norris Chesley, associate editor of the *News-Journal*, wrote a widely circulated profile of Martin Luther King under the headline, "What Manner of Man Is Leading America's Negro Movement?" Mabel Chesley was a dedicated civil rights activist. She had taken on Sheriff Willis McCall, from neighboring Lake County, one of the most overtly racist sheriffs in Florida. She lost her small newspaper due to her courageous opposition to the sheriff, and after the paper failed, she was hired by Herbert Davidson, editor of the *News-Journal*. She found her voice under his tutelage. In answering her own question, she wrote, "To his lowliest followers, he is virtually a saint." She then outlined his demands: "We want desegregation of all public facilities; we want merit employment on the part of the city and county, a policy that is fair to our people; we want the appointment of a biracial committee, with two-thirds of its Negro members to be appointed by SCLC; we want all charges dropped against all participants in demonstrations who were peaceful and broke no unjust laws."[11] The citizens of St. Augustine were soon to learn a great deal more about this man and his determination to end segregation in their city.

It was vital that I have someone in St. Augustine whom I could trust. Since becoming state attorney I had become friendly with George Allen, a talented investigative reporter for the *Daytona Beach News-Journal*. George had covered a number of cases I had recently tried, including the Effie Norris murder trial in St. Augustine. We had become close friends and I knew I could trust him completely. During the Norris trial, I had sought a theme for my closing argument, one that would convey to the jury, in a dramatic way, the guilt of the defendant. The evidence of her guilt was built on strong circumstantial evidence; however, in a first-degree murder case the jury wants something more definite if they are to convict the defendant. On the last evening of the trial, before closing arguments were to commence the next morning, George and I were walking from the courthouse. He suggested I use a metaphor to explain my theory of the evidence. "Why not call the evidence 'footprints of guilt.' Use this theme to describe the conscious and unconscious acts of the defendant that will create a path of evidence leading the jury to the conclusion she was guilty of murdering her boyfriend." Weave a comparison, he urged, between the similarity of the boyfriend's poisoning and the poisoning of the other two victims. Let those footprints lead the jury to a guilty verdict, just as footprints lead an investigator from a crime scene directly to a guilty person. I admired George Allen's honesty, intellect, and his dedication to journalism. He was able to analyze complex situations, was highly ethical, and had shown sound judgment in all my past dealings with him. George would be an ideal companion during the racial conflict in St. Augustine.

On Tuesday, June 9, I stopped by the *News-Journal* to talk with the managing editor, Tippen Davidson. I asked him to assign George to St. Augustine. I needed someone who could be objective in reporting the news, preferably someone I had worked with in the past. I explained my plans and said this was an opportunity for the paper to obtain a firsthand report of the drama unfolding in St. Augustine. Tippen was not enthusiastic about the idea. He did not want to jeopardize the integrity of the paper and was concerned that my close association with George might impair the impartial judgment he required of all his reporters.

I explained how I intended to handle the crisis and eventually prevailed upon him to allow George to come with me to St. Augustine. He made it clear, however, that he would not allow any compromise of his duties as a journalist; he had to have the freedom to write anything he wanted without censorship on my part. I agreed that everything would be on the record. George Allen became one of the first "embedded" journalists in the civil rights movement.

On that same day, Judge Simpson issued several orders that had a significant impact on future demonstrations. He entered an order not only overturning the city's recent ban on night marches but also restricting the confinement of demonstrators in outdoor holding pens. (The sheriff, who had enlarged the outdoor holding compound before Judge Simpson prohibited its use, was now caught in a bind. The county jail was overflowing with demonstrators and the county had no place to house newly arrested demonstrators.) He also ordered that bonds of fifteen hundred to three thousand dollars set by Judge Mathis be reduced to a hundred dollars. If appearance bonds had remained in the higher amounts the demonstrations might have been canceled. He further ordered all juveniles released to their parents pending court appearances. This order reversed Judge Mathis's controversial decision remanding arrested minors to juvenile authorities as wards of the state.

These rulings sent a message to Judge Mathis about the federal court's view of the right to free speech and to petition the government for redress of grievances. It also sent a message to city officials: federal courts would keep a sharp eye on how demonstrators were treated by city and state officials. Grumbling was immediately heard among state and local authorities.

The most important of all the orders, the one that would cause the most trouble for law enforcement, required Sheriff L. O. Davis, Police Chief Virgil Stuart, Mayor Joe Shelley, and "all other officials in St. Augustine" to permit "peaceful and orderly demonstrations by marching in and about the city of St. Augustine and its public streets, sidewalks and parks at any hour in the night time." In rendering the opinion, Judge Simpson wrote, "If law enforcement agencies are willing to let people move in and take over the downtown area it is time for the state to take over. I think the state has the power to police a little place like St. Augustine."[12] This last remark was akin to waving a red flag in the face of a bull.

Tobias Simon hailed the orders as "precedent setting." He explained, "Until now, state courts had been using their powers to suppress the activities of demonstrators. . . . No one has the right to set bail as these people did, in amounts big enough to keep demonstrators in jail or bankrupt the organization trying to free them." These tactics, he continued, were being used "by city officials in an effort to break the spirit of the demonstrators."[13] Judge Simpson restricted bail to no more than one hundred dollars for each offense but he would not move the cases to federal court as Andrew Young had requested. The bonds, some of which had been forfeited to the county, were posted by Charles Cherry, a civil rights activist and businessman in Daytona Beach.

On Wednesday, June 10, the day after Simpson's orders, and despite a heavily armed escort, violence broke out again during a march by some four hundred demonstrators. In response, Governor Bryant ordered twenty additional Florida Highway Patrolmen into the city. This raised the number of state troopers in St. Augustine to 320, all under the command of J. W. Jourdan, the deputy inspector of the Florida Highway Patrol.

It should have been clear to officials in St. Johns County that if peaceful demonstrations were disrupted by the more virulent elements in the community, especially KKK members, the violence might well escalate beyond anyone's control. This would surely bring federal authorities into St. Augustine. When Judge Simpson refused to move Mary Peabody's case to a federal court, city officials had been elated. His most recent orders brought defiance and criticism from St. Augustine's political elite.

King made swift use of the order prohibiting law enforcement from interfering with peaceful nighttime demonstrations. Within hours of the order's being issued, more demonstrations were held. One, led by Andrew Young, occurred on the night of the tenth, with demonstrators marching two abreast through the old city. The requirement that demonstrators be permitted to march at night through the old section of St. Augustine was the most controversial and the most dangerous of Simpson's directives. The march was peaceful at first. But on the return trip, as demonstrators were passing by the old slave market, small bands of hoodlums began hit-and-run tactics, singling out white demonstrators for attack. One white marcher was surrounded by the angry mob and kicked and beaten as police officers tried to break up the attack. A number of demonstrators required medical attention. Initially, the few policemen in the area were caught off guard, but the undermanned officers quickly recovered and broke up the attacks.

The crowd began to throw rocks and bricks at the demonstrators, and despite the best efforts of law enforcement, the violence almost got out of hand. Tear gas was used, but still the crowd would not disperse. What could have become a riot was finally quelled, but it was a portent of the violence that was sure to follow Judge Simpson's order if someone in authority did not take control. It had been an extremely tense night, and in response, Sheriff Davis made a bizarre appeal to the citizens of St. Augustine urging them to sign up as deputy sheriffs. He intended to recruit two thousand untrained citizens to deal with the mounting violence, a foolhardy and potentially dangerous decision. I immediately conveyed my concerns to the governor. It was clear to me that Judge Simpson was determined to intervene directly in St. Augustine if state or local officials were unable to control violence and protect the demonstrators.

With the arrest of King and Abernathy, the Monson Motor Lodge became the focus of the demands for desegregation of private accommodations. Located in the center of the old city, just around the corner from the old slave market and near the old fort, which was a major tourist attraction, the motor lodge was used for meetings as well as business lunches. Civic clubs and other organizations met there weekly. The Monson now became not only a magnet for demonstrators but also a target for Klan violence. Sandwiched between the county courthouse and the city business district, this relatively small space would daily be crammed with hundreds of law enforcement officials, demonstrators, and a much larger group of Klansmen, newsmen, and onlookers.

Though the claim that slaves had once been sold at the park was disputed by many in St. Augustine, the park's symbolic power was not lost on King. The park was bordered by King Street on the south, the Catholic cathedral on the north, the Bridge of Lions on the east, and the most famous attraction in the city, the Castillo de San Marcos, on the north. Up Avenida Menendez, a short distance to the northeast, was the historical heart of the city. This area, with its narrow streets and alleys, was where the quadricentennial celebrations were to be held. It afforded scant protection to the army of marchers that King had mobilized in St. Augustine, many of whom were children. In the center of the area was the Monson Motor Lodge, which soon became the heart of King's daytime demonstrations and an icon in his message of racial equality: the elaborate celebration planned by the city could not be held here without eliminating segregated businesses. The symbolic value of the area was not lost on the Klan either, and it too staked out the area, gathering nightly at the park to harass demonstrators as they marched to the old city's center. This relatively small area afforded excellent cover for the KKK's guerrilla tactics.

Here, in the heart of St. Augustine's historic district, both sides would make their stand. The world would surely notice, as would the U.S. Senate. Democracy was headed for a showdown between the moral and legal force of the First Amendment and the South's ardent belief in states' rights.

For the past several days, I had been commuting to St. Augustine from Daytona Beach, a distance of some fifty-five miles. When the demonstrations began to take place at night, I had to consider moving. With the arrest of King and his companions on June 11, I ended my commute and moved to St. Augustine. George and I checked into the Monson Motor Lodge. Mary, with our six children, was scheduled to check in the following day. The children would have their summer vacation amid strife. As it turned out, this was not a smart move. But I didn't realize that the threat of violence would spill over into my personal life.

George and I settled down to implement the strategy we had discussed for ending the crisis. The time for a peaceful resolution was quickly running out. We needed to take immediate action.

While King remained in jail, Sheriff Davis refused to allow anyone in the press to interview him. Pictures of King behind bars and stories about his incarceration might arouse sympathy, possibly even among people who were not ardent supporters of the civil rights movement. And such publicity would surely bring more demonstrators into St. Augustine. King was a master at playing to the news media, and Davis had felt the sting of adverse publicity about his tactics, especially his decision to feed baby food to young people confined in outdoor pens at the jail. This rather petty act had drawn negative press reports and public criticism from around the country. But his contempt for those arrested was favorably received by many in St. Augustine.

George suggested I ask the sheriff to let him interview King in jail. We needed to find out exactly what he wanted from the community. The plan was to tape-record King's conversation, with his consent, so we could determine if there were any reasonable grounds on which we could negotiate to end the demonstrations. I contacted the sheriff and told him I wanted George to be allowed to interview King. He agreed. I waited at the Monson Motor Lodge while George went to the jail for the interview.

I believed King's goal was to end segregation in public accommodations, and I was in sympathy with this goal. I had learned as a student at Guilford College that without power, rarely can people change social conditions. George had a different assessment of King's motives. He thought King's purpose was to put pressure on Congress to ensure passage of the public accommodations act. He believed King had selected St. Augustine as the site to accomplish this goal. "The last thing King wants," George reasoned, "is to end the demonstrations." The marches were hurting the city, especially its tourist industry, which was vital to the city's financial well-being. King's goal, George believed, was to keep the spotlight on St. Augustine's segregated businesses, such as the Monson Motor Lodge, until Congress passed the public accommodations act. "King will leave St. Augustine when Congress passes the bill," he predicted.

I wasn't so sure. Once you let loose violent emotions like those fermenting in the city, they cannot easily be turned off. King might be stuck in St. Augustine long after the civil rights bill had passed. Ending the demonstrations now was my goal—and doing so without loss of life or property. But this posed a paradox: ensuring the right for peaceful demonstrations meant allowing the Klan to demonstrate, provided they did so without violence or threats.

I had studied the legal aspects of using peaceful demonstrations to advance civil rights and prepared a legal brief on the issues involved. When could state government restrict that right? If local government interfered with this constitutionally protected right, I was sure the federal courts would step in to protect it unless the state could show the absolute necessity of doing so. Martin Luther King had led demonstrations in Albany, Georgia, in 1961–62. When the first demonstrations began in St. Augustine in 1963, Albany's prosecutor called me about my use of the grand jury. I had begun my legal research on this issue earlier that year, and I sent a copy of my brief to him.

In the case of the *Schenck v. the United States* (1919), the defendant had been convicted of conspiracy to cause insubordination by publishing a pamphlet against military conscription when the country was at war. A majority of Justices upheld the conviction. In that decision Justice Holmes made a statement of great importance to the right of free speech. His "clear and present danger" analysis gave life to freedom of assembly and freedom of speech, with the caveat that "the most stringent protection of free speech would not protect a man falsely shouting fire in a theater and causing a panic." Before the government could suspend First Amendment rights, a showing had to be made that a clear and present danger existed, but that danger could not arise from lack of law enforcement. The decision required states to use all their powers to protect the right of demonstrators to peacefully assemble and petition the government for redress of their grievances.

If local and state law enforcement agencies were unable to keep the peace, they must ask the federal government for help or face the prospect that the federal government would move unilaterally to uphold the right. No southern governor would ask for assistance from the federal government under such conditions. A governor always had the option to call out the state National Guard, but in doing so he ran the risk of having the guard federalized as President Eisenhower had done in Little Rock. In the South, such an act amounted to political suicide, and I was sure Governor Bryant wasn't going to run that risk.

There was no question in my mind as to what I should do. As state attorney it was my sworn duty to protect the rights of peaceful demonstrators, including the Klan. Throughout the South, from the Montgomery bus boycott in 1955 to Birmingham in 1963, King had relied on local officials to interfere with this basic, constitutionally protected right. Once the right had been denied, he would call upon federal courts for protection. The pattern was the same in St. Augustine. Judge Simpson had cited the principle in his most recent decision allowing nighttime demonstrations. In the sure knowledge that officials in St. Augustine would follow the same strategy used by other officials throughout the South, King brought his demonstrators to St. Augustine.

Insofar as I was able, the right of King and the SCLC to demonstrate, to protest, and to seek redress of their grievances would be protected in St. Augustine. This would be the first time such protection had been accorded civil rights activists in the South. No other state official had stepped forward to protect the constitutional rights of demonstrators protesting the South's Jim Crow laws. Images of white law enforcement officers using dogs, clubs, and fire hoses to break up demonstrations were an inseparable part of segregation in the South, images that had horrified most Americans and many others throughout the world. All this coalesced into a powerful political tool, and King knew if he could maintain the pressure, Congress would have to act. I was certain he expected St. Augustine to engage in the same brutal practices. I was just as determined to ensure the demonstrators' First Amendments rights.

Sending George Allen, a newsman, not an elected official, to interview King was a bit tricky from a political standpoint, but I hoped to quell the outcry from the local political power structure by positioning the grand jury as a barrier between the mayor's stance and Judge Melton's order. At this point I had not fully reckoned with the extent to which lack of local leadership would aid the Klan. As it turned out, the Klan would dictate the course the city would take during that long, hot summer. The void created when city officials refused to negotiate with King or other SCLC members left the field wide open for the Klan's violent tactics.

Throughout the city people were saying that the Klan had just as much right to demonstrate as did the civil rights activists. Some businesses even helped the Klan by collecting funds to support the Ancient City Gun Club. It would be the Klan I would eventually have to control. On what grounds could I restrict the Klan's right to peacefully assemble? Their violence usually occurred at night and was clandestine. The cowardly hit-and-run tactics were conducted by individuals who quickly faded into the night, making it almost impossible to detect or to stop them. A way would have to be found to restrict the Klan's activities.

I asked George when he met with King to reassure him that I wanted to be part of the solution, not part of the problem, and to explain why I had asked for the impaneling of the grand jury. I outlined to George the steps I was willing to take in order to meet King's demands. I envisioned a biracial committee of five blacks and five whites to start the negotiations that would end segregation in St. Augustine. I would also take steps to protect the demonstrators.

The grand jury not only had the power to indict individuals for crimes but also had the moral authority to deal with any matter that affected the general health and welfare of the community. Grand juries had never been used for this purpose in the South, but armed with broad powers a grand jury could become a powerful tool for resolving violence. If a majority of its members chose to appoint a biracial committee, there was little the mayor or anyone else could do to stop it from adopting this course of action. I had used grand juries in Volusia County to force the school board to maintain public schools in good repair. I asked jurors to inspect the physical condition of all public schools in the county as well as other public property. A detailed report as to the condition of each property, down to missing light bulbs, was included in the grand juries' presentations. A scathing report on the deplorable condition of a school or other public building had a way of concentrating the attention of public officials on their responsibility to maintain such structures; an adverse report usually brought quick action from public officials. Why couldn't the same idea be used for racial disputes? Peace and tranquility in St. Augustine certainly affected the community's health and welfare. I reasoned a grand jury could be used to bypass the local power structure and create a biracial committee that could respond to the grievances of the black community.

I waited at the motel for George to return from his interview. The jail was a short distance away, just off highway U.S. 1 toward Nine-Mile Road. George returned later in the day and we listened to the tape recording of his conversation with King. "This was the first time I have ever interviewed a person in his shorts," George laughed. It was extremely hot in the jail and King had stripped down to his shorts, which, George said, were blue.

I recognized King's voice on the recording. It had the same rhythm and lilt he often used when speaking with reporters. "St. Augustine is the most segregated city in America," he said, yet "no one in authority will talk to me about the segregation policies of the city." Somewhat flustered, he said,"I am prepared to talk to anyone in authority who could help." Then he quickly added, "I'm prepared to stay in the city until those in authority change the policies of segregation, if it takes all summer." Listening to this phrase, "if it takes all summer," was the line used by General Grant in 1864 when his drive to capture Richmond stalled. Confronted by Lee's strategic retreat and defensive stand at Spotsylvania, Grant said he was prepared to "fight it out here, if it takes all summer." A hundred years later King would use the same phrase fighting very much the same war. King's tactics were the same as Grant's: keep the pressure on until victory was achieved.

King said he would only halt demonstrations if "a good faith effort" was made by the grand jury. He asked for four things: integration of motels, hotels, and restaurants; hiring of black police officers and firemen; dropping charges against those arrested for demonstrating; and formation of a biracial committee. Most of these requests were beyond my power or the power of a grand jury to grant, but it was a start. At least we knew what King's demands were.

George and I discussed the demands and after digesting his request, decided that George should return that evening with a request of King: would he be willing to voluntarily appear before the grand jury? No subpoena, just a voluntary appearance. Please reassure Dr. King, I said, that this was not a trick; he would not be placed under oath. He would merely make whatever statement he wished to make to the grand jury and be willing to answer questions the jurors might have about his goals and his organization. This last request was important. Many in St. Augustine genuinely believed the civil rights movement was controlled by or at least being manipulated by the Communists. I wanted the grand jury to get to know this man, to listen to his reasons and his motives. I wanted each member to judge those motives for himself.

When George returned from his second meeting, he said King agreed to accept the invitation, "provided it was a good faith grand jury." He was anxious, he told George, that the grand jury would not be used to impede the demonstrations or seek to indict those in the movement through some devious legal maneuver. I would make sure this did not happen.

George and I talked late into the night on how to proceed when the grand jury met the next day. I knew I had to convince King that I could be trusted. I was sympathetic to his cause and from an early age had tried to improve race relations. He had no way of knowing this and there was no time to try to educate him now.

King was scheduled to receive an honorary degree from Yale University over the weekend, but first he had to appear before Judge Mathis on Friday, June 12, to be arraigned and released on bond.

The grand jury was impaneled the morning King was arraigned. Upstairs in the main courtroom of the county court house, Judge Melton told the jury that it was responsible only to the court and it "need have no fear of anyone" in performing its duties.[14] We set King's appearance before the grand jury for three o'clock that afternoon. After he appeared before the grand jury he was to be transported by the Highway Patrol to Jacksonville for safety reasons. He was scheduled to return to St. Augustine on Tuesday, June 16, after receiving the honorary degree from Yale.

As King was being arraigned early on Friday morning, I met with the grand jury to explain what I intended to do. The purpose of this first meeting was to draft a statement, or "presentment," of principles to guide the grand jury in its investigation of the disturbances and to demonstrate the grand jury's good faith in the attempt to negotiate a settlement. I also wanted to set a moral tone for the grand jury and establish a positive atmosphere for negotiations during its deliberations. Once the statement of principles was adopted, it would be difficult for the grand jury to fail to do something meaningful to end the demonstrations. In establishing the principles to guide the jury's deliberations, I urged members to issue an appeal to all citizens to help relieve racial tensions.

After deliberating, it did so, and I released the presentment to the press. Signed by R. Aubrey Davis, its foreman, it read the "Grand Jury shall endeavor to establish meaningful lines of communications through which the two race groups involved may establish mutually acceptable solutions."[15] The grand jury was committed to the endeavor but I still needed to convince a majority of its members to appoint a biracial committee. Though twelve was the minimum number needed to put the resolution into force, for practical purposes the decision would have to be unanimous.

We were to take King's testimony at 3:00 p.m. Shortly before this time, King, Ralph Abernathy, and William England, the Boston University chaplain, appeared before Judge Mathis and pleaded not guilty to criminal trespass charges. This time they posted bond. Meanwhile, demonstrations and mass arrests continued; that same day, twenty-three demonstrators were arrested for trying to desegregate several restaurants. Time was fast running out for a negotiated settlement.

Attorney General Kynes was also busy. He filed a motion in federal district court in Jacksonville to allow state officials to reinstate a ban on night marches. The hearing on the motion was scheduled for the next day, Saturday, before Judge Simpson, who was giving preference to civil rights cases. They were being moved ahead of other cases on his docket. Since his refusal to move Mary Peabody's case to federal court, he appeared to have changed his opinion on the quality of justice available to the demonstrators in state courts. The basis for the hearing was an attempt by the state to establish that a clear and present danger existed if night marches were allowed to continue. It was a tough constitutional standard to meet, and I had doubts, at this point, about whether the state would succeed.

In addition to Martin Luther King, I had requested that other witnesses voluntarily appear before the grand jury, including Mayor Joe Shelley and Attorney General Kynes. Kynes was to give the jury the state's position on setting up a special police force to incorporate local officers into a unified command headed by the Florida Highway Patrol under Major Jourdan. This was a step I had asked the governor to take. The attorney general would be before the grand jury for more than an hour.

I had little time to think through the fast-moving events, but so far our strategy seemed to be working. At three in the afternoon an uproar swirled around the courthouse as King appeared to testify before the grand jury. The area was packed with reporters awaiting his arrival. Security in the courthouse was tight as the grand jury and I waited on the second floor of courthouse for the arrival of the man who had almost singlehandedly brought the entire city to a standstill. Before King arrived and before the grand jury went into secret session, I talked to its members about their responsibilities on this historic occasion. I said it was imperative that we try to bring order to the city and stop the violence that was spiraling out of control. I emphasized the need to be courteous to Dr. King no matter how individual members felt about him. He was a guest of the grand jury. I challenged the jurors to rise to the occasion and be on their best behavior when Dr. King testified. My efforts weren't notable for their success, but I had to try.

I had never seen King in person. He had a mythic aura about him; a leader whose courage and determination had been seared into my mind as someone of imposing physical stature and vitality. When he appeared at the door and was ushered into the courtroom by the bailiff, I was surprised. He was a rather small, quiet man, immaculately dressed in a dark blue suit, and much younger than I had imagined. I had given much thought as to how to greet him; I desperately wanted to set a positive tone for this historic meeting. Before the grand jury went into secret session, I rose and walked to the open door of the courtroom. In a voice loud enough that members of the grand jurors could hear, I said, "Dr. King, my name is Dan Warren; I'm the state attorney for the Seventh Judicial Circuit. I have been a longtime admirer of yours and I want to welcome you to the St. Johns County grand jury." This statement seemed to confuse him, but he quietly acknowledged my greeting as we shook hands, and the grand jury went into secret session. He would testify for more than three hours.

I wish I were at liberty to disclose the exchange between individual grand jury members and King, but testimony before a grand jury is secret. When the grand jury finally went into recess, one of the jurors spoke to me as we were leaving the courtroom, saying, "He ain't no different from any other blue gum nigger from South Georgia." It was going to be a long, hot summer.

As King left the grand jury room, he looked extremely tired, and when asked by reporters what happened during the session he replied, "As you know grand jury proceedings are secret and I was sworn to secrecy." With that, he left the courthouse amid a throng of reporters and onlookers.

King was to be moved to Jacksonville for his safety and he was quickly driven away from the courthouse by a state trooper. As he looked out the rear side window of the caged police cruiser, a large German police dog seated beside him peered menacingly over his left shoulder. An enterprising photographer snapped this memorable scene of King, seated in the rear seat, with the large police dog beside him. This image was flashed all over the world, giving millions of viewers a graphic perception of police insensitivity. All the hard work we had put into an attempt to create a picture of fairness and understanding by the citizens of St. Augustine was destroyed in an instant by that single photograph. It was not an auspicious start for the grand jury or for resolving the crisis.

Later that Friday night, the Klan opened its countercampaign, with some four hundred Klansmen marching in a demonstration. Police officers, mostly Florida state troopers, were stretched to the limit of their ability to keep the peace. J. B. Stoner urged white marchers not to engage in violence as they marched through the black community. Hundreds of blacks lined the sidewalks in complete silence as the robed Klansmen marched through their neighborhoods. I was deeply concerned that unless we could keep the marchers separated, the antagonists would eventually collide somewhere along the route. I was not concerned about violence from the SCLC, but I knew Klan violence might be hard to control even with Stoner's admonition against violence. King's demonstrators were disciplined, nonviolent marchers. The Klan, an organization founded on hate, mistrust, and bigotry, presented a real and present danger.

The author talks with Farris Bryant, Florida's governor, in Daytona
Beach in 1963. From the author's collection.

Demonstrators stand in front of the St. Augustine Chamber of Commerce in 1963. Courtesy of *Daytona Beach News-Journal*.

Sheriff L. O. Davis, *standing*, reads an arrest warrant to Mary Peabody, the mother of the governor of Massachusetts and a cousin of Eleanor Roosevelt. With her are, *clockwise*: Robert Hayling, Esther Burgess, and Hester Campbell. Courtesy of Melvin Thomas.

Dan Warren, his wife, Mary, and their children pose for a family portrait in 1964. From the author's collection.

Klan leader J. B. Stoner addresses supporters in the St. Augustine city park during 1964 demonstrations. Courtesy of the Florida Department of State, State Library and Archives of Florida.

Martin Luther King examines a bullet hole in the window of a St. Augustine house he was to occupy. King was not present when the shot was fired. Courtesy of Associated Press.

Martin Luther King encourages young demonstrators in June 1964. Courtesy of Melvin Thomas.

Civil rights activists rally at a St. Augustine church in June 1964. Courtesy of Melvin Thomas.

Connie Lynch exhorts hooded Klansmen from the back of a pickup truck, June 1964. Courtesy of the Florida Department of State, State Library and Archives of Florida.

J. B. Stoner speaks at a Klan rally, June 1964. Courtesy of the Florida Department of State, State Library and Archives of Florida.

Martin Luther King and Ralph D. Abernathy speak with motel manager James Brock just before their arrest on June 11, 1964. Courtesy of Associated Press.

St. Augustine demonstrators wait to begin their march on June 11, 1964. Courtesy of *Daytona Beach News-Journal*.

Injured demonstrator being assisted on June 11, 1964. Courtesy of the *Daytona Beach News-Journal.*

Motel manager James Brock pours muriatic acid into the pool during the "swim-in" at the Monson Motor Lodge on June 18, 1964. Courtesy of *Daytona Beach News-Journal.*

A policeman dives into the Monson Motor Lodge pool to arrest "swim-in" demonstrators on June 18, 1964. Photograph by Horace Cort. Courtesy of Associated Press.

From left to right: Joe Jacobs, assistant attorney general; Jimmy Kynes, attorney general; the author; and James Brock, the motel manager, examine firebomb damage at the Monson Motor Lodge on June 25, 1964. Courtesy of *Daytona Beach News-Journal.*

State troopers in full uniform form a protective barrier around civil rights activists trying to use the St. Augustine public beaches on June 25, 1964. When Klansmen made an attempt to break through and attack the demonstrators, the troopers applied force sufficient to "meet and overcome the resistance offered." Courtesy of the Florida Department of State, State Library and Archives of Florida.

6   Little Children Shall Lead Them

It could have been a scene from a different time, a different country. Racists lashing out blindly against ideas they feared, solely on the basis of physical attributes they had been programmed to hate. The scene reminded me of Pathe newsreels from the 1930s depicting the racial hatred taking place in Germany. It was ironic to see the same intense bigotry that the United States had fought against during World War II being repeated in our own country.

Holstead "Hoss" Manucy, president of the Ancient City Gun Club, was the organizing force behind the local segregationists. A semiliterate farmer and moonshiner, he became the main spokesman for the segregationists and for the Klan. "If them niggers march, we're gonna march," he told a national audience from his platform in the city's central park.

I shall never forget the contrast between Manucy's hate-filled cohorts and the first SCLC demonstration I witnessed. That scene of peaceful protesters will be etched in my memory forever. It literally made the hair on the back of my neck rise and sent chills down the length of my spine. The demonstrators, with small children in the lead, some holding hands, slowly emerged from the shadows of the night, marching silently two abreast in perfect step. As they made their way out of the darkness, flanked by heavily armed and helmeted policemen, they moved in a slow, steady march toward the muffled sounds of screaming Klansmen. Their eyes opened wide, darting to and fro, were filled with fear. From the distant park the faint sounds of the white mob rose and fell in cadence with the soft sounds of marching feet, giving grounds for the fear I saw in the children's eyes. But on they came. They reminded me of a stream of bombers headed into a maelstrom of flak, a scene I had observed many times during the war.

I marched with them that night, in the rear, surrounded by a number of law enforcement officers. I elected not to wear a helmet, as a gesture of respect to the marchers' bravery. That night I realized I would have to send Mary and the children home. This was no place for a vacation. I drove my family back to Daytona Beach on the following morning, June 13, and did not attend the hearings in Jacksonville. Judge Simpson denied the state's motion to limit night marches, as I expected he would.[1] It looked as though I was going to be occupied for a long time in St. Augustine, perhaps for the rest of the summer.

The ruling allowed King to continue staging marches at night through the very heart of old St. Augustine despite the danger; however, it also allowed the Klan to march at night into the black section of St. Augustine. Judge Simpson, in remarks made shortly after issuing his order, took direct aim at law enforcement: "I suggest real enforcement would arrest these hoodlums everybody seems afraid of and would stop any violence."[2]

His comments touched the heart of the legal issue. If local law enforcement was incapable of maintaining the peace and arresting those in St. Augustine who created the violence, Judge Simpson would be forced to intervene. But the complex issue of how to deal with the Klan's hit-and-run tactics, carried out at night as they slipped quickly back into cover of darkness, was not an issue that he addressed. He did not seem to realize the problem that his order created for law enforcement. We would hear more of this later when Governor Bryant was cited for contempt for suspending night marches contrary to Judge Simpson's order. I would also find myself at the center of this controversy. But up to this point, the demonstrations had been noisy but relatively peaceful, although surrounded by hate; except for isolated incidents by the Klan, no one had been seriously injured.

Because of the covert tactics the Klan employed, law enforcement was hard pressed to deal with the situation, especially when violence occurred in isolated areas of the county. It was impossible for police to be at every location where violence might occur. Judge Simpson was obviously out of touch with the realities of the situation in St. Augustine. We simply did not have enough law enforcement officers to keep the peace in the city, especially at night. So far we had managed to keep the demonstrators separated, except in the city center; even on these occasions we had managed, but just barely, to control the intense emotions that often erupted.

It was Judge Simpson's implied threat to call upon federal forces if local officials could not control the violence that finally attracted the governor's attention. I knew the governor would never allow the federal government to control local law enforcement, but I was equally sure that if the governor failed to maintain the peace, the judge would call upon federal authorities to intervene.

I had only been in St. Augustine since the previous Monday, and my days and nights were filled with the delicate task of coordinating grand jury meetings and talking with people I thought might be helpful in controlling the growing threat of violence. I was getting a crash course in the practical art of politics, one that would test my understanding of the intricate nuances of the legal rights each citizen enjoyed under the First Amendment.

On Saturday, June 13, after Judge Simpson upheld his order allowing marches to continue at night, some two hundred segregationists once again marched through the Lincolnville section of the city. Klansmen, flying the Confederate battle flag along with a huge banner that read "Don't tread on me," were accompanied by a contingent of heavily armed law enforcement officers. This time, the residents lined the street, laughing and singing, "We love everybody."[3] It was rather comical, with Klansmen being the subject of derision from an amused black community. There were no incidents, but police officers were exhausted, having escorted three marches by blacks and two by whites in five days.

On Sunday, in New Haven, Connecticut, Martin Luther King received an honorary degree from Yale University. In paying homage to King, the speaker predicted that "generations of Americans yet unborn will echo their admiration of you. As your eloquence has kindled the nation's sense of outrage, so your steadfast refusal to countenance violence in resistance to injustice has heightened our sense of national shame."[4] This view had yet to reach folks in St. Augustine.

I informed the governor that the state troopers were exhausted. I also described the escalating problems we were encountering. As the attorney general had suggested, I urged him to remove state troopers from the sheriff's control. The sheriff's lack of professionalism, as well as his association with Manucy and members of the Klan, disturbed the more professional members of the Florida Highway Patrol, who had expressed to me concern over the sheriff's ability to handle the growing violence. On Monday, the governor issued an order organizing all state law enforcement officers into a special force. Using the same emergency powers he had used for my appointment, the governor made J. W. Jourdan, deputy inspector of the Florida Highway Patrol, the commanding officer of this special police force.[5]

To emphasize the importance of this appointment, the governor flew to St. Augustine. At a press conference he introduced each of us to the press, voiced his concern over the situation, and outlined the measures he was taking to control violence. His order placed under unified command the Highway Patrol, the Board of Conservation, the Beverage Department, the State Sheriff's Department, the Game and Fresh Water Fish Commission, and investigators from the governor's office and that of the attorney general, as well as those from city and county agencies. Jourdan and I set up headquarters in the National Guard Armory, as did Joe Jacobs of the Attorney General's Office and Elmer H. Emerich, a former FBI agent now working for the governor.

Earlier, Sheriff L. O. Davis had flown to Tallahassee in the governor's private plane for a conference. Davis was an interesting character. A populist by nature, he resembled the caricature of a bumbling lawman, which reflected what the community wanted with respect to law enforcement. He also wanted to be liked, with the tragic result that during the crisis he chose to please the white majority in St. Augustine, especially the Klan.

After I had driven my family back to Daytona, I returned on Monday. I brought along a pistol, the first time I had carried a gun since World War II. I kept it in an open brief case on the front seat of my car. St. Augustine would surely turn deadly in the weeks ahead.

Local business leaders adopted a resolution that alleged the city had been chosen for unknown reasons "as a battleground for invading forces

representing extremists on both sides of the racial question . . . that is creating an image of the city of St. Augustine which is totally unfounded
and untrue."⁶ The resolution did not help in resolving the crisis, but I felt
that we were making progress. My efforts to create a biracial commission were paying off, especially with H. E. Wolfe working in the background. The members of the grand jury had agreed to appoint a biracial
committee and I was trying to find ten individuals who would agree to
serve. There seemed to be an air of hope in the community. A group of
businessmen, headed by state senator Verle Pope of St. Augustine, were
meeting informally to discuss the attitude the business community should
take if the civil rights bill passed, and I was hopeful the biracial committee would be appointed before the week was out.

Some members of the press were even downplaying the turmoil that
was taking place in the city. Bernard J. Roswig, a United Press International reporter, wrote an article titled "Tell Tourists to Come to St. Augustine," which the *St. Augustine Record* ran on the front page. "If this
oldest city in the nation is on your summer vacation schedule, it really
isn't necessary to change your plans because of racial violence that has
erupted here," he wrote. "Just stay clear of King Street between Washington and the old slave market after dark. That's where all the conflict
has occurred between young whites and Negro demonstrators. But on the
Bay sea wall a few hundred yards from the action you would never know
what was happening." The article was preceded by a note that read: "Most
newsmen and TV announcers here give many biased opinions of St. Augustine's racial unrest. So it is a delightful change to read a different news
story about this oldest city."⁷ This "unbiased opinion" had a difficult time
competing with facts.

Some motel owners were saying privately that they were now willing
to integrate, if they had adequate police protection. The economic costs
of the demonstrations affected both races. The impact on the tourist industry, on which the local economy depended, was substantial, as was the
cost of providing for additional law enforcement officers who had to be
housed and fed. Part of the cost for maintaining the large presence of officers in the community had to be paid by the county, a fact that did not sit
well with the county commissioners or the taxpaying public. The demon-

strators, who had little financial support for housing and meals or the cost of bonds for those arrested, also faced financial hardship.

Jackie Robinson soon joined the demonstrations. Speaking to an integrated audience, he told the crowd, "President Johnson should use action instead of words." Inserting politics into the fight, he said, "I ask you to register so we can vote Democratic because if the Republicans nominate Barry Goldwater that will say to Negroes: we don't want your vote."[8] The first black to breach the racial barrier in major league baseball, his prestige among blacks was equal to that of Martin Luther King, and his appearance on the local scene boosted the morale of the demonstrators at a time when the demonstrations seemed to be losing momentum.

The civil rights bill was a major political issue for both parties. This was a presidential election year, and both parties were acutely aware of the political significance of the issue, including Senator Barry Goldwater, who was seeking his party's nomination for president. In a rather surprising move, he voted against curbing the civil rights filibuster, a maneuver that played well in St. Augustine and apparently with some members of the Republican Party. Senator Goldwater seemed certain to win the nomination when the Republican convention was held in July. Ultimately, passage of the civil rights bill would undermine the hold that conservative Democrats held over the South, eradicating the Solid South and paving the way for the transfer of political power in the South to the Republican Party.

On Monday, June 15, at 10:30 p.m., demonstrators again marched peacefully to the park. There were few whites in the park that night and those that gathered there were asked to leave before the demonstrators arrived. C. T. Vivian led the march and assured those in the movement that "the demonstrations are broader than the attack on segregation. We are struggling as much for poor whites as we are for Negroes."[9] On Wednesday afternoon, public beaches at St. Augustine were successfully used by blacks without incident, and that same afternoon the grand jury was working hard in hopes of finishing its recommendation to create a biracial committee by Thursday.

On Tuesday, Martin Luther King returned to the city. He promised to stay until segregation had been abolished and to return to jail if necessary to accomplish his goals. That night he spoke to a group of rabbis who had responded to his plea to religious leaders throughout the country to lend their moral support to the cause. Many Jewish leaders would play an important role in the civil rights movement. Other people were also part of the effort, including whites such as Sarah Patton Boyles, wife of a University of Virginia professor, and William England, a chaplain at Boston University. Arriving in carriages driven by black drivers, racially mixed groups asked to be admitted to restaurants. After being ordered to leave, they waited in front for the police to arrive and arrest them. The drivers were also arrested, an act that was prominently reported by news organizations in stories and pictures. Since King's arrest the previous Thursday, some 180 demonstrators had been arrested. The county jail was overflowing and the costs for housing and feeding those arrested was growing rapidly. Not one Klansman had been arrested.

In a surprise move, segregationists organized another peaceful march through a predominately black neighborhood. Commenting on the new tactic Holstead Manucy, the leader of the march, said, "We wanted to see if white people would be afforded the same rights the federal courts have given the Negroes."[10]

The economic costs to the community continued to increase. Business in the city was down by 50 percent, with restaurants and motels hardest hit. Though vacancy signs appeared all over the city, negative effects on the motel industry were partially offset by the number of law enforcement officers who were housed in motels throughout the city. It seemed to come as a surprise to those who were planning the city's quadricentennial celebration that many foreign visitors invited to the city might not be white. There was a dawning realization that dignitaries from around the world with different skin color and ethnic backgrounds might attend the festivities.

The black community was also feeling the pinch. Many had been fired from their jobs, and the number of demonstrators in jail who had been required to post bonds created a financial problem for the movement. Bondsmen generally charged 10 percent of the face value of the bond, plus security of some kind. Some people were afraid they would come out of the campaign with nothing really accomplished and heavily in debt. No financial woes seemed to afflict the Klan. It continued to collect contributions from business establishments that had set up collection jars by cash registers throughout the city.

The possibility that a biracial committee might be appointed by the grand jury and that demonstrations might move from streets to the conference table, offered a ray of hope. Demonstrations, however, were continuing, and on Wednesday night, June 17, three hundred marchers, including a group of Jewish clergymen from nine states, began a two-mile night march through the dark, narrow streets of the old city.[11] When they reached the Monson Motor Lodge, they paused and held a prayer service. I marched that night with law enforcement officers assigned to protect the group. Abernathy urged the marchers to continue on through a white residential area. "If they come through our neighborhood, we can go through theirs," he said, referring to the Klan's march through the black community.[12]

No violence marred the march that night. The few white spectators, perched atop cars and trucks along the march route, watched silently and sullenly as the demonstrators passed by. But the Klan perceived the march as a challenge. And the protection afforded the demonstrators by law enforcement that night did not sit well with the editors of the local newspaper or their readers. In a front-page editorial in the *St. Augustine Record* titled "Two Sides to the Coin," the newspaper took the governor to task for allowing demonstrators to hold a prayer meeting and stage demonstrations on private property. "The state police force has apparently assumed power here which borders on making the city a police state," read the editorial.

Surely they had the authority to have kept the demonstrators marching instead of invading private property at this late hour of the night. They have assumed the power to clear the Plaza, a public park, of citizens when the integrationists march and demonstrate at night and to stop and search automobiles and pedestrians without search warrants to protect the demonstrators. Yet, these same demonstrators were allowed to bring their threat of violence through a peaceful neighborhood and also to demonstrate on private property late in the nighttime after a leader of the demonstrators had publicly declared that they were changing their tactics because there were not enough people in the downtown area—these citizens having heeded the appeals of authorities to stay out of the area to avoid adding to the threat of violence.

The editorial concluded with the comment that " the rights of law abiding citizens should not be abridged in [the] process."[13] This was the first criticism we had received from the local power structure for our efforts to protect the demonstrators. It would not be the last.

The grand jury was scheduled to return its presentment the next day, and hopefully it would include the appointment of a biracial committee. H. E. Wolfe had come through with his promise of help and had convinced five whites to serve. Five blacks had also agreed to serve. We labored through the morning, threshing out the final details of the report. It was close to noon and the day was very hot. The windows on the second floor of the courtroom were open in the unair-conditioned room, and the sounds from the old city could be heard. The Monson Motor Lodge was only a block away and shortly before noon, we heard sirens and angry shouting. Something was happening. The grand jury decided to take a break and find out what was going on.

A near riot was taking place at the motor lodge. Seven black demonstrators, six men and one woman, had jumped into the motel's swimming pool among the white guests. As news cameras rolled, the manager, James Brock, rushed to the pool, shouting for the intruders to get out. When they refused, he ran inside, returning with two one-gallon jugs of muriatic acid. With exaggerated gusto he dumped the contents into the pool. As he ran excitedly around the edges of the pool, he continued yelling at the uninvited guests to leave. News cameramen had a field day. The frantic actions of the manager would be televised on the six o'clock news for all the world to see—a city gone berserk. This rather comical scene, arranged primarily for its news value, played out while Martin Luther King watched from across the street. That it occurred at the moment the grand jury was considering the appointment of a biracial committee was unfortunate. And its impact on the jury's decision was anything but comical.

Television was a potent, relatively new visual medium for conveying fast-breaking news to the American public. But there were no satellite uplinks to permit live broadcasts; in order to make the nightly news, film had to be driven to Jacksonville, where it was processed and then distributed to major news networks. For an incident in St. Augustine to be featured on the six o'clock evening news by NBC, CBS, and ABC, the event had to take place no later than noon. The "swim-in" had taken place just before twelve o'clock, assuring that it would be the lead story on most news broadcasts that evening. King had a fine sense of timing, and it wasn't lost on the hard-working grand jury. The motel manager's frantic, comical antics were beamed into millions of homes across the nation. It was high comedy. But the members of the grand jury were not amused. The pressure on them these past few days had been intense, and although I am not at liberty to reveal what went on in the grand jury room, the jury's actions after this incident speak for themselves.

On June 19, the day after the swim-in, the grand jury agreed to name a biracial committee of five whites and five blacks. But it insisted that the committee would meet after a thirty-day cooling-off period, during which time there would be no further demonstrations. King immediately rejected the offer. He called the report "a very disappointing and unwise recommendation."[14]

I was disappointed and puzzled by this response, as were many in the news media. King's call for the appointment of a biracial committee when we first approached him in the St. John's county jail had been widely reported. When he accepted the invitation to appear before the grand jury, he said he wanted a biracial committee "to study the problem" and that he would be willing to work out "some kind of adjustment period to accomplish this."[15] He was not willing to wait a year or six months, he quickly added. Now that he had what he demanded, he had rejected it without any comment except that it was an unfortunate decision. Why had he rejected it without offering an explanation or proposing another solution? It puzzled many of the reporters, and some began to question his motives. The next day, King softened his stance slightly and agreed to call off the demonstrations for one week. The jury foreman, R. Aubrey Davis, issued a defiant response: "This Grand Jury will not be intimidated," he said. "We will not negotiate. We will not alter our presentment."[16]

As comical as the swim-in was, its effect on the grand jury was most

unfortunate. And King's quick rejection of the cooling-off period sty-
mied any further attempt to open lines of communication between the
demonstrators, the grand jury, and the community. It did, however, play
into the hands of the KKK. In anticipation of other swim-ins, Holstead
Manucy and some kindred souls captured several large alligators, placed
them in the back of pickup trucks, and parked close to the Monson Motor Lodge, ready to dump the gators into the swimming pool if another
attempt was made to integrate it. The defenders of Whites-only bathing took great pleasure in displaying their new weapon to newsmen, who
were quick to share the event with the worldwide viewing public. It was
one of the top stories on the TV networks that evening.

The lines were now firmly drawn; soon Klansmen from all over the
South were headed to St. Augustine to fight to maintain the "purity of
the white race." And now the failure of those in power to find a solution
to the grievances of blacks and the unwillingness of the local churches to
speak up would have tragic consequences for all citizens of St. Augustine.
In this moral and political vacuum, the voice of the Ku Klux Klan would
prevail, leaving the Klan, by default, the spokesman for the citizens of
St. Augustine. In the coming weeks, that venomous, hate-filled voice
would besmirch the proud image of the city. The festivities intended to
celebrate the glories of the past would become an occasion for the Klan
to spread its creed of violence and hold the nation's oldest city hostage to
its message of hate.

The most important thing for me was that I had failed. I had failed
to understand or even consider the national implications of King's movement. Despite George Allen's argument to the contrary, I had held to the
naive and parochial view that the events unfolding in St. Augustine were
only of local importance. In reality, St. Augustine was merely a symbol of
the plight of blacks in a segregated society. The crisis actually had little
to do with segregation in one city. The real issues were much larger and
far more complex than how St. Augustine's business community was affected. Hugh Morris, president of the Baptist Deacons Convention, had
put his finger on an important change in the attitude of blacks toward
segregation when he spoke to convention delegates in Daytona Beach on
June 24, 1963. "There is the emergence of a new Negro, one with courage
and determination, whose patience has become exhausted, and he has de-

cided that 100 years is long enough to wait for freedom, and he will wait no longer."[17]

I was to see that courage and determination in the dedication demonstrators exhibited in St. Augustine: They would wait no longer for freedom. And in the end this determination would help Congress muster the votes necessary for passage of the 1964 Civil Rights Act. Martin Luther King would not succeed in changing the character of southerners, but he would succeed in helping to change the nation's laws.

We had reached a stalemate, and the mood of the community matched that of the grand jury members. The demonstrations were taking a heavy economic toll on St. Augustine and on the state. Summer was the most profitable season for many businesses, and economic losses in 1964 were considerable. But few individuals in the community were willing to speak out. To do so they would risk not only the violence of the Klan but also the condemnation of community leaders.

The Civil Rights Act of 1964 was signed into law by President Lyndon Johnson on July 2. James Farmer, head of CORE, knew firsthand the importance of the interstate commerce portion of the act. He had risked his life in 1961 leading a group of freedom riders on interstate carriers across the South.[18] Commenting on the effects of the bill, Farmer said, "It may well be the single most important act of our Congress in several decades and gives hope to Negroes that the American people and government mean to redeem the promises of equality, and to an even chance to enjoy the blessings of liberty." Moreover, he added, it was "a challenge to men of goodwill in every part of the country to transform the commands of our law into the customs of the land."[19]

At the moment there were few men of goodwill in St. Augustine. What should have been a triumphant celebration for King, Farmer, and others who had waged the long fight for passage of one of the most important pieces of civil rights legislation in the history of this country turned into an ugly confrontation with the Ku Klux Klan. The voice of moderation and conciliation was almost silent. When Senator Pope, along with a group of local businessmen, made a public statement that they would abide by the recently passed civil rights legislation, every window in the building that housed his insurance agency was smashed. His office was right across the street from the county courthouse where law and order should have prevailed. This was the Klan's response to those who dared disagree with them—even when that disagreement took the form of obeying the law of the land.

The churches remained silent. And Governor Bryant issued an ill-conceived statement that the passage of the civil rights bill was "a great injury to national unity." He called on the civil rights demonstrators to cease, saying, "it is my hope that with this legislation those persons who are committing criminal acts in Florida in the name of civil rights will cease doing so in order that we can be about the task of reestablishing the peace and harmony which has been our tradition."[20] The fact that not a single civil rights demonstrator had committed any unlawful act during the demonstrations gave little credence to his statement. And it certainly did not help solve the escalating crisis in St. Augustine.

On the night of June 19 an unusually large number of Klansmen gathered in the park while police officers assembled behind the Wax Museum, awaiting the demonstrators who had assembled for a march some blocks away. They were expected to arrive at any minute. Sheriff Davis sought me out. The situation is very dangerous, he said, and "if the marchers take the route along the park where the Klan is rallying, someone is going to get killed. I don't have enough men to control the crowd." This startled me, and I told him he should "make the marchers go down Bay Street," a popular name for Avenida Menendez. "Don't let them go by the Klan." He responded rather prophetically, "If I do, I'll be held in contempt of court." He then asked, "Will you defend me?" I quickly replied, "Yes." As it turned out I was unable to keep that promise because the governor and his advisers decided I would be the chief witness for the state in the subsequent contempt hearings It was obviously impossible to represent L. O. and also be a witness for the state. L. O. was very angry when I told him what had been decided but there was nothing I could do to change the situation.

Meanwhile, I waited in the darkness for the arrival of the marchers, chatting with a young police officer holding a leash that tethered a huge German shepherd police dog. As we talked quietly, I could feel the tension in the air. A gentle breeze was blowing from the bay only a block away, but the faint rebel yells coming from the park had an ominous sound as we waited, pondering what might happen. Faint shouts could be heard as J. B. Stoner, the Klan lawyer from Georgia, and Connie Lynch, the fundamentalist preacher from California, whipped the crowd into its usual frenzy.

Quietly, out of the darkness, the tread of marching feet could be heard, so soft at first that the sound was hard to detect. In a moment a group of people with small children in the lead came slowly out of the darkness, two by two, holding hands as they marched silently toward the assembled Klansmen. It was an inspiring, heroic moment. I fell in behind the marchers, along with the police. As we reached the Bridge of Lions, a scuffle took place when L. O. refused to allow the demonstrators to turn onto Cathedral Street, which led past the waiting Klansmen. Andrew Young, leading the group, resisted the sheriff's order not to march past the Klansmen and was quickly hustled into a police cruiser, vigorously protesting our interference with Judge Simpson's order.

Klansmen now began to leave the park and dart through back alleys to intercept the demonstrators. As we approached the Monson Motor Lodge, the hidden Klansmen began hurling rocks and bottles at the group. Two Klansman ran toward me, fists raised in anger, yelling that I was an FBI agent. I was sure I would be assaulted, but L. O. Davis, walking a short distance behind me, intervened, explaining to the angry men who I was. They sullenly melted back into the yelling mob. It was a frightening experience, not unlike ones I had experienced during the war. I was scared then, and I was scared that night. But what left the strongest impression on me was the sight of young children, leading the march with eyes wide open, obviously afraid, too, but fighting for a principle just as important as those I had fought for during World War II.

There were no more incidents that night, and as the marchers moved safely past the old city, I was walking back to the motel when an FBI agent fell in beside me. I knew him from the meetings we had held with police officers at the armory; he had been introduced to me by Sheriff Davis. We fell into conversation as we walked, reviewing the potential violence that had been so narrowly averted. I told him of the near attack by two white segregationists who thought I was an FBI agent. He laughed. We spoke about my work with the grand jury, and he told me that the FBI had some sexually compromising tapes of conversations between King and a white woman from California. He indicated the tapes could be made available if the grand jury wanted to hear them. Rumors had circulated around town that King was having affairs, but this was my first contact with anyone who claimed to have proof. I declined the offer. I wasn't interested in smearing King's reputation; I was interested in resolving the crisis.

7   State versus Federal Control

The rerouting of the demonstrators was in direct violation of Judge Simpson's order allowing night demonstrations. I immediately contacted Governor Bryant and reported to him why we had taken this action. The next day he issued an executive order banning night demonstrations in St. Augustine.[1]

The text of the order was important. After recounting his duties as the supreme executive under the constitution of the state of Florida, the governor said he was charged with the duty "to take care that the laws be faithfully executed and [had] the dominate interest in protecting the people against violence." The findings of facts contained in the executive order were premised on a number of factors: "that the physical layout of the routes used by these demonstrations consists of narrow streets bordered by shrubbed and wooded areas without sufficient light dangerous to persons, property, and lives of the citizens in this area; . . . that the law enforcement has been strengthened to its maximum since June 9, and that additional enforcement sent into this area would not in any way alleviate the circumstances creating the danger to peace and order; . . . that the Grand Jury of St. Johns County, after having met and attempted to conscientiously find a solution to the problem . . . there was no good faith effort on behalf of some to attempt to find a solution." He then decreed that "it shall be unlawful for any person to . . . march, parade, . . . or assemble between the hours of 8:30 p.m. and sunrise in St. Johns County." [2]

The order set the stage for a direct confrontation between the power of the governor as the state's chief executive and the authority of the federal court as manifested in Judge Simpson's order permitting night marches. It was a classic First Amendment confrontation: the state's right to control purely local law enforcement matters versus those rights guaranteed under the U.S. Constitution. We would soon have to defend the governor's understanding of his authority under Florida's constitution versus those of Judge Simpson's under the U.S. Constitution.

There was no question in my mind of the need to suspend night marches through the old city. I was ready to defend the order I had given Sheriff Davis to divert demonstrators from marching past Klansmen gathered in the park and perhaps hidden throughout the old city. Senator Verle Pope welcomed the governor's action. Holding a press conference on Saturday, June 20, 1964, he told assembled newsmen that he had asked the governor "to invoke full provisions of a 1954 emergency act which gives the governor authority to halt demonstrations and marches, establish curfews and regulate meetings and demonstrations."[3]

Not everyone in the city approved of the action taken by the governor or the local senator urging the governor to take such action. This was especially true of the mayor. Expressing surprise that a press conference had been held without his knowledge, he lashed out at Pope. "Senator Pope's move is entirely politically motivated in an effort to second guess local officials." He added that "evidently Senator Pope did not feel city and county officials were capable of handling the situation with[out] the help of the governor."[4]

The *St. Augustine Record* ran an editorial titled "A Clear and Present Danger?"

> For nearly a month now our city has been plagued with nighttime demonstrations that have incited normally peaceful citizens to riot or near riot. Federal judge Bryan Simpson has refused on two separate occasions to allow the city or the state to prohibit further night-time marches and demonstrations. Evidently the judge feels that there exists no "clear and present danger to life and property." We submit that if Judge Simpson had accompanied Negro or white marchers during the past several weeks down some of our darker streets abutting totally darkened alleys and houses, his judg-

ment would be completely reversed. Racial agitator M. L. King has refused to accept in behalf of local Negro citizens a 30-day cooling off period at the end of which the county Grand Jury will reconvene to appoint a 10-man bi-racial committee. Yet King continues to cry that a bi-racial committee is what he wants. . . . However he insists that he shall dictate the terms. Perhaps in Birmingham, Oxford[, Miss.], and, maybe even Washington, D.C., King is a big man with a great deal of influence. However, in St. Augustine, King is just another racial agitator, who really isn't interested in the rights of local colored citizens, but is vitally interested in their money and his personal power.[5]

King's legions of disciplined demonstrators marched that night in defiance of the governor's order. The Klan did the same. On Sunday, four blacks and a white were arrested for attempting to integrate the morning service at a Methodist church. Later that evening demonstrations began anew in the city. The battle would soon shift to the federal courthouse in Jacksonville where the issue of state versus federal control of law enforcement in St. Augustine would play out.

Public beaches in St. Augustine were segregated. But despite this long-standing custom, in the past few days demonstrators had used the public beaches. The Klan now concentrated their efforts on keeping blacks off those beaches. At least the demonstrations would take place during the day, curtailing the hit-and-run tactics the Klan had used so successfully at night. However, state law enforcement officers were now required to maintain the peace not only at the beaches during the day but also in the city at night. Soon, a twenty-four-hour operation was in place; it required more men and more equipment.

Our forces were scattered all over St. Augustine, but individual units could be assembled in fairly short order as long as demonstrations were centered around the park. The public beaches, however, were located on Anastasia Island some distance away, accessible from the mainland only across the Bridge of Lions. The ability to assemble the forces necessary to protect the demonstrators, especially on short notice, was greatly impaired.

The first two wade-ins at the beaches had taken place without incident, but the growing number of Klansmen flooding into the city turned this area into the next battleground. The Klan was a well-organized force with excellent two-way radio communication allowing members to talk with each other and avoid areas where our forces were concentrated. KKK members in pickup trucks, flying the Confederate battle flag from whip antennas, were seen racing from one area to another in search of trouble.

A fight broke out on Monday, June 22, as nineteen demonstrators trying to wade in the surf were attacked by Klansmen. Dozens of officers were quickly on the scene and stopped the violence. Six Klansmen were arrested as they attempted to chase the demonstrators out of the surf. Some Klansmen were thrown to the ground and handcuffed. During the melee a cameraman from Denmark was injured when he was hit in the face by a shirtless Klansman who then ran away. This was the second incident that day at the public beaches. Vivid scenes of renewed violence were aired on national television that night; it appeared the violence would escalate to new heights.

Klan members responded with a show of force. Approximately 275 segregationists waving Confederate flags marched past 120 demonstrators that included a few white supporters. The groups passed each other on opposite sides of the street. This was one of the few demonstrations that did not erupt in violence. A few Klansmen yelled obscenities; as usual there was no response from the civil rights demonstrators.

As expected, Andrew Young filed a petition with the federal court on Monday afternoon, June 22, seeking the issuance of an order of contempt against those officials who had defied Judge Simpson's ruling. It did not take Simpson long to issue the contempt order. By Monday evening, Governor Bryant, Sheriff Davis, highway patrol chief H. N. Kirkman, and St. Augustine police chief Virgil Stuart had been instructed to show cause why they should not be held in contempt of court.[6] The legal issue was joined and now the federal court would decide who controlled the demonstrations.

As if in response to the "show cause" order, the *St. Augustine Record* published in its entirety an editorial from the *Tallahassee Democrat* titled "The Time and Place to Stand." It urged the governor to fight the order. "The Governor of Florida should ignore the summons of a Federal Judge to defend himself against a possible contempt of court hearing. . . . Practicalities of the situation are subordinate to legal fundamentals, but it is pertinent the federal judge's series of orders and statements from the bench in Jacksonville had done nothing to restore domestic tranquility at St. Augustine. They may have aggravated the situation. . . . Sometime, somewhere—and soon—a stand must be made against this recurring attempt of our federal judges to make and direct enforcement of the laws as well as to interpret them and settle disputes which arise under them."[7]

King called on both the White House and the Department of Justice to intervene. In a press release, he voiced his concerns that "there seems to be a conspiracy between the police forces and Klan-like terrorists."[8] There was no conspiracy, as far as I could determine, but the sheriff's close association with Manucy and certain members of the Klan certainly gave the impression there was one.

Upon receipt of the order, Governor Bryant dispatched a Highway Patrol Cessna 182 to the St. Augustine airport. I flew to Tallahassee for a conference with the governor, his attorneys, and the attorney general. That evening we gathered in the basement library of the attorney general's office at the old state capitol and planned our legal strategy to defend the governor's right to restrict demonstrators from marching at night through the old section of St. Augustine. The hearing was set for the following Friday, in Jacksonville. The ruling issued by Judge Simpson directed the named respondents to appear before the court and "show cause" why they should not be held in contempt of court for violating the court's order. The burden of proof is on those named; they must justify their actions.

One of the governor's attorneys from St. Petersburg led the discussion. Everyone there knew that Judge Simpson would not tolerate defiance of a legal order issued by him, even from the governor. However, some in the room were of the opinion that Judge Simpson would not dare hold the governor in contempt. I wasn't so sure about this and expressed my doubts with their position.

The first question we addressed was whether the governor should attend the hearing. His position was that by attending the hearing he might concede jurisdiction to the federal courts and the powers held as chief executive of the state. The governor, an unrelenting states' rights advocate, was not willing to concede this power. Bryant made it clear he would not attend the hearing. He would assert his right as chief executive of the state of Florida to control purely local law enforcement matters under the Tenth Amendment.

It was finally agreed the attorney general would appear and argue that the federal court lacked jurisdiction over the governor to control law enforcement decisions made regarding St. Augustine in the exercise of his constitutional duties. He would claim the action the governor had taken in restricting nighttime demonstrations through the old city was strictly a matter for state law enforcement not the federal government. I was uncomfortable with this jurisdiction argument but for the moment did not express my concerns. I did not believe this argument would succeed nor did I think it would impress Judge Simpson. I saw the issue as one controlled entirely by decisions of the U.S. Supreme Court involving First Amendment rights.

The next question was a strategic one: the legal approach we should use to defeat the court's order to show cause. The burden of proof would be on us to show "a clear and present danger" existed that night. We had the facts to support our decision to interfere with the route the demonstration had chosen. We could show that the danger to the demonstrators arose not from our failure to supply sufficient law enforcement but entirely from the route the demonstrators had chosen for their march. No one, including the federal government, could ensure the demonstrators' safety under those circumstances.

An attorney for the governor proposed that we use the doctrine of nullification and interposition to oppose Judge Simpson's order. I was shocked: interposition? This was the same excuse southern leaders had used to justify seceding from the union, one that had brought on the Civil War. Under this antiquated argument, the federal government had only those powers expressly granted to it by the various sovereign states, and when the government exceeded this authority, there being no common arbiter, any state had the right to interpose its sovereign power and nullify the action. The argument, first advanced by John C. Calhoun of South Carolina in 1830, was premised on the theory that rights not delegated to the federal government under the Tenth Amendment were reserved to the states. Local law enforcement was one of these rights and, therefore, the states could interpose their sovereignty over that of the federal government.

I thought the doctrine of nullification had been put to rest when the South lost the war. The nullification argument was, of course, a political move on the governor's part, one that resonated well with the sentiments of a majority of Floridians. He would pay homage to the Lost Cause myth so dear to the hearts of many southerners. It was a popular political move but, to my way of thinking, totally unrealistic. The First Amendment stood in the way.

I have never been very diplomatic when arguing a point of law. That night I bluntly pointed out that this issue had been laid to rest when the North won the Civil War. I argued that we could successfully respond to the "show cause" order by proving to the court that a clear and present danger existed to the demonstrators, including small children, as they passed through the dark, narrow backstreets of the old city. No one, I argued, could have ensured the safety of the demonstrators under those circumstances. Snipers hidden along the parade route could have fired on the demonstrators and nothing, not even the awesome power of the federal government, could have prevented injury and mayhem. The assassination of President Kennedy had surely proven this. For all its might and despite all its precautions, the government had not been able to stop the assassination of the president, in broad daylight, in the heart of a great city. How, then, could state and local law enforcement forces have protected from snipers' fire a group of people marching along a dark, narrow way in St. Augustine?

My views were not welcome, but after debate, we decided to use the arguments I set forth. I would testify to the facts that had created the clear and present danger—ones I had personally observed. In the final analysis, this issue became our main defense. I was confident it would succeed and that Judge Simpson would not hold anyone in contempt. Despite this, the governor insisted we use an ancillary to the interposition theory as one of our arguments. He would not concede jurisdiction to the federal courts. We had worked late into the night, and at the end of the session a few of the individuals present were invited to the governor's mansion for a late night snack. Pointedly I was not included. But the governor was greatly concerned over the possibility of being held in contempt and later the next day, in an aside, he handed me his private, unlisted telephone number and asked that I call him as soon as I finished testifying, no matter how late the hour.

On Thursday we drove to Jacksonville and checked into the Robert Meyers Hotel, where Joe Jacobs and I had a room together. The hotel was directly across the street from the federal courthouse. Later that evening, we learned that a mob of white segregationists had gathered in St. Augustine. They were angry because a white teenager had been clubbed by a state policeman when the teen had broken through police lines at a beach in St. Augustine. Some demonstrators, including children, had also been injured; thirty had required treatment at the local hospital. The possibility of a conspiracy between Manucy and the Klan was buttressed by a statement he made during a news conference. He said the attack may have been caused because excessive force was used in arresting some of the Klansmen at the recent swim-in.[9]

The next morning, our party, including the attorney general, met for breakfast in the hotel dining room. Seated at a table next to us was a group of businessmen from Jacksonville that included Ed Ball, the richest man in Florida. His sister had married Alfred I. DuPont who established the DuPont empire in Florida. Upon DuPont's death in 1935, Ball had been appointed to administer his brother-in-law's estate and with it control of the vast DuPont empire in Florida. Ball's money and influence had helped elect Farris Bryant governor in 1960.

Ball was also given credit for the defeat of Senator Pepper by George Smathers in 1950 and was said to control many of the state's political leaders. Farris Bryant had confided to me, just before the election in 1960, that Ed Ball's influence would help him be elected governor. Ball's business interests included the Florida East Coast Railway, whose corporate offices were located in St. Augustine, the St. Joe Paper Company, one of the largest private landowners in Florida, and the Florida National Banking system. Most days he could be seen having breakfast, lunch, or dinner with his political and business associates at the hotel. Calling across to our party, he said, "Tell the governor if 'Cowboy' puts him in jail, I'll go bail." Judge Simpson, who was from Kissimmee "cow country," was often referred to by the nickname "Cowboy," but never, never to his face.

Ed Ball had undoubtedly been influential in Simpson's appointment to the federal bench.

When we crossed the street and entered the federal courthouse the hallway was filled with reporters, milling around, waiting for the hearing to start at 9:30. It was scheduled to last for two days. The courtroom was packed with spectators and lawyers anticipating the governor's appearance. It was a massive room with high ceilings and impressive walnut paneled walls. Above the judge's bench hung the great seal of the United States of America, inscribed with the phrase *fiat justitia*, "let justice be done." In Roman times the mandate of the Caesars guaranteed justice for all citizens of Rome, wherever they might live within the far-flung Roman Empire. Under our system there were two sovereigns in the courtroom that day with two different approaches to administering justice, one of which would define how the demonstrations would be conducted in St. Augustine.

As the proceedings began, a game of cat and mouse took place between the judge and the attorney general. The judge wanted to know why the governor was not present in court. He wanted assurances from the attorney general that the governor had been properly served and had personally read the order. All the lawyers in the courtroom, and most of the news reporters, knew that this line of questioning was designed to lay the groundwork for holding the governor in contempt. The hearing began on Friday, and that night, as if to emphasize his executive power, the governor toured "strife-torn St. Augustine" and called up eighty more law enforcement officers to help prevent further racial violence. He issued a statement that he was considering "banning all demonstrations day and night."[10]

The attorney general, who was also named as a party in the contempt proceedings, argued that Judge Simpson did not have the right to countermand an executive order of the governor. Since the legislature had enacted legislation giving the governor power to issue such an order, it had the legal effect of a duly enacted state statute and only a panel of three federal judges could declare a Florida statute unconstitutional. "The Governor of Florida has the dominant interest in preventing violence and disorder in the state not the federal government." It was purely a state matter, he argued. "The State is the natural guardian of the public against violence, not the federal government. No act of this court should be interpreted to leave the state powerless to avert such emergencies." It was a classic Tenth Amendment argument. Judge Simpson did not seem impressed.[11]

At this point in the hearing there was little question in my mind that the judge was laying the groundwork to support an order holding the governor in contempt, and Kynes's arguments, I believed, would not be successful. This was high drama. The courtroom was as tense as any I had ever seen, but it was exhilarating to be part of this historical moment in the history of the state.

The hearing then proceeded to the taking of testimony on the issue of the necessity of state officers to interfere with the designated route of the demonstrators and the constitutional right of the governor to enter a order prohibiting night marches. This required sworn testimony from witnesses. In all, we subpoenaed some twelve witnesses to testify on behalf of the state to support the governor's contention that his ban on night marches was necessary to maintain law and order and that the demonstrators presented us with a clear and present danger sufficient to suspend First Amendment rights. One of the first witnesses on this issue was a young wildlife officer. Shortly after he was sworn in, he was escorted from the room by a federal marshal, quickly followed by the attorney general and a flock of reporters. A major crisis was obviously in the making. The officer had testified that his shirt had been torn in a scuffle with a demonstrator when the officer attempted to arrest him.

This was serious. If true, the credibility of King's claim that the demonstrations were peaceful, and therefore protected under the First Amendment, was at stake. I knew from personal experience that discipline among the demonstrators was excellent. Throughout the entire time demonstrations had been going on, often under the most adverse conditions, I had never witnessed or heard of a single demonstrator fighting back or engaging in disruptive conduct or abusive language of any kind. This was in spite of the torrent of abuse hurled at them by the Klan and other hoodlums. If it could be shown the officer's shirt had in fact been torn by one of the demonstrators, King's central constitutional argument was in trouble. This had happened to Hayling and the NAACP when Judge McRae ruled the petitioners had not come into court "with clean hands" because of Hayling's threat to "shoot first and ask questions later."

Judge Simpson ordered the witness to produce the shirt. When he replied he had sent it to his wife in Tampa to be mended, Judge Simpson had the witness escorted out of the courtroom under guard. He ordered marshals to proceed immediately to Tampa and retrieve the torn shirt, without alerting the wife or allowing the officer to place a phone call. The State asked permission to speak to the witness in private. Simpson consented. Tobias Simon, King's attorney, raised no objection.

Since I had been at the demonstration when the incident allegedly occurred, I was allowed into the conference room with the attorney general and the witness. I doubted the truth of the wildlife officer's assertion. We would certainly have been notified if such an incident had occurred. During questioning, he admitted he had lied; there was no torn shirt. The only thing to do was to convey this rather startling information to the judge and the other parties at once.

We talked first with Tobias Simon, explaining what had happened. Perjury, or testifying to an untruthful act or statement, can be purged if recanted during the same proceeding. However, it can also support a criminal contempt conviction. To our surprise, Tobias went to bat for the witness. He did not want him punished; he stated he knew the intense pressure the witness was under and if he recanted his testimony in open court, King would be satisfied. We then sought a private meeting in chambers with Judge Simpson.

It was a tense moment. The judge was not happy about a witness testifying untruthfully in his court. He gave every indication that he intended to hold the young man in contempt of court, but Tobias made an impassioned plea on King's behalf that the young man not be punished. Finally the judge agreed. Mabel Chesley, the *News-Journal* editorial writer covering the proceedings, was incensed and expressed her displeasure to me, but in view of King's position there was little she could say about the matter, except to report what had happened in the newspaper, which she indignantly did.

During the proceedings, I met with Mabel and a number of ministers from Boston University in a private conference room at the federal courthouse. L. Harold DeWolf, a distinguished theologian and King's mentor at Boston University, had come to St. Augustine, along with others, in an attempt to help resolve the crisis. I was continuing in my efforts to have a biracial committee appointed, and we met during the hearings to explore other avenues for easing the tension in St. Augustine. Meanwhile, the situation in St. Augustine continued to worsen. On Thursday night, a mob of hundreds of whites again attacked the civil rights demonstrators. Fights had broken out as demonstrators again attempted to integrate the public beaches and were attacked by Klansmen. In Congress, objections by southern congressmen to the Senate's version of the civil rights bill was sent to the rules committee, where it would be delayed, although for no more than ten days, as the debate over a meaningful civil rights bill continued.

At long last, late Saturday night I was called to the stand. After two days of lengthy and often acrimonious questions by both sides, with caustic comments about the good faith we had used to suppress the violence, tempers were short and both sides seemed to be spoiling for a fight. My direct examination began with the attorney general asking about the role I had played in diverting the marchers. I testified to the dangerous events that led to my taking this action. I had kept notes of the time and place of each incident I had observed and also noted the number of law enforcement officers on hand to provide protection for the demonstrators. I testified that I had been in the march that night. And although at the rear, I had firsthand knowledge of the danger that existed. I testified to the reasons for diverting the march, describing the area where the marches were being held and stressing the fact that this area posed a considerable threat from snipers. I pointed out that demonstrators, including small children, could easily have been injured or killed by someone hiding in ambush. I finished my direct testimony by heatedly stating, "Hoss Manucy is not going to take over law enforcement in St. Johns County as long as I am state attorney."

On cross-examination, Tobias Simon suggested that my attempts to soothe racial unrest in the city were nothing more than a ploy to obstruct King and that I had given in to the pressure of the Klan. I vigorously denied this totally false suggestion and testified to the good faith efforts we had made in attempts to reach a peaceful solution to the impasse. Tobias then accused me of being in cahoots with the sheriff and using the grand jury as a ploy to aid the Klan. This was of course not true; however, it revealed how King had completely misread my efforts to resolve the matter peacefully. My last comment about Manucy may somehow have led Tobias to suspect that I was cooperating with the Klan. Or he may have been referring to the statement issued by the grand jury calling on "all citizens to desist from any acts that would add to the racial unrest." For whatever reason, I was puzzled by this line of attack.

I had been trained, as a trial lawyer, not to respond in anger to provocative questions but to field each question, no matter how insulting, with measured restraint, always giving a firm but unemotional response. I am a rather emotional man and have struggled for years to control my quick temper, but before I could respond to Tobias's question, L. O. Davis blew up. Rising from his seat at the respondent's table, he vehemently denied the accusation, shouting it was a lie. The proceedings came to a halt as Judge Simpson sought to maintain order, but L. O. refused to be silenced. Judge Simpson joined in, accusing officials in St. Augustine of doing absolutely nothing to control the explosive situation. I could not restrain myself, and I joined the fray. Pulling out the pocket diary I had kept during the entire time I had been in St. Augustine, I recited the time and place of the steps we had taken to control the situation, including my June 19 meeting with King at Puryear's office, a fact not publicly known until now.

After Judge Simpson finally got the hearing under control, the questioning returned to me. Tobias attempted to go on to another matter but I stopped him. Turning to Judge Simpson, I addressed the court. "Your Honor," I said, "I haven't had an opportunity to reply to the last question," the one that had provoked the sheriff, and I asked permission to respond for the record. Judge Simpson seemed a little annoyed but he nodded for me to continue. Looking Tobias straight in the eye, I calmly said, "No."

When Tobias finished his cross-examination, I was excused as a witness. I paused, again struggling to control my emotions, and said I wanted to give additional testimony about the danger night marches presented. "I would like to address the court on this issue," I said. It was very late, close to midnight, but the courtroom was still filled to capacity. For a moment I thought Judge Simpson was going to hold all of us in contempt.

Judge Simpson was a tall, gangly man, with rugged features like those of a working cowboy, one who had been on the open range too long. He had an unruly shock of white hair that defied all efforts to be combed into place. With a deep, weary sigh, he leaned far back in his chair, closed his eyes, and said, "All right, Mr. Warren, you go right ahead."

I took a deep breath, and as calmly as my pent-up emotional state permitted, I began: "I don't care if you call out every marshal at your disposal." I paused for effect. "Or if you call out the 101st Airborne. You cannot protect the marchers. If they are allowed to march in the old city at night we cannot ensure their safety. There are a hundred places where a sniper can hide and kill a marcher. There are small children in the march and there is no way we can protect them." I paused again, slightly longer this time. "I have six children of my own." And looking Judge Simpson straight in the eyes, I quietly added, "I don't want the blood of any of these children on my hands."

There was dead silence in the room and I thought Judge Simpson would surely hold me in contempt. He remained in the reclined position for a long time, contemplating that thought. Then, leaning forward slowly, he said, "Thank you, Mr. Warren. That was bothering me too."

At the end of my testimony, Judge Simpson recessed court saying he would rule on the motion by Tuesday. As I left the courtroom, Andrew Young ran after me. When he caught up, he said, "You killed us, Mr. Warren. The one thing we could not justify was the fact that young children were among the marchers." I said good night to Young and went to place the call Governor Bryant had requested. He must have been by the phone for it rang only once. When I told him of the exchange I had had with Judge Simpson and Andrew Young, he said, "God bless you, Dan," and then quickly added, "I will never forget this."

I was exhausted. After three weeks in St. Augustine, I needed a break. I headed for home.

Francisco Rodriguez, regional vice president of the NAACP, blasted King. In a statement released in Tampa on June 28, he said: "Unlike other areas, the St. Augustine savagery was not inevitable." He went on to say, "To those who ask me, why have demonstrations continued even after

passage of the civil rights bill [is certain], I have no answer. With pain-
ful reluctance, I am driven to the conclusion that those at the helm in the
city of antiquity now look away from the goals that we have immemori-
ally sought and have become obsessed with the burning ambition to bring
St. Augustine to its knees. This would be only of transitory interest were
it not for the fact that the entire struggle for human rights is being jeop-
ardized by what seems to be on one hand the yearning to demonstrate for
the sheer sake of demonstration and on the other the irrepressible impulse
in the heart of one man to have his name written on the skies as the 'super emancipator.'" He identified Martin Luther King as the man he was
referring to.[12]

This political rivalry between the veteran NAACP and the upstart
SCLC was not about their mutual goals but rather about the methods
used to achieve those goals. However, the criticism, at this rather precarious moment of the civil rights movement in St. Augustine, created a
stir among most whites in the city, who perceived the criticism as a personal rejection of King. And most of them, especially the political leadership, agreed with Rodriguez's sentiments. The fact that the tactics being
used by King were questioned by a high official of the NAACP was all
the ammunition locals needed to brand Martin Luther King as an inter-
loper, with a sinister agenda to destroy the city's image, and someone who
did not even have the support of the NAACP. These comments, coming
from an official of the NAACP at a critical time in the civil rights movement, revealed a growing division of style among some in the movement
as to how to eliminate segregation from society. Many citizens in St. Augustine agreed with the "super emancipator" sentiments.

The editors of the *St. Augustine Record* did not let up in their relentless
criticism of the movement. In an editorial titled "Governor, Local Officials Show Courage Not Brawn" the editor stated that "the question to be
answered in Judge Simpson's court is not one of civil rights. On the contrary, it is one of Federal Power v. State Power. If Simpson again rules
against the city, county, and state, he will in effect be saying that his decisions are the ultimate in the state of Florida and therefore he may control
all people under his appointed domain on any constitutional question."
The editorial pointed out the dangers of continued violence: "Continued

violence by mob action in the streets can only hurt the chances of our officials in court. Civil disobedience during the trial of our officials can greatly influence the court's action."[13]

The hope of peace that had seemed to prevail earlier disappeared as demonstrations continued and the city's mood changed from one of cautious hope to anger. On Saturday night, the twenty-seventh, violence broke out again. A white youth was wounded in both legs by shotgun pellets as he rode in the back of a pickup truck in a black neighborhood. Several blacks said their cars had been fired on and some were now fighting back.

On Sunday it rained, but a rally held by the segregationists went on. Klan spokesmen J. B. Stoner and Connie Lynch announced they planned to stay in St. Augustine as long as King remained. That same day, elders at the First Methodist Church turned a group of six blacks away when they attempted to attend the eleven o'clock service.

The Klan was now well organized, well coordinated, and even more dangerous, which we knew from having infiltrated their nightly meetings. We had recruited a young wildlife officer who was able to attend their meetings and keep us advised of their plans. Pickup trucks raced from one trouble spot to another. Their constant chatter over the CB radios was being monitored, enabling us to track the movements of their leaders.

I spent Sunday at home alone with my family but could find little mental peace. I had been taught that all individuals are equal in the sight of God, and over the years, as I grew to maturity and gained experience, I was more and more in sympathy with the poor, the downtrodden, and especially the blacks caught in the vice of hypocrisy in a country founded on the principles of equality. Morally inoculated by my parents' teachings of respect and tolerance for others, I had not been infected with the virus of racism.

I was stung by the unfair criticism of my efforts to solve the racial problems in St. Augustine and especially the pointed suggestion that I was in a conspiracy with the Klan. I knew my intentions were honorable and the question had obviously been designed to provoke me, but even so, it hurt. To have someone insinuate that I was a tool of the KKK was too much.

There was, however, a kernel of truth in a question posed by Judge Simpson: "Did anyone, from the governor on down to local officials, do anything other than to hope that Manucy would stop—did anyone, from the governor on down, appeal to him and his bunch to stop?" This question went to the heart of the matter that existed in St. Augustine. I knew the answer was no. In fact little had been done, especially by local law enforcement, to go after the ringleaders of the terrorists. The Klan had virtually taken over St. Augustine, as shown by the many businesses that were now collecting money to support the segregationists. Manucy's Ancient City Gun Club had taken on the folk status of "Manucy's raiders" and become local heroes to many in the community, a role Manucy played to the hilt.

Almost every restaurant had a collection jar soliciting money for the segregationists, and Manucy and his lieutenants made daily rounds collecting those funds. Klansmen were pouring in from all over the country to aid in the fight, and every act of violence that occurred in St. Augustine could be attributed to the Klan. In short, Manucy, Stoner, and Lynch had become the spokesmen for St. Augustine, and no one, including me, had challenged their authority to do so. Judge Simpson had hit the nail on the head, whether I liked it or not.

It was true we were still short of sufficient state troopers to completely control the situation, and the out-of-town law enforcement officers stationed in St. Augustine were very tired. There was little question in my mind the sole objective of most of these men was to maintain law and order in St. Augustine not to assist the Klan. Somehow I had to take a firmer stand against the Klan. This was not the time to be smarting from a wounded ego. Something needed to be done about the situation and I intended to do it.

I was back in St. Augustine on Monday, June 29. Tippen Davidson told me George Allen would have to come back to Daytona Beach and Mabel Chesley would cover events in St. Augustine for the *News-Journal*. I prevailed on him to let George stay a little longer and finally he agreed.

On the previous Monday, a series of demonstrations occurred at the public beaches when demonstrators and some white supporters tried to swim. They were attacked by about fifteen Klansmen armed with wooden survey stakes that they used as clubs. A few law enforcement officers at the scene broke up the melee before it got completely out control and arrested a number of Klansmen engaged in the free-for-all. Several hours later another altercation took place between swimmers and about twenty-five whites. This time, the only weapons were fists; a number of individuals engaged in the fight were arrested.

I was in my office at the National Guard Armory in St. Augustine on the following Monday. After the threats toward me made by two white toughs during the violence on June 19, Major J. W. Jourdan had assigned a young state trooper as my bodyguard. I was going over some matters with Joe Jacobs, the assistant attorney general, when the trooper told me there was someone in the lobby who asked to talk with me. "He's only wearing a bathing suit!" he said.

I found C. T. Vivian waiting in the lobby. He asked if I was in charge of law enforcement in St. Augustine and I replied, "Well, I'm the state attorney, so I guess I am." Flashing a nervous smile, he replied, "I want to go swimming." Smiling back, I said, "You're properly attired, so be my guest." He was prepared for this reply, and answered, "You don't understand, Mr. Warren. Every time we try to go swimming the Klan beats us up." Vivian was a tall, thin, rather nervous man, about my age, and as we faced each other, he constantly paced back and forth while still looking directly at me. Except for this apparent sign of tension, he was completely self-controlled. He certainly posed no threat to me, but the trooper assigned as my bodyguard, abruptly stepped in between us: "Don't get too close to Mr. Warren," he said. I waved him off with the assurance that "Reverend Vivian and I understand each other." Then I spoke directly to Vivian. "Will you agree to cooperate with me?" He replied, "It depends on what you mean by cooperation." I said, "If you will give me forty-five minutes, I'll ensure that you can go swimming and no one will bother you." He agreed and left. I realized this was a test to determine if we would enforce the law and protect the demonstrators.

This was the time to use the authority the governor had given me. I quickly dictated an order to Jourdan, which my secretary Clara Tillotson typed. It read substantially as follows: "Pursuant to the power invested in me by Executive Order of the Governor, you are to immediately take sufficient troopers under your command to the public beaches of St. Augustine, and there you are to maintain law and order. You are to provide protection for all individuals who desire to swim in the ocean or to use the public beaches of St. Augustine. If anyone attempts to interfere with another's right to use the public beaches, you are to advise them of this order. If anyone fails to obey this order, you are to use such force as is necessary to meet and overcome the resistance offered." I signed the order along with Joe Jacobs.

Jourdan acted immediately. In short order he had rounded up sufficient troopers to accompany me to the public beach. They were in place within the time agreed, ready to deal with the Klan. I was sure his officers would follow the order to the letter. They too had had enough of the Klan. The state troopers assigned to St. Johns County were disciplined law enforcement officers who had been on duty for more than a month and by now knew how to control threatening crowds.

The officers, with dogs held on leashes, escorted some thirty civil rights demonstrators into the surf. In parallel lines the officers formed a human chain and in full uniform waded into the water to form a protective barrier around the demonstrators. When the demonstrators started entering the water, a number of whites, waiting in parked pickups and cars along the beach, grabbed wooden survey stakes that had been hidden in truck beds and car trunks. Wielding these as weapons, the Klansmen made an attempt to break through the line of officers. The officers were ready, and some were aching to deal with the Klan. Using billy clubs they applied the force sufficient to "meet and overcome the resistance offered" that I had directed against the startled Klansmen. The Klansmen were soon scattered. A number were injured in the scuffle, and one was admitted to the local hospital. The rumor quickly spread that some of the attackers had been hospitalized and one might die. Klansmen were incensed, but the point had been made. Their reign of bullying was over. The next day the headline of a New York newspaper read "Fla. Gets Tough with Klan."

Jimmy Kynes called, and in an emotional voice said, "We're proud of you, Dan." I wasn't proud; I was angry. For despite this show of strength, the violence continued. Young white hoodlums drove their pickup trucks defiantly through the city at night looking for trouble. The Klan began gathering almost nightly outside the city, where the burning of a cross was the grand finale to their rallies of hate. Klansmen from as far away as Cincinnati arrived in St. Johns County to support their brothers in terror.

Fortunately, our decision to infiltrate the inner circle of Klan meetings paid off. We knew what they were planning. J. B. Stoner and Connie Lynch, who were conducting the nightly meetings on a vacant lot just outside the city limits of St. Augustine, off U.S. Highway 1, had been seen drinking coffee and conferring with Sheriff Davis at the courthouse. These meetings spelled trouble for the professional law enforcement officers we had assembled in the county. But the governor had ordered a crackdown on the violence and more law enforcement personnel were flooding into town. We now had the trained forces necessary to deal with any situation.

On Thursday night a small group of Klansmen broke through the ranks of state troopers guarding the demonstrators, but instead of attacking the demonstrators they assaulted the troopers. The Klansmen seemed to concentrate on officers who had protected the swimmers at the Monday wade-in. I was sure the officers attacked had been deliberately targeted by the Klan. Staying up most of that night taking testimony from witnesses, I bypassed the normal arrest procedures and filed "direct criminal information" against William Thomson for assaulting a state trooper.

This seldom-used procedure had the desired effect. In the past, when warrants were issued, probable cause hearings had to be held before either a justice of the peace or Judge Mathis to determine the sufficiency of the evidence. The procedure for filing a direct criminal information has the same effect as a grand jury indictment: initial probable cause was determined by me. Although the defendants had the right to question the sufficiency of the information, a circuit judge—not Mathis or Marvin Geer, who was the justice of the peace—would hear the evidence supporting probable cause. It was important that the Judge Melton rule on this vital issue, not Mathis or Geer.

In a press release, I warned the Klan we would not tolerate any more of their violence and at least ten other direct informations were forthcoming. It was the first major step against the Klan, one that directly challenged their reign of violence. The Klan got the message. They would respond in the usual way, with threats of violence against anyone who attempted to challenge them, as I would soon find out.

Although Judge Simpson had indicated he would make a ruling on the contempt issue by Tuesday, no ruling was forthcoming from his office that day. His secretary said he was tied up with other cases; a decision probably would not come for a day or so. It was an indication, at least to me, that no order would be forthcoming. Some have speculated the reason Judge Simpson did not issue a ruling on the contempt charges was due to assurances from state officials they would crack down on the Klan, but I knew he must be having problems with the sufficiency of the evidence to support such a drastic remedy as contempt, and I did not expect a ruling anytime soon. Judge Simpson was one of the fairest, most decent judges I have ever met. I was sure that any decision he made would be based on the evidence, not on an alleged promise by state officials to provide more enforcement. I felt certain the evidence was so persuasive that Judge Simpson would not enter an order of contempt against the governor or anyone else. As it turned out Judge Simpson never did rule on the issue. Eventually it was dismissed.

In the week following the Klan's attack on the state troopers both sides began to draw back, seemingly spent. After nearly a month of often violent confrontations during which we had narrowly averted one disaster after another, both sides began to move cautiously.

I welcomed the reprieve; I too was exhausted. I had returned to the practice of driving back and forth from my home in Daytona Beach. The hour's drive, often late at night, was taking its toll. We lived in Daytona Beach Shores, on a rather isolated section of the beach. The house was exposed to anyone who might want to harm my family; all they had to do was drive along the beach at night and firebomb the house. The Klan was grumbling about the latest arrest of one of their members and my threat to file direct informations against others. Connie Lynch was heard to complain there was a Trojan horse in their midst. He was correct. The young wildlife officer we had planted in their ranks continued to give us vital intelligence as to the Klan's plans and activities.

8   Exodus with Honor

The failure of Judge Simpson to promptly rule on the contempt citation was seen as a victory for the state. The judge's decision to defer a ruling on this critical issue had placed King in a rather precarious situation. The Klan was growing stronger and now the attorney for the Florida southeast district of the NAACP was attacking King. Francisco Rodriguez had labeled King a "super emancipator," which had created a sensation in St. Augustine. Somehow, King had to find a way out.

On the afternoon of June 19, George Allen and I had been seated in a booth at the Monson Motor Lodge Restaurant when an Associated Press reporter approached us. "Dr. King asked that I deliver a message to you," he said. "Would you be willing to meet with him? He said it could be off the record and no one need know."

Without hesitation I replied, "Please tell Dr. King I will meet him any time, any place, day or night, public or private. Just name the time and place." A few minutes later, the reporter returned. He had talked with Dr. King. "He would like to meet with you in Dr. Puryear's office at Florida Memorial College at seven o'clock this evening." I immediately agreed.

Shortly after 6:30, George and I headed out of the parking lot of the Monson Motor Lodge to meet Martin Luther King. Florida Memorial College was located on a few bleak, barren acres of land on the western outskirts of the city. We were met by Royal W. Puryear, King, and some of King's aides. It was a hot, stifling evening, and the confines of the small office added to the discomfort. There was no air conditioning and as we crowded around Puryear's small desk, I was sweating profusely. King, immaculately dressed as usual, looked, as we say in the South, "cool as a cucumber." I joked that when he received full equality he would find you could not survive without air conditioning in Florida. King smiled and began the meeting by expressing his concerns with the grand jury report. "Mr. Warren," he said, "the grand jury's thirty-day cooling-off period has created insurmountable problems for me." I retorted that the swim-in at the Monson Motor Lodge exactly when the grand jury was finishing its report had hardened the attitude of most of the members, and I added that his rejection of their good faith effort to appoint the committee had created problems for me. I pointed out that the grand jury was the most responsible body in the county and their decision not to negotiate the thirty-day cooling-off period was nonnegotiable.

He appeared frustrated and quickly replied, "You don't understand, Mr. Warren, there are those in the civil rights movement," he said, mentioning more militant elements, "who don't think America is worth saving. They want to burn it down." He continued, "I don't want to burn America down; I want to save America."

"Dr. King, you don't have to preach to me, I have been in the civil rights movement longer than you have," I replied. I recounted the efforts I had made during my student days at Guilford College in an attempt to integrate Greensboro's social services and my close association with Mary McLeod Bethune when we formed a committee in an attempt to bring blacks into the political process. This rather presumptuous statement was a knee-jerk reaction to King's rejection of the grand jury's offer to establish a biracial committee, something I had labored long and hard to achieve.

The appointment of a biracial committee had been a sincere attempt by the grand jury to solve the racial conflict in St. Augustine. I pointed out to King that those who had been selected to serve were respected members of the community, headed by Andrew J. McGin, president of the local chamber of commerce. I told him of the help we had received from H. E. Wolfe, who had used his considerable influence to convince individuals to serve on the committee. The five blacks who had agreed to serve were also community leaders; they included Royal Puryear, president of Florida Memorial; Otis Mason, principal of a high school in Hastings, just outside St. Augustine; and Elzora Martin, a member of the local NAACP executive board. I explained that by rejecting the grand jury's proposal King had made it impossible for me to negotiate with its members.

King was silent. He showed the same emotion or lack thereof as when I had introduced myself during his appearance before the grand jury. That stoic stance puzzled me. I wanted desperately to convince him that I was on his side, but I needed some response from him, not his silence.

We then talked of other things, the Klan's violence and the failure of community leaders to talk with him or anyone in the SCLC. We discussed the danger of using small children in the demonstrations and of the fact that the Klan had the support of many in the community who were contributing money collected by local businesses to support the Ancient City Gun Club.

He asked me to intercede on behalf of local blacks who had been fired from their jobs with business leaders, and he wanted a guarantee from me that blacks would not be harassed if a truce were declared. I told him I would do everything in my power to provide adequate police protection. I also said I was working on a plan to deal effectively with the Klan but I could not guarantee him I could persuade the community's political leaders to cooperate, even if a truce were declared.

Others joined in the conversation, and after an hour, King wearily said, "Mr. Warren, I want out of St. Augustine, but I must come out with honor. I have never lost one of our maneuvers." The importance of this statement was not lost on me. George and I had discussed this very fact almost from the beginning. With this statement the meeting was over. We shook hands. I said I would do what I could to alleviate his concerns but it was going to be difficult.

As George and I drove away, I was deeply troubled. The truth was I had given little thought to what might happen if more militant groups moved into the area, but I had to concede it was a frightening prospect. King's remark that he wanted out of St. Augustine was the most troubling. The violence taking place in St. Augustine wasn't something you could easily walk away from, with or without honor.

George and I had discussed this very issue when we first came to

St. Augustine. George had been right. Demonstrations in St. Augustine had merely been the means for achieving a greater goal, passage of the Civil Rights Act. Now that that had been accomplished, King was desperately seeking a way out of St. Augustine. I was worried about what such a move would mean for those like Hayling who had fought for the cause and had to remain in St. Augustine after the SCLC left. After leaving the meeting with King, George and I drove around aimlessly, pondering the implications of what had happened and what our next move should be. The Klan was the key. We talked about how best to deal with the violence that had been unleashed by the Klan.

We had kept the operation to infiltrate the Klan a secret; only a few individuals in law enforcement knew about it. The project had provided some useful information but so far we had not decided how best to use the information we had acquired. I discussed with George what we had learned. We had identified the leaders of the Klan, the ones who played the most important roles in its daily operations, including the communications expert who had arrived from Georgia. Klan members had a rather elaborate communication system that allowed them to keep in touch with each other and effectively avoid areas where we had concentrated our law enforcement efforts. The communications expert serviced the two-way radios, but of more immediate importance to us was the fact that his wife had accompanied him to St. Augustine. We knew she was playing fast and loose with Holstead Manucy while her husband was busy elsewhere; her husband did not know about it. We decided to tell him everything.

George and I also discussed the nightly burning of crosses on private property. We now knew the property was owned by a baking company in Tallahassee with a local office in St. Augustine. Joe Jacobs had checked with the secretary of state and obtained the name of the resident agent who operated its local baking company in St. Augustine.

The most difficult part of our plan, at least for me, was the decision to ask the Klan to call off their night marches into black neighborhoods. George suggested that since Manucy was running the show we should approach him and ask that demonstrations be called off. I was reluctant to deal with him, but George reminded me of the remarks Judge Simpson had made during the contempt hearings: no one in authority in St. Augustine had made any attempt to speak with members of the Klan and ask them to stop. As unpleasant as this course of action was for me, I decided to give it a try.

The next day, I stopped by the sheriff's office at the courthouse. I found him as he was leaving the courtroom. "Hold on," I said, "I need to talk to you." We stepped back into the vacant courtroom and I explained that we had to convince Manucy to call off the that night's march. "Would you try to get him to agree?" Much to my surprise, he didn't hesitate. "Sure," he said, "I'll go talk to him now."

The sheriff soon got in touch with me. Manucy had not agreed to call off the march, but he did agree to meet with me. Where did I want the meeting to be held? Joe Jacobs and Elmer Emerich, the governor's investigator, were staying at the Holiday Inn on U.S. Highway 1 so I told him that would be the best place. "Tell him I'll meet him at 7:30 tonight." The Klan was scheduled to begin the march at nine o'clock, and this would give us just enough time to have it called off, provided Manucy agreed. I contacted Joe Jacobs and also the attorney general to outline our plan. It was agreed that the attorney general would be by the telephone in Tallahassee so if Manucy balked at calling off the march, we could have the attorney general talk with him. He would have a hard time saying no to the attorney general.

I had first met Manucy in 1963 at the funeral of William Kinard, the young man who had been killed while a passenger in a car driven by Manucy's son in the Lincolnville section of St. Augustine. I had also seen him from time to time in the sheriff's office at the courthouse, where he seemed to spend a lot of time. His recent fame had lifted him to a new status in the community: from convicted moonshiner to folk hero. It was quite a step up the social ladder but Manucy was no Robin Hood. He was racist to the core. His sudden importance in the county had made him a man of some importance, but his easygoing manner masked the pent-up hatred he held for blacks. His new status as a folk hero in St. Johns County made him an important source for television newsmen who sought him out to obtain sound bites to spice up their stories about the racial violence in St. Augustine. This made Manucy an important spokesman for the Klan. And this was the man I had to deal with because, in the absence of true leadership, he had been co-opted as an unofficial leader of the community. His cooperation was essential to the peace, if not the dignity, of the city.

Joe Jacobs, Elmer Emerich, George Allen, and I conferred before the meeting. The plan was to write a script for Manucy to read to the assembled Klan in the park that night, if he agreed to call off the march. We wanted to make sure that any statement made would be free of racial slurs, a tall order for a man like Manucy. I knew the Klan meeting that evening would be covered by television eager to capture the visceral hatred of the Klan. They could count on Klan leaders to spew well-rehearsed racist slogans to a national audience. Allowing Manucy to play the race card on national television, while appearing to comply with the grand jury's request to refrain from further violence, was a risk I did not want to take.

Manucy arrived, accompanied by one of his lieutenants, a small, thin man with a clubfoot. I explained what we wanted him to do and asked that he call off the march. He protested. "I can't do that, Mr. Warren," he said. "This is a democratic club. The membership would have to vote on it first."

I challenged him. "Come on, Holstead, I thought you ran this organization, and now you tell me you have to ask someone else to call it off!"

He faltered, "I can call it off, but it ain't going to go over too well with the members."

"Look," I said, "the grand jury has asked all good citizens to help keep down the violence. Are you going to go against the grand jury's request?"

"Well," he replied, "everyone's ready to march."

Playing my trump card, I replied, "The attorney general of the state of Florida is on the phone in Tallahassee waiting for your word the march has been called off. You go talk to him and tell him you won't do it."

He was stunned and could only stammer: "The attorney general?"

"Yes," I replied, and directed him to the next room where Joe was holding the phone with Kynes at the other end of the line. We could hear only Manucy's side of the conversation, which consisted of "Yes, sir," "Yes, sir, I'll do it," "Thank you, sir."

Emerich had a typewriter in the room, one used to write his daily reports for the governor. George quickly typed the statement we had agreed to use, and I handed it to Manucy. Fumbling with his glasses, he seemed to have difficulty reading the short statement. We suddenly realized he couldn't read. "These damn glasses they gave me in the pen ain't no good," he stammered. "Just tell me what you want me to say."

I had a sinking feeling about Holstead's making a statement on his own and feared it would end in disaster, but we had little other choice. We verbally went over the statement with him, reminding him that millions would be watching on national television and to be on his best behavior. Although he assured us that he would, his behavior, unfortunately even at its very best, was socially challenging. We had reached an agreement, and to celebrate Holstead took out a pint of moonshine stashed in his hip pocket and said, "Let's have a drink." He took a swallow, and passed it around. I declined as politely as I could.

George and I decided to walk down to the park that evening to watch.

There is something primeval about a mob, the way it reacts to timeless savage instincts. There is a raw brutality that seems to draw strength from each member and then mutates into a hundred forms of malevolence as the crowd absorbs the common bond of mutual hate. That night the mob allowed us to see a reflection of a community's failure "through a glass darkly." When Manucy arrived, J. B. Stoner and Connie Lynch had the assembled crowd of some five hundred Klansmen at fever pitch.

When time came for the march to begin, Manucy took the stand and hushed the crowd. In the most commanding voice he could muster, he said, "The grand jury has asked all us good citizens to help hold down the violence. So, we ain't going to march tonight." There was a thunderous roar of disapproval from the angry crowd of Klansmen, who shouted in unison, "No! No!" They wanted no part of the grand jury's request. The shouts grew louder, "We're gonna march!" Boos rent the air and Holstead had a hard time calming the crowd. Someone yelled, "There's a fifth column among us!" Finally, Manucy quieted the crowd. There would be no march through the black community that night. But Manucy couldn't keep from having the last word. "If them niggers march," he yelled into a bank of television cameras and to the rest of the world, "we're gonna march!" The attempt to mold Holstead into a good citizen, heeding the request of the grand jury, had missed its mark. We sadly shook our heads and walked away.

In my talks with the governor, he had spoken of the possibility of appointing a biracial committee himself, but he was very secretive about the idea. "It's hush, hush, at the moment," he said. The committee named by the grand jury had never met; in fact, some of those who had agreed to serve had backed out. In effect, there was now no biracial committee and the idea of the governor's appointing one seemed to me a way out of the impasse. I hoped he would have more success than I was having.

On Thursday, June 30, when the governor announced the appointment of a committee and said that Martin Luther King had declared a truce I was relieved. In making the announcement, the governor said, "Whether we agree with the civil rights bill or not—and I do not—it is time to draw back from this problem and take a look down the long road at the end of which, somehow, we must find harmony."[1] When the governor had first taken office, he had announced that members of a civil rights committee established by former Governor Collins had been reappointed, when in fact, the committee had been allowed to expire. Finally, I thought, a biracial committee has been appointed. Later I was to find out it was a hoax.

King announced that he was calling off the demonstrations for two weeks. In announcing "victory," he said, "The purpose of our direct action was to create a crisis, a tension, to bring our case out in the open, so they would talk about it. . . . Now they have agreed to it." He was quoted in the *News-Journal* as saying that "[the] committee will begin immediately to discuss ways to solve the racial problems of St. Augustine and grapple with the just grievances of the Negro Community." With that remark, he left St. Augustine. He returned only one more time, when he threatened to take to the streets again but never did. The governor never released the names of the four individuals allegedly appointed to the committee. Mayor Shelley was incensed that the governor would appoint a committee over his objections. When confronted, the governor replied, "The truth of it is, I haven't formed a committee in St. Augustine."[2]

George Allen had been right. Now that the civil rights bill had been signed into law by the president, Martin Luther King was ready to leave St. Augustine. Many blacks in the community, including Hayling, were incensed that King had called off the demonstrations. His group had not been consulted, and they were the ones who had been fighting the battle since 1963.

On Saturday night, July 4, about 250 Klansmen, carrying Confederate flags with the U.S. flag turned upside down, marched through St. Augustine. There was no violence that night, but the long, hot summer was not over. There would be a high price to pay for failed leadership on both sides. Although demonstrations had been going on long before King arrived on the scene, the local movement seemed to lose its cohesion after King's departure. But the Klan was not ready to give up.

On July 2, Tobias Simon released a statement in Miami asking Judge Bryan Simpson to quash the petition he had filed seeking to hold Governor Bryant in contempt. "We took this action," he said, "to show our good faith and aid in the genial feeling that is beginning to pervade the area."[3] Tobias was seriously misinformed if he believed a "genial feeling" prevailed in St. Augustine. The Klan had virtually taken over the city. Masked by the banner of the Ancient City Gun Club, it had the support of many of the white citizens in the county, and with King's abrupt departure, collection bins overflowed with cash, funding the Klan and allowing "Hoss" Manucy to thrive and prosper.

Although there were acts of violence, leaders of the Klan had yet to step over the rhetorical constitutional line of "shouting fire in a crowded theater." Individual members certainly stepped over this line, but these incidents, which occurred mostly at night in hit-and-run attacks, were almost impossible to predict or to stop. These clandestine acts of violence—such as smashing windows at Senator Pope's insurance company, throwing rocks at a business owned by a member of the grand jury, and shooting into the homes of sleeping blacks—were carried out in the darkness of night. Absent a case of conspiracy among Klan members, one that could be tied to Manucy, Stoner, or Lynch, the Klan could continue their verbal harassment under the protection of the First Amendment. Time and local citizens continued to defend the Klan and its leaders, saying they had as much right to demonstrate as King and the SCLC. The mistaken belief by many in the community that the violent conduct of the Klan was equivalent to the peaceful demonstrations of the SCLC strengthened the growing power of the Klan. Somehow it had to be stopped.

George and I discussed the problem of the Klan at length the night after I met with King. George was about to begin a series of articles, a survey of the events he had witnessed in St. Augustine. The first of the articles was scheduled to appear in the *News-Journal* on Wednesday, July 1. In the article, he would review the unrest, pinpoint the causes, explore the lessons we had learned, and examine how the attempt to stop the demonstrations through negotiations and bring an end to segregation had failed.

When certain members of the biracial committee advocated by the grand jury resigned, that failure seemed complete. I suspected some of them had had this in mind when they agreed to serve. I couldn't prove this, but even so, it left a sour taste in my mouth and I was extremely disappointed. In the climate of hate and distrust that prevailed in the community, it was extremely doubtful a functioning committee could ever be formed. Ironically, the situation in St. Augustine was far worse than it had been when I first arrived. The temporary standoff was just that, temporary. I was under no illusion the situation would improve when the truce ended on July 14. The fears I had expressed to George when I first arrived in St. Augustine were coming true, though there was little solace in being proven right.

At a rally on June 30, King told a jubilant crowd that a victory had been scored. It would prove to be a hollow victory for the many dedicated individuals who had gambled everything they had to support the movement. Hayling had risked "his last dime" to be free from segregation, and now he and many others were left alone to face the ongoing hostility of the Klan.

The announcement by James Brock that Monson's Motor Lodge would abide by the law was a major step in the right direction, even though he appeared to pander to the Klan by quickly adding, "we're not capitulating to anybody. . . . We had no other choice." On Wednesday, July 1, a group of St. Augustine businessmen met to discuss the civil rights legislation scheduled to be signed into law by President Johnson the next day and pledged to abide by the Civil Rights Act. For the moment racial peace returned to St. Augustine.[4]

Governor Bryant began pulling out many of the special state police assigned to St. Augustine. I thought the crisis was over, especially with the governor's assurance that the still unnamed biracial committee would start to work soon, and I made preparations to return to Daytona Beach for a much needed rest.

I relished these few days of peace with the hope it would last. But be-

fore I threw myself into the task of clearing the many cases that had accumulated around the circuit and needed immediate consideration, my
family needed my attention. July 4 was the date of the annual Firecracker
400 held at Daytona International Speedway. Our family, especially the
boys, loved automobile racing.

In 1952, as a young city commissioner, I was instrumental in promoting the speedway and since 1953 had been a member of the Speedway
Authority, a public body created by the legislature to oversee the lease of
public land on which the track was built. My position on the authority
and my friendship with Bill France Sr. gave us access to the track. My
family always looked forward to this annual outing, especially the festivities that preceded the race. We had the best seats in the house, on the finish line in the Sir Malcolm Campbell Grandstand, and before the race we
had a cookout behind Club 92, a local restaurant owned by a friend, across
the street from the speedway.

We always invited friends from the racing fraternity to join us. It was
an all-day event where we could relax and enjoy this fast-growing sport
that was proving to be extremely popular, especially in the South. Lurk-
ing in the back of my mind was the volatile situation that still existed in
St. Augustine, one that could be reignited at any moment by a spark of
violence. The possibility of having to return at a moment's notice was
constantly with me, but for the time being I relaxed with my family and
friends.

In Jacksonville, Klan attorney J. B. Stoner announced the KKK would
march on Saturday, July 4, despite an announcement by Manucy that the
rally had been called off. Stoner claimed hundreds would participate, but
his claim was exaggerated. Even though the march was relatively small,
the ritualized festival of hate held afterward in the woods was a sure sign
the Klan had not retired from the field of battle.

Yet there were also hopeful signs. James Brock, acting as spokesman
for the St. Augustine Hotel, Motel, and Restaurant Owners Association,
made a statement to the press: "We want to do everything we can to get
our community back to normal with harmonious relations between the
races."[5] Brock was a decent man caught between the violence of the Klan
and the unwillingness of community leaders to find meaningful ways
to end segregation. His whole business enterprise was built around the
Monson Motor Lodge and the demonstrations threatened his financial

stability. He would pay a high price for advocating harmony among the races.

The first in the series of articles George Allen had written on the St. Augustine racial crisis appeared in the *Daytona Beach News-Journal* on July 1. In this article, he assessed the situation we had encountered in early June, reviewing the events that had occurred over the past month. Allen highlighted seven individuals who played key roles in the crisis: Martin Luther King, Holstead Manucy, Farris Bryant, James Kynes, L. O. Davis, Bryan Simpson, and me. He revealed to his readers the story behind the headlines. This account was based on his unique position as a reporter, an eyewitness, and one of the architects of the plan for resolving the crisis. The full story had not previously been revealed to the public. He detailed the meetings we held with King and Manucy, the hopes we had cherished, and then the disappointments we experienced as events spun out of control. Tippen Davidson, the *News-Journal*'s managing editor, need not have worried; George Allen's journalistic integrity remained intact. He told the story as only he could tell it: someone who had been an integral part of it from start to finish. In revealing the details of the drama that unfolded in St. Augustine, he discussed the lack of leadership from the community's elected officials, the unheeded warnings given by the grand jury in 1963, and the adamant refusal of community leaders to appoint a biracial committee. He highlighted the dilemma King faced when the grand jury offered to appoint a biracial committee, the acceptance of that offer by segregationists, and the consequences of King's unexpected rejection. The rejection threatened to bring about the collapse of the civil rights movement in St. Augustine and George reasoned that King knew a failure in St. Augustine would undermine the confidence his followers had placed in him.[6]

The accuracy of this assessment was revealed by the criticism that had been leveled at Martin Luther King by Francisco Rodriguez, the vice president of the NAACP in Florida. The debate over the best strategy for eliminating segregation and achieving racial equality had been going on for more than seventy-five years. The debate was still going on in 1964, and Martin Luther King was not immune to criticism from those who disagreed with his approach.

In the second article, published July 2, George wrote of the collision between King, the Klan, and "Hoss" Manucy, the self-styled general of Manucy's raiders: "Standing on the sidelines were city and county officials, unwilling to voice moderation for their own individual reasons, including fear of personal or political retaliation by irate super-racists." In the third and final article, published on July 3, George wrote that the middle ground for compromise disappeared in the tragic consequences of inaction. "Race-baiters brought in from Georgia and Alabama," he noted, "climbed atop a picnic table in the town square on Thursday night. . . . Under the glare of television lights, backed up by fluttering Confederate flags, and cheered on by hundreds of men, women and children, [they] loosed tirades against everyone who sided with what the racists called 'niggers, Jews, Catholics, the Communist-dominated Supreme Court, Martin Luther Coon, and the Federal Bureau of Integration.'" He wrote of our meeting with King and our meeting with Holstead Manucy and described other efforts we had made to resolve the crisis.[7]

The 1964 Civil Rights Act was signed into law on Thursday, July 2. It mandated equal treatment for all customers in hotels and motels with five or more rooms; in eating establishments, including lunch counters and cafeterias; in theaters, movie houses, concert halls, sports arenas, stadiums, and other places of public entertainment; in short, in any facility that served the public. It also prohibited segregation in public schools. The act finally brought relief to the nation from the terrible tragedy of segregation, and barriers throughout the South began to fall, though new forms of racism more difficult to define would appear. Racism wasn't just about public accommodations or desegregated schools. It was, above all else, about equal opportunity. Nonetheless there was a decided change throughout much of the South as business leaders acknowledged the need to comply with the law. And indeed, the new law had bite. States and municipalities that discriminated in education or other public programs could have federal funding cut off. Some southern congressmen called this the most severe provision of the act, but it proved to be an effective way to end segregation.

President Johnson named LeRoy Collins, former governor of Florida, to head the Community Relations Service, which had been created to help local communities resolve differences over discrimination. During his last term as governor, Collins had begun to moderate his view on race, and after his term as governor ended in 1960 he had publicly displayed a substantially more liberal stance. Secretary of Commerce Luther H. Hodges was also assigned to the Community Relations Service. He was the former governor of North Carolina and also a moderate on race relations. The two mediators set out on July 7, 1964, to tour southern states and explain the new law to local leaders. It was a daunting task. They were received not as emissaries of the president but as southerners who had abandoned their roots, which in a sense they had. They met strong resistance almost everywhere. In Florida, Governor Bryant said he had no duty to enforce the new law and did not intend to make use of former Governor Collins to help Florida with desegregation.[8] He did tell all Florida sheriffs that "violence cannot and must not be a part of our response" to the new law.[9]

Associated Press reporter Paul Wills wrote an article titled "Warren's Role as Peace Seeker in St. Augustine Strife Reviewed." The story was given wide publicity in many newspapers in the South. My hometown newspaper, the *Greensboro Daily News*, published an article on the role I played in helping resolve the crisis. I received numerous responses to these articles, not all of them favorable. Wills correctly quoted me as saying the key to maintaining peace in St. Augustine was to control the militant segregationists who were resisting integration throughout the South. "They must be made to realize that they will not be permitted to influence local law enforcement. As long as I am state attorney they are not going to exert this influence."[10] The chance to back up this statement came the same day this article appeared and would bring death threats to my family and me.

Sunday, July 5, was a lovely day and people had gathered on Vilano Beach Bridge to fish. It was a popular spot, especially as the tide changed. That day eight young hoodlums sealed off both ends of the bridge, which connected St. Augustine to Vilano Beach. This group of white racists, with bicycle chains wrapped around their hands, mercilessly assaulted all the blacks who were fishing on the bridge, including a woman and a child. One elderly man was thrown into the river below.[11]

This outrageous and savage attack, committed in broad daylight, exemplified racism in its most vicious and brutal form. Upon receiving the news that afternoon, I immediately returned to St. Augustine. But before

I left Daytona Beach, I called my friend Phil Chanfreau, the official court reporter for the circuit and asked him to assign one of his best court reporters to accompany me. We would take statements from any witnesses who could identify the individuals who had committed this raw act of violence. We arrived in St. Augustine just before dark and I set up an office in my assistant's law office on St. George Street. Law enforcement officers were instructed to keep searching for witnesses and to bring them to my office so statements could be taken and direct informations filed for the arrest of those involved. So began an all-night search for witnesses.

We were in luck. Officers had earlier interviewed a young sailor from the Jacksonville Naval Air Station who had witnessed the attack. He had had engine trouble in his small boat as he was fishing in the Tolomato River. Tying his disabled boat to the fenders guarding the approaches to the bridge, he mounted the ladder from the fender to the road just as the brutal assault took place. He rescued the elderly black who had been thrown from the bridge into the river. We contacted the commander of the naval air station and requested that the young sailor be brought back to St. Augustine. He arrived around three o'clock in the morning and with his help we were able to identify several of the assailants. Armed with this information I prepared criminal charges and had those he identified arrested that same day on felony charges of assault with intent to murder.

By morning, we had located five of the individuals who had carried out the beatings and the assault on the elderly black man. One was a juvenile; two were known members of the Klan; two others had just been convicted for breaking and entering and were free on bond awaiting completion of their presentencing investigation reports. Bail was revoked for the convicted felons and they were immediately taken before Judge Melton, where they were sentenced to jail for the burglary convictions. I again used direct criminal informations to charge the suspected assailants. Early the next day I held a press conference and warned that "criminal acts by one person against any other person will not be tolerated by this office. Marauding in the name of segregation will not be overlooked." I called for an end to racial violence, saying, "There currently exists a cooling-off period voluntarily agreed to by the leaders of the Negro community. This cooling-off period should apply equally to all citizens."[12]

Retaliation was not long in coming. The young wildlife officer who had infiltrated the KKK reported that at a Klan meeting that night members were plotting to kill not only my family and me but also the attorney general and his family. He emphasized that the threat was serious. I made immediate arrangements to protect my family in Daytona Beach as well as the attorney general and his family. For the remainder of my stay in St. Augustine, officers were stationed at our home and my children remember to this day the sound of the officer on the sundeck atop our house as he walked back and forth during the night. It was a tense time for our children, the youngest of whom was only four. It was a harsh lesson to learn at such an early age, that such hatred exists. And it is one they will never forget.

In the ensuing trial, the Klan, in an attempt to intimidate me, packed the courtroom. Sheriff Davis, fearing for my safety, suggested I use the back entrance to the courthouse during the course of the trial. I remembered the lesson taught by my father, the Klan was a hate group made up of cowards, and I told the sheriff "it will be a cold day in hell when the Klan makes me run for the back door." During the course of the trial, at every break, I plowed through the crowd of Klansmen spilling out of the courtroom and deliberately ate in the restaurant where they gathered for lunch. I responded to their taunts of "nigger lover" with a smile. Once during a break in the trial, as I descended the main stairway in the courthouse, groups of Klansmen were gathered at the foot of the stairs, talking. They apparently didn't see me, and one Klansman said, "I don't like the son of a bitch either, but I would sure hate to have him mad at me." I hoped he was referring to me. Two of the assailants were acquitted; three were convicted, but of lesser offenses.

On July 8, the *News-Journal* ran an editorial, written by Mabel Chesley, highlighting the efforts I had made to settle the racial crisis in St. Augustine. The banner headline read, "We're Proud of Dan Warren." It was a flattering editorial. Knowing Mabel, I suspected she had talked to Martin Luther King about our meeting and was encouraging me to try again. Even so, it was good to know my hard work trying to deal with the tense situation was being recognized by my local newspaper. The editorial pointed out the truth of my position in St. Augustine: "It is good to have seen this man's sound instincts of right conduct in action. He certainly was intensely unpopular with certain redneck elements in St. Johns County."[13] That was an understatement of the intense hatred the Klan directed toward anyone who attempted to integrate St. Augustine. Frankly, I didn't care about my popularity or lack of it. My mother and father had taught me right from wrong, and this counted more than whether I was popular.

The Monson Motor Lodge was integrated peacefully on July 7 when ten civil rights workers, divided into groups of twos and threes, began testing businesses to see if they were complying with the law. The businesses that did comply were soon confronted with picketers from the Klan, including J. B. Stoner and Holstead Manucy. On Monday night, July 13, five men attacked Robert Preiskil, a civil rights attorney from New York, and Henry Twine, a St. Augustine civil rights activist, outside the Congress Inn then fled before police arrived.[14] Gangs of whites began roaming the city, harassing and assaulting blacks they found abroad after dark. Manucy was heard to brag that the tactics were working, and fired by this initial success, he and his cohorts began pressuring other businesses to deny blacks service, threatening them with their picket brigades if they refused. Clearly, it was only a matter of time before all-out violence would begin anew.

Segregationists began picketing businesses that were opening their doors to blacks. One businessman said, "We're damned if we serve them [Negroes] and damned if we don't." Another said the white picketers "were much more effective than their Negro counterparts." Holstead "Hoss" Manucy claimed that picketed restaurants had "voluntarily agreed not to serve any more Negroes."[15]

On Thursday, July 16, I drove all night to take Mary and the children to Greensboro to stay with my family for the remainder of the crisis. I returned on Saturday, the eighteenth. Just before I left Greensboro, W. R. Weaver, a reporter from the local newspaper, called and asked that I grant him an interview. He was interested in what had happened in St. Augustine. When he arrived, he asked for my impressions of the crisis. "I have seen films of Hitler and the hate displayed by Nazi Germany during World War II," I said. "I was shocked [to see] the same hatred and screaming mobs in St. Augustine. It is hard to believe such things can happen in America." He asked for my impressions of Martin Luther King. I said that I was impressed with his integrity, but disagreed with his plan to create a crisis in St. Augustine. "You must not create a crisis without assuming responsibility for its consequences."[16]

I had said the same thing to King when we first met and at that time he had replied, "Civil disobedience has been recognized since the Boston Tea Party." I countered this position by saying "this is not the eighteenth century. We've come a long way since then." At least I thought we had, but the debate on how to end segregation had been going on in this country since the Civil War with violence as a constant companion. I wasn't sure we had advanced very far since then. I expressed my hope that the situation in St. Augustine could be peacefully resolved, but it was not to be.

On the seventeenth, King threatened massive new demonstrations within a week if civic leaders did not take steps to "end the terrorism of the Ku Klux Klan. . . . We're not going to let the Ku Klux Klan run St. Augustine. If it can be solved by negotiation, good; but if it means we must once more put on our walking shoes, we will do it that way. We are determined to be free . . . even if it means physical death."[17] King did not follow through with the promise to take to the streets again. But the violence continued. On the eighteenth and nineteenth, it broke out again as roaming groups of whites attacked blacks.

King expressed his frustration over this turn of events in an interview with Mabel Norris Chesley of the *News-Journal:* "I pray that I shall never have to demonstrate in St. Augustine again. I have been at this thing since Birmingham, and I would like to get out from under the tension."[18] There was little question that he was extremely tired. The demonstrators were also growing weary, and King's threat to start new demonstrations drew little support. Hosea Williams, one of the leaders of the civil rights movement with King, pleaded for volunteers and threatened to leave St. Augustine if more demonstrators did not come forward. Speaking to a group of about forty blacks, he said, "If I can't do anything in St. Augustine, I can better use my time in Alabama." When he asked for volunteers only two raised their hands. This disappointing response apparently shook Williams. "If our efforts peter out tomorrow, I'm going to kiss you all goodbye."[19] Then he, too, left St. Augustine.

To add to the mounting distress, the city now became the headquarters of the National States' Rights Party, which was running J. B. Stoner for vice president. He was paired with John Casper of New Jersey, its presidential candidate. On Sunday, July 19, at a Klan rally in St. Augustine, Stoner told some 150 Klansmen, "The way to white supremacy is to rid Congress of those who voted for the civil rights bill and get that nigger-loving Lyndon Johnson out of Washington" as he struck a match to a copy of the recent civil rights bill and set fire to a huge cross the Klan erected on private property three miles south of the city. We had been waiting for this opportunity.[20]

On Tuesday, July 21, two more blacks were beaten, and on July 24 the restaurant at the Monson Motor Lodge was firebombed. A crude bomb made from a soda bottle containing a flammable liquid was thrown through the window of the restaurant, igniting a fire and causing considerable damage to the motel and restaurant.[21] The Klan ensured that "normal and harmonious relations between the races" in St. Augustine would be thwarted as long as possible, and those who attempted to bring peace to St. Augustine would be punished.

I called the attorney general. The Klan was becoming more brazen in its defiance of the civil rights bill and of the civilian authorities in St. Augustine. I told Kynes it was time we did something about the Klan. I suggested he fly to St. Augustine, which he did the next day. I met him at the airport and on our drive into the city I outlined the plan I had in mind. We had witnesses to the fact that Stoner lit the match when the Klan set fire to the cross on private property. It was owned by the baking company in St. Augustine. We discussed using an old statute, passed in 1933, which made it a crime to burn a cross on private property without the written permission of the owner. The wildlife officer who witnessed the event had identified the other Klansmen on the platform at the time.

On our drive into the city, I suggested we stop by the bakery and have a talk with the resident manager. My plan was to walk into his office unannounced, place him under oath, and ask if he had given written permission for the Klan to burn the cross on company property. If he had not, I intended to have Stoner and those on the platform arrested. Joe Jacobs, Kynes, Jourdan of the highway patrol, and I marched into the manager's office. I introduced the attorney general and myself, then without further ado, I solemnly asked him to raise his right hand and placed him under oath. Had he given written permission for the Klan to burn a cross on the property? I asked. Visibly shaken, he said they didn't ask. "They just told me they were going to use it." That was enough.

I had arrest warrants issued for J. B. Stoner and the others on the platform. The Klan's communications expert who had been brought in from Georgia was asked if he knew his wife was running around with Holstead Manucy. He didn't. We told him. He immediately gathered up his equipment and his wife and left town.

I held a press conference to announce the arrests. "There will be additional charges tomorrow relative to violence in St. Augustine," I said. "We are going to vigorously pursue lawbreakers until peace returns." The governor, who had been notified of our plans, added, "These nightriders cannot be prevented in every instance, but we expect to pursue them vigorously."[22] The next day I filed felony warrants charging two white segregationists, Paul Cothran of Jacksonville and Bill Coleman of St. Augustine, with tossing a threatening note, weighted with a brick, through the window of a company that sold concrete and ceramic tile. It read, "Fire niggers or go out of business."[23] We found that Connie Lynch had made a false affidavit when he received his Florida driver's license in Jacksonville. I called my friend Eddie Booth, the Jacksonville solicitor, and Lynch was arrested.

In an ominous turn of events, those testing the power of the civil rights law attempted to be served at twenty-eight businesses open to the public and were turned away from twenty-three. It was apparent that many establishments in St. Augustine would not comply with the law. Klan marauders continued to stalk blacks at night, and on July 18, four blacks were beaten as they walked along U.S. 1. Later, a car was overturned outside the emergency room of the local hospital. A young black had driven to the hospital to be treated for injuries resulting from an attack. He had been escorted by officers through a crowd of angry whites gathered outside the hospital; when the police left, his car had been vandalized.

In a speech on Sunday, July 19, his first since the violence began, Governor Bryant called upon all Floridians to abide by the law. Speaking at the dedication of the new Marion County Courthouse in Ocala, he recalled the progress made over the past several years to bring blacks into the mainstream of American life. "Within the lives of everyone here the problems of civil rights have taken forms they never took before. Only a decade ago we assumed that education and goodwill would in time provide an answer with which all men could live, that individuals and communities [would] be permitted to work this out for themselves."²⁴ The governor had finally heard the "firebell in the night" to which Thomas Jefferson had referred in 1819. It was a bit late, for there was little goodwill left in St. Augustine.

The pressure on King must have been great, for now an additional problem began to threaten his movement. Civil rights leaders from around the country called upon him to back off, fearing the civil disobedience campaign was hurting the Democrats' chances in the 1964 elections. Senator Barry Goldwater, soon to be the Republican presidential nominee, was using the antagonism toward the new civil rights legislation to curry favor in the South. Segregationists were gaining in popularity as the impact of the new law began to be felt. King was at his wit's end. According to Mabel Chesley, he told her, "If you know of any other channels we can explore to bring this thing to an end, please let me know. If anyone can reach the power structure and persuade it to call off the Klan, we will welcome it."²⁵ There were few in the power structure who *could* call off the Klan and none who were willing to do so.

The moratorium called by King did not sit well with local civil rights leaders in St. Augustine. Hayling, speaking only for himself, was quoted as saying, "Dr. King cannot tell us what to do on the local level. We will not give up our gains and go away and hide our heads. This is one of the few places in the United States where there is a citywide effort to buck the civil rights laws. We brought Dr. King into the movement in St. Augustine. This was delivered to him on a silver platter."²⁶ Others in the civil rights movement also challenged King's call to curtail mass demonstrations. At a meeting of six of the nation's civil rights leaders, unanimous agreement could not be reached on whether to curtail demonstrations until after the national election. John Lewis, chairman of the Student Nonviolent Coordinating Committee, and James Farmer, national director of the Congress for Racial Equality, refused to go along with the moratorium.²⁷

On July 20 a way out of the St. Augustine impasse would be found in two lawsuits filed in the federal district court in Jacksonville. In the first, eight plaintiffs asked the court to enjoin the Knights of the Ku Klux Klan and the Ancient City Gun Club from using pickets and threats of violence to prevent businesses in St. Augustine from complying with the new law. In the second suit, King asked the court to take jurisdiction of the more than three hundred cases growing out of the demonstrations in St. Augustine. These cases were still pending before Judge Charles Mathis Jr. of St. Johns County.[28]

The move came just in the nick of time. On the twenty-second, the Klan held its biggest rally yet in St. Augustine. The crowd, estimated at close to six hundred, was told by Connie Lynch that the KKK was the last army of white men and that since the passage of the civil rights bill the ranks had grown enormously. On that same day, Judge Simpson threw out a renewed motion to have Governor Bryant held in contempt. He ruled (as I had expected) that the governor of Florida could not be put under an injunction because "a cop on the beat turns his head."[29] He complied with the request for an injunction against the Klan and the Ancient City Gun Club. He also issued a protective order keeping hundreds of civil rights protestors from being tried in state court. The effect of this order was to move to federal jurisdiction all the cases against demonstrators that were pending in state court.

Another suit sought to compel thirty restaurants to open their doors to blacks. The defendants in these two cases were divided into two classes. The motel and restaurant owners were class one defendants, and Holstead Manucy and other Klansmen were designated as class two defendants. The taking of testimony began immediately on the merits of these two suits. James Brock, besieged operator of the now infamous Monson Motor Lodge, testified to his frustration in attempting to comply with the new law and demanded the court get Holstead Manucy and the picketers off his back. After two days of testimony, Judge Simpson moved swiftly and entered an order that blacks had to be served at two St. Augustine restaurants, Rusty's and the Santa Maria. Both owners testified that the fear of violence had influenced their decision not to serve blacks.[30]

Hearings continued, and on the twenty-eighth, Holstead Manucy took the Fifth Amendment some thirty times as attorneys for King sought to show a conspiracy existed among segregationists to violate their clients' civil rights. The only question he would answer was whether he had ever been convicted of a crime. Judge Simpson ruled he had to answer this question. Everyone in the courtroom knew Manucy had been sentenced to two years in the federal penitentiary for making moonshine, so no one was surprised when he admitted he had been convicted of making 'shine.[31]

Lawyers for the SCLC continued to chip away at owners of recalcitrant establishments who refused to serve blacks after the civil rights law went into effect. Their questions centered on an alleged conspiracy that existed between members of the Klan, and James Brock testified that in July, when he opened his restaurant to blacks, Holstead Manucy, Jack Coleman, and others picketed his motel for three days. Brock reported that he asked Manucy to stop picketing his business and to get the others off his back, but Manucy replied that he didn't control the others. Brock insisted that he did, saying, "You are the kingfish with these people." Then he added, "It didn't help."[32] Picketing continued, and when Brock, justifiably frightened by Manucy and the Klan, was pressed to name the others, he pleaded with the judge not to require him to answer the question. "You put me in an unpleasant position when you ask me this. I am a little bit afraid to be talking like this." Simpson ruled that he didn't have to reply. The other picketers were later identified as Dixon Stanford and J. R. Woodall. Dixon Stanford was one of those who had been riding with Kinard when he was shot and killed in 1963. Judge Simpson provided Brock with a bodyguard for the remainder of the trial.[33]

Other restaurant owners testified they too were afraid. "I was scared, I don't mind admitting it," said Louis S. Connell, operator of the Santa Maria Restaurant. After all the testimony had been given, Judge Simpson enjoined the businesses named in the complaint from further violations of the law. The first ruling by a federal judge under the new Civil Rights Act, it was a dramatic breakthrough that would end segregation in St. Augustine and eventually throughout the South. In years to come, this ruling and others like it would be the main tool for breaking the back of segregation throughout the country.

On August 6, 1964, the next phase of the lawsuit began. It involved class two defendants, the Ku Klux Klan, the National States' Rights Party, the Ancient City Hunting Club, and twelve individual defendants. The plaintiffs sought the court's relief from the defendants' interference with implementation of the Civil Rights Act in St. Augustine.

On that same day Martin Luther King again claimed victory in defeating segregation in St. Augustine when he triumphantly displayed a copy of Judge Simpson's order requiring fifteen local restaurants to comply with the new civil rights law. He also claimed victory over the Klan and Manucy. King challenged the citizens of St. Augustine to accept the judicial decree and welcome the opportunity to live together in peace and harmony in a climate of justice.[34]

King's idea of justice was obviously different from that of Judge Mathis. But on August 7, Judge Simpson would bring some measure of justice to those defendants who had been required to post high bonds set by Mathis. He ordered the state to return the bonds forfeited by the judge. Many of the bonds had been posted by Charles Cherry, a Daytona Beach businessman. Their cases were moved to the federal district court in Jacksonville where they were ultimately dismissed.

Diehards in St. Augustine continued to resist, and on Friday, August 14, Judge Simpson entered a "rule to show cause" to the owners of the Empire Inn and Palms Congress Inn, requiring them to demonstrate why they should not be held in contempt of court for failure to allow blacks to register as guests. On Tuesday, August 25, 350 residents organized a Citizens' Council in St. Augustine, dedicated to combating the dangers of racial integration. Among the attendees were Justice of the Peace Marvin Griffin, Sheriff L. O. Davis, and Tax Assessor Percy Talethorp.

The last of the special state officers finally left St. Augustine and in a telephone conference with the governor, I praised the courage and dedication of those who had served so valiantly during the crisis. I urged him to have letters of commendation placed in the personnel file of every state officer who had served in St. Augustine. He agreed. They had been the true heroes in this bitter struggle, in contrast to law enforcement generally throughout the South. I was proud to have been associated with these men who had served our state so well under very difficult conditions. They deserved all the praise the governor could give them.

I also asked the governor to allow me to travel to New York to review the film that had been taken by NBC of the violence in St. Augustine. I thought it might be useful if we could develop a case of conspiracy. He agreed, and later I traveled to New York with two of my sons to view, once again, the graphic scenes of the violence the Klan had created in St. Augustine. It was a bitter reminder of the price we pay when good men fail to act.

When the crisis finally subsided, Andrew Young dropped by my office in Daytona Beach to thank me for my help during the crisis. He wanted to make sure there would be liaison between the SCLC and my office in the event further disturbances occurred in St. Augustine. We talked about the struggle that had taken place, and I compared his work in St. Augustine to that of an ambassador. I had just finished reading Robert Murphy's memoir *Diplomat among Warriors,* in which he had written of his experiences as President Roosevelt's wartime ambassador. I gave my copy to Young and wrote an inscription on the flyleaf. It read, "When the history of the civil rights movement has been finally written, Andy Young's name will be listed as an Ambassador for Peace." We spoke of several matters and discussed our upbringing. He knew I had attended Guilford College, a Quaker school, and told me his college roommate was a Quaker. Just before leaving he asked if there was a restaurant in Daytona Beach where he and his wife could have dinner without causing a disturbance. I immediately invited them to have dinner with Mary and me at one of our favorite restaurants. He thanked me, but declined. It was clear to me he too was dead tired and only wanted to go home without further ado. Like King, he had had enough of strife.

The battles King, Young, and thousands of others fought did defeat segregation, although it will take years before their goals can be fully realized. When President Carter appointed Young U.S. Ambassador to the United Nations, I wrote a note reminding him of the book I had given him, and of the inscription I had written. He did not reply, and our paths never crossed again.

Later that year, I was in Washington with my friend Bill France exploring the possibility of running for the congressional seat being vacated by Congressman Sid Hurlong. I stopped by the House of Representatives to watch committee hearings on Klan violence. Also attending was C. T. Vivian and we greeted each other as old friends. Bill France and

I also stopped to visit with former governor Bryant, who had been appointed the Federal Emergency Management Agency's planning director by President Johnson. We invited the governor to have dinner with us, but he declined, saying he had too much to do. When we returned to our hotel there was a message from the governor saying he would be able to have dinner with us, after all, and we met later that evening.

It was an interesting evening. Governor Bryant was rather fussy, often pompous, and slightly regal, but he was considered by many to be the best administrator ever to occupy the governor's office in Florida. Always soft-spoken, this evening he spoke in a near whisper that made the conversation seem conspiratorial. Choosing his words carefully, he told us he had just come from a national security meeting with the president and while it was still a secret, tomorrow the president would announce the call-up of fifty thousand more troops to fight in Vietnam. We would, he said, "now take the war to North Vietnam." I was appalled at the prospects of an all-out war and replied that if he did, we would rue the day it happened. I told the governor that we had no business fighting a war in Vietnam. Governor Bryant accused me of being unpatriotic but I held my temper. Later, I joined others in sending a telegram to the president protesting our involvement in Vietnam.

As the evening wore on the conversation turned to St. Augustine. For the first time I told Governor Bryant of my meeting with King and his statement that he wanted out of St. Augustine. Bryant was shocked and angry, demanding to know why I had not told him of this conversation at the time. I replied that it was not relevant to solving the problem. The governor disagreed; had he known this fact, he said, he would have reacted differently. At the time, I did not know of the deception used by the governor when he announced the phantom biracial committee. I had not wanted to politicize the delicate negotiations I had undertaken with King, and I knew if I told the governor of King's desire to leave St. Augustine, that's exactly what he would have done.

However, the governor was grateful for my service in St. Augustine. Later, he called and offered to appoint me to a new circuit judgeship the legislature had recently created in the Seventh Judicial Circuit. I declined. He was flabbergasted. "I don't understand you, Dan. I'm handing you a judgeship on a silver platter, and you won't take it. There are a dozen attorneys knocking at my door trying to get this appointment. You think about it and call me tomorrow." I did, and when I called the next day, I told him I wasn't cut out to be a judge. I had to advocate a position, and I couldn't do this on the bench. In the late fifties Governor Collins had appointed me to fill out the unexpired term of a judge he had removed for malfeasance. From this experience, I knew I did not have the temperament to be a judge. I have had no further contact with the governor since then, and though he invited me to a reunion of his administration, I declined. I had no further contact with King or any of his associates either, but I have not forgotten what took place in St. Augustine during those long, hot summer days and nights when violence ruled the city, when so few heard or heeded the critical firebell in the night.

Recriminations soon began. King's attorney, Tobias Simon, was under investigation by the Florida bar on complaints he solicited cases during the civil rights struggle in St. Augustine. Fred Karl from Daytona Beach, later a state senator and a Florida supreme court justice, also a friend of mine, defended Simon. Soliciting legal business is a violation of the rules of the Florida Bar, but if the individuals who made the complaint thought they could intimidate Tobias Simon they were sadly mistaken. His courage and personal integrity were well known among lawyers throughout the state and the threat of disbarment merely aroused his tenacity. He relished the opportunity to defend himself against the charges and filed a response setting forth the facts of his involvement in the 1964 struggle, pointing out he had worked without a fee. In typical First Amendment style he asked that all hearings on the complaint be held in public, something St. Augustine did not need or want.

The charges, brought by Donald E. Buck, the St. Johns County prosecuting attorney, and Fred A. Brinkoff Jr., chief juvenile counselor assigned to Judge Mathis's court, alleged that when demonstrations first began and massive arrests were made, Tobias had solicited the young demonstrators to hire him as their attorney. This was laughable because Tobias was working without a fee of any kind, but the complaint gave him the opportunity to question the secrecy of bar grievance hearings. At that time, as now, hearings on complaints against attorneys were investigated and held by local grievance committees composed of attorneys from the county where the alleged violation occurred. The committee would make a probable cause determination on the merits of the complaint before the bar made formal charges, which would then be made public. Hearings were always conducted in secret until probable cause was determined. Tobias wanted the public to be in on the proceedings from the beginning. He petitioned the Florida supreme court to open the hearings to the public and to make public the preliminary report, which had already been completed.

The supreme court ordered that hearings not be held by the Florida bar until it decided whether the bar's transcript of the preliminary investigation should be made public. Tobias wanted to have everything in the open, including the original transcript, but J. Lewis Hall, attorney for the bar, objected: he likened the hearings on grievance matters to a grand jury investigation, which, he argued, were always conducted in secrecy.

This brought the press into the picture, and the media clamored for release of the transcript of the preliminary hearing. On December 17, 1964, the Florida supreme court ruled the bar's investigations were secret and could not be revealed until formal charges were made. They never were. In May 1965, the Florida bar dismissed the charges without further comment.

On Monday, December 14, 1964, the U.S. Supreme Court ruled on a case involving people who were arrested during peaceful demonstrations throughout the South. It was the intent of Congress, the court ruled in a 5 to 4 decision, that the new Civil Rights Act was retroactive. This ruling meant that demonstrators who had been arrested but not yet tried—estimated to be close to nine hundred throughout the South—could not be prosecuted. All the cases were dismissed. But fallout from the demonstrations continued. On December 16, the Florida supreme court reversed an order by circuit court judge Melton that had dismissed twenty-two appeals from the 1963 demonstrations. The order was based on the court's finding that city ordinances prohibiting public meetings without first obtaining permission were unconstitutional. The supreme court, ruling that the appeals should have been allowed under general state law, reinstated them.

The struggle continued. On January 12, 1965, Judge Mathis refused to decide eight cases before him, ruling he might be held in contempt of the federal court that had enjoined him from proceeding with the cases.

Tobias Simon asked the judge to quash the charges based on the supreme court's recent ruling, but county attorney Donald Buck objected. "I don't know what cases were sent to federal court," he said. "I know some names came back, but these people may be in other cases still in federal court." He challenged Tobias Simon to prove the cases he wanted dismissed had not been removed to the federal court. "It will be a cold day in hell," Tobias replied, "when an attorney for a criminal defendant has to prove to a judge that he has jurisdiction." Judge Mathis continued the cases "until such time as it appears injunctions against this court are not operative under these circumstances."[35]

On and on it went, around and around, with neither side willing to call it quits. The division in the community had become so complete that state courts no longer wanted to proceed with the prosecution of the demonstrators, yet the courts still refused to dismiss the cases. Slowly, in other cities throughout the South, attitudes began to change, but not in St. Augustine. The bitterness was deep and would remain so for years to come.

Governor Collins observed that federal facilitators were quietly and unobtrusively working with leaders in Selma, Alabama, and other southern cities, urging whites and blacks to work together and resolve their differences. On February 18, 1965, the Florida supreme court struck down a state law prohibiting blacks and whites from living together. Moderates in the South and elsewhere were being heard, and slowly the damage and ill feelings from the demonstrations would heal. Through churches and other organizations. people of goodwill worked to open doors of opportunity to blacks, but reconciliation was a long, slow process.

There were pressing problems around the circuit, and St. Augustine had taken virtually all my time for more than two months. It had been an exhausting experience for me and for my family, with each day bringing new and dangerous challenges. But through it all, I felt we had maintained steadfast dedication to protecting the rights of the demonstrators. There was no question in my mind I had done all that I could. Still the haunting memory of my meeting with Martin Luther King on that Friday afternoon in Royal Puryear's office remains.

Only later was I to understand the dimension of his dilemma and the wisdom in King's statement, "I want out of St. Augustine, but I must come out with honor." There wasn't much honor for anyone in St. Augustine, but there is no question in my mind that King come out a winner and with honor.

Passage of the Civil Rights Act would finally bring real change to the South, change that is still ongoing. We can thank Martin Luther King and the people who dedicated themselves to the cause of human rights for the change. King may not have changed the character of many southerners, but he changed the vision of America to one that included blacks in America's dream of freedom and justice for all.

Racial violence flared once again in St. Augustine in late 1965, and questions would be asked about the manner in which Governor Bryant and I handled the racial crisis. A legislative investigative committee would want to know the names of members on the confidential biracial committee. Governor Bryant refused to reveal the names.

Before 1964 ended, King had written a book, *Why We Can't Wait*. He had also received the Nobel Peace Prize in Oslo, Norway—a fitting tribute to a brave man.

9   Recrimination and Recovery

In January 1965 I received a letter from Harold DeWolf, dean of the School of Theology at Boston University. He had been Martin Luther King's faculty adviser when King received his doctorate in theology. He issued an invitation for me to speak in February to the students and the combined faculties of the College of Law and the School of Theology. He suggested a theme: the moral dilemma of a southern prosecutor during times of racial crisis.

St. Augustine had been an emotionally draining experience for me and members of my family, one that I was not keen on reliving so soon after it had occurred. However, I was deeply troubled as to why so many of the civic and church leaders of the city had failed to respond to the moral issue segregation posed for the city, especially in planning a birthday party to celebrate the four hundredth year of its founding, while excluding a quarter of its population from the party. I felt this issue ought to be addressed.

Mary and I talked over the invitation and quickly concluded I had to accept. Though raised as a Methodist, she was from a Quaker family and devoutly believed in human rights for all mankind. Most in her family were pacifists. Her mother, aunt, and brother had all attended Guilford College, where I had done my undergraduate work. Mary was a leader in the integration of public schools in Volusia County and one of the first to volunteer to teach at formerly all-black schools integrated after *Brown v. Board of Education.* Mary, with her usual exuberance for causes she espoused, was excited about the prospect of my speaking at Boston University, regardless of the political consequences. She encouraged me to accept, which I did.

DeWolf had suggested that I might wish to speak "off the record." How he expected to accomplish this, I don't know. As it turned out, the speech was covered by the local news media, both television and newspaper. In any case, I rejected his offer, believing it would be dishonest to distance myself from the implications of the speech I intended to deliver. My assessment of the disaster that occurred in St. Augustine should not be hidden from the people I represented. What happened in St. Augustine need not have happened, and I knew the breakdown in leadership was a warning to all individuals in our society that failure to address social ills has consequences for everyone, especially in a representative democracy. The peace and stability of society are entrusted to civic and political leaders, whether elected or not. Holding public office is a public trust, and fidelity is due to each member of the community. The raw facts of the failure to fulfill this trust, as I perceived them, should be on the record.

In deciding how to develop the moral issues involved, Mary and I decided the principal issue was why the civic and religious leaders of a distinguished city had failed to recognize the role blacks had played in the founding and building of St. Augustine. Ignoring the request of a quarter of the population to be part of such a historic event as the four hundredth. year of its founding was nearly incomprehensible. I decided to outline, fact by ugly fact, all I had observed during the racial crisis in St. Augustine, including the absence of leadership by elected officials, by the business community, and particularly by many of the local churches.

I was willing to accept my share of the responsibility for the failure, since I was the elected state attorney. I had to reveal exactly what happened during the eight weeks I was in the city attempting to deal with a situation whether it tarnished my reputation or not. I gathered newspaper clippings and my own papers and notes made during the crisis, and relying on my still-fresh memory, I began to write the story of St. Augustine as I remembered it. I did not tell anyone I was writing the history of my experiences, but just before we departed for Boston, I delivered a copy to Mabel Chesley, one of the editors for the *Daytona Beach News-Journal*. I asked if the newspaper would consider publishing the speech. The last thing I wanted was for the citizens of St. Augustine to be caught by surprise; they had a right to know exactly what I was saying in Boston.

I need not have bothered with it. The Citizens' Council of St. Augustine obtained a copy of my speech and paid for a full-page ad in the *St. Augustine Record,* where it was published. They too wanted the citizens of St. Augustine to know what their state attorney was saying about them.

The St. Augustine chapter of the SCLC also obtained a copy, apparently from the *News-Journal,* and distributed a reprint of the speech with an open letter to the business community in St. Augustine. It read, "As interested local citizens of the nation's oldest city, we realize that a city divided against itself cannot stand, not to mention thrive and prosper. There is little doubt that the former wonderful name and image of the nation's oldest city has been besmirched and smeared by a small anti-democratic, neo-fascist control element. . . . With the Holy Easter Season upon us and the city's many anniversary celebrations approaching, let us ask ourselves this question: How can I contribute toward making our city a city sharing in the Great Society; a city thriving in the mainstream of American life; a city of Peace and Prosperity; a living symbol of democracy?" It then counseled: "With this question in mind, we ask you to let your conscience and your better sense of judgment be your guide."[1]

Again they appealed for the right of blacks to participate in the upcoming quadricentennial celebration.

If the necessary steps can be taken in the next couple of weeks to help the Negro of St. Augustine exercise his constitutional rights and participate in the many activities of the city government and the Quadricentennial Celebration, there will be no grounds for renewed demonstrations and civil rights activities that possibly would spoil the plans and operations of the Quadricentennial Celebration. To this end, we of the St. Augustine Chapter of the SCLC feel that we can quote Chancellor Edward Litchfield of the University of Pittsburgh, a member of the Quadricentennial Commission: "The significance of the St. Augustine Quadricentennial Celebration is not measured alone in its years. It is important, too, as a symbol of the spread of Western culture into this hemisphere. An essential part of that culture is our belief in the value, the dignity and therefore the equality of all men."

The letter appealed to the public conscience: "It would be a repudiation of that culture, a reflection on that symbol and a mockery of that event were this nation, through the sponsorship of a presidential commission, to hold a national and even international celebration in a community in which any of our people are denied the unmistakable full measure of their citizenship." The Citizens' Council of St. Augustine included excerpts from this letter in their ad.

The speech had been well publicized in Boston and the hall was packed, with people standing in the aisles and lining the walls of the auditorium. Esther Burgess was on the speaker's platform with me. She was the wife of an Episcopal bishop and had traveled to St. Augustine with Mary Peabody in March 1964. They had been jailed while attempting to integrate the restaurant of the Ponce de Leon Motor Lodge.

I was apprehensive as to how my speech would be received, particularly by the students. Many had been in the civil rights movement and I knew from experience that college students can be a very tough audience. I began by expressing concern for accepting a speaking engagement in Boston, considering the rather undignified reception Mrs. Peabody and Mrs. Burgess had received in St. Augustine. Amid much laughter, I continued, "But I was reassured when I remembered the warm welcome I received from the citizens of Boston on May 24, 1945, when our troop transport docked at Commonwealth Pier in Boston Harbor, the first of millions of veterans to return to the United States after the end of the war in Europe."[2]

This comment set the tone for my remarks, and soon I drew strength from the warm feeling emanating from the audience. I used a style of delivery I had perfected during closing arguments to juries and had committed the speech to memory. This required only an occasional glance at the written text, which made the delivery natural and spontaneous. Striding around the podium and speaking in the southern dialect of my birth, I gave an informal and animated speech. The crowd was young and enthusiastic. They responded with laughter and applause at some of the humorous moments, such as when we informed the Klan's communications expert of his wife's carryings-on. I soon felt completely at ease.

I posed the question: How could the city fathers of St. Augustine have allowed radical elements, such as Holstead Manucy, Connie Lynch, J. B. Stoner, and the KKK, to become the voice of the city? It presented, I said, a riddle that defied reason.

I outlined the violent reaction of the community to peaceful demonstrations and the emergence of the Klan, noting that many community leaders seemed to believe the violence of the Klan was a fitting response to the demonstrators' demands. I stressed the silence of the churches and the absence of their moral authority. I spoke of the raw hatred displayed by the Klan in the very heart of the city, at the front door of St. Augustine's Roman Catholic cathedral. The Klan's voice, I said, was the loudest of all. Collection jars placed in business establishments to support the Ancient City Gun Club and other violent elements loose in the city testified to the widespread public approval of the Klan's activities.

Why, I asked, would the community totally reject the plea of a fourth of its population to participate in the quadricentennial celebration? Blacks had played an important role in the building of the city from the time of its inception and had at one time enjoyed equal status as a free community. I suggested an answer: The failure of city leaders to appreciate or understand the need in the heart of every human being for respect.

Continuing, I said, "From the first verbal encounter between the demands of the black community to participate and the failure of the community to respond, there arose in the background the rallying cry of the KKK. Unrecognizable at first, it swiftly infected the whole of community life, drowning out any voice of moderation that might have been raised to counter it.

"The Klan did not surface immediately," I explained. It was "Manucy's raiders," under the banner of the Ancient City Gun Club, that first came on the scene. The outrages of the night riders, the young white hoodlums roaming the city and shooting into residences and businesses, were seen by many as an appropriate response to "uppity Negroes." "At first," I continued, "the night riders, the burning of crosses, the throwing of fire bombs, and later the cowardly shots into homes of sleeping Negroes were looked upon as just reward for those who asked for social and economic change."

And then, I confessed, the unthinkable happened: "[Within] a fortnight the Klan [had] gained respectability and acceptance in the community." I told of the efforts of the grand jury to establish a biracial committee and of the failure of the community's leaders to respond. I stressed the terrible consequences a community must pay for failure to respond to the clear signs of a gathering catastrophe. "The policy of hate, the hallmark of the Klan, began to shape a new and terrible future for a proud city that had much to offer, but no one was willing to offer it." I was referring specifically to the mayor's statement, "We have no biracial committee here because it could do nothing we have not already done."

I went to the heart of the legal issue involved, one that was vital to the freedom of every human being. "Dr. King and his Southern Christian Leadership Conference had been down this road many times before, at Birmingham, at Albany, and in other cities throughout the South where the knowledge and know-how had been gained. It was to be used to its most effective advantage in St. Augustine, to accentuate the civil rights bill and to implement its passage in the Congress. A solution to the St. Augustine impasse was not Dr. King's immediate goal," I argued. "Morality was his issue. His weapon was the sure knowledge that if he presented a clear-cut violation of the constitutional rights of his followers federal courts would uphold him in his fight."

I honed in on the inherent immorality of segregation and the deaf ear most of the churches gave to the issue. "After the first encounters, with the open acts of violence by the Klan and its followers, the community began to take notice, but not action. The voice of the church, as has so often been the case in the past, remained silent. The cry was repeated that if only Dr. King and Mrs. Peabody would leave St. Augustine, the matter could be settled." Here, the crowd came alive, and wave after wave of enthusiastic clapping shook the rafters of the hall.

I continued, "It is more difficult to be a moderate than it is to embrace the extremes of either side, because total acceptance of the position on either side is expected, and any deviation is met with cries of 'Uncle Tom' or 'nigger lover.' And so it was in St. Augustine that the voice of moderation was branded as treason, and as the situation became more acute, a moderate voice became the weakest of all. The voice of moderation held its breath as the 'Reverend' Connie Lynch called upon Martin 'Lucifer' King to go back where he belonged and to leave St. Augustine to the true white children of Jesus Christ."

There was hardly a stir or even a breath to be heard in the hall. "What are the lessons to be learned from St. Augustine?" I paused for a long time. "You may say," I continued, "that the moral test of courage presented an unusual task for the church and the political leaders and does not present a true picture of everyday life. I contend that St. Augustine presented no greater challenge to the leaders of the churches and to officials of the city than is presented every day in every city across the land. It is true that the spotlight of the nation may not bare to the world the tragic results of moral inaction, and the time for action is a personal decision. But the challenge is there nevertheless."

I closed the speech with my belief as to the true meaning of Martin Luther King's movement. "Yesterday," I began, "while en route to Boston, I read last week's issue of *Time*. It told of a dinner held recently in Atlanta by local citizens to honor Dr. King, who had received of the Nobel Peace Prize. Dr. King, moved to tears, told the assembled dignitaries that the tragedy of the civil rights movement has been 'the appalling silence and indifference of the good people.' And then he prophesied that 'our generation will have to repent not only for the words and acts of the children of darkness, but also for the fears and apathy of the children of light.' And he said something else that moved me greatly: 'This hour represents a great opportunity for white persons of good will, if they will only speak the truth, and suffer, if necessary, for what they know is right.'

"As a southerner," I concluded, "I cannot permit the Klan to become my voice because I am silent. If the South is to bear the burden of the Klan, it must also shoulder the responsibility of enlightening the rest of the world that it does not bear it in silence."

Spent, I sat down. Wave after wave of thunderous applause stunned me, and finally DeWolf asked that I rise in response to the applause. I was overwhelmed by this ovation. I had poured out my own frustrations and feelings, and the response was overwhelming. It stroked my ego, but in a deeper sense, it liberated me from my doubts. The Bible verse my parents had taught me was correct: "And ye shall know the truth, and the truth shall make you free" (John 8:32). The truth had indeed set me free.

After I spoke in Boston, Mayor Shelley, in a press release, asked if I could answer a few questions for him. "First," he queried, "you as state attorney for the Seventh Judicial Circuit are the top law enforcement officer for this circuit. How was it that you expected St. Augustine and its officials to run certain individuals, namely, Connie Lynch and J. B. Stoner, out of St. Augustine, when you yourself were unable to do anything about it? I think it is because you realize that there are no laws under which you could have acted."[3]

The mayor had other questions. "As I understand it, the Grand Jury is a purely investigative body. . . . Under your discretion, [it] not only recommended the appointment of a biracial committee, but assumed a political function in appointing that committee itself. In doing this, it bypassed the elected officials of the community. . . . Do you think that the above-mentioned extremist measures indicated some degree of radical control outside the community of St. Augustine? I feel sure that the questions which I have outlined above will be of very great interest to the people of Volusia County, as well as St. Johns, Putnam and Flagler counties, which comprise the Seventh Judicial Circuit."

He wasn't through. "This points up the need for a State Legislative Investigative Committee to thoroughly analyze and study such action as that which occurred in St. Augustine last summer and inform the State Legislature what corrections are needed so that communities have some protection against such individuals. . . . It was only after Judge Simpson's unexplainable and unjustifiable injunction against the city officials of St. Augustine and the Governor of the State of Florida that Mr. Lynch and Mr. Stoner made their appearance on the scene and things began to get out of hand." Apparently the mayor had a short memory. Lynch and Stoner had arrived before Judge Simpson's injunction was handed down. I took note of his veiled threat that the public would react unfavorably to any attempt I might make to seek reelection.

I framed a careful but challenging reply.

I made the remarks at Boston University after due deliberation and with a sincere desire to seek an answer to the St. Augustine impasse, and with the same sincere hope that it would provoke the officials of the city to search their hearts as to the causes and take action so that St. Augustine could be spared any further turmoil. I do not expect you to share my views, but what I do hope will happen is that you, as an elected official of St. Augustine, will take some leadership to assure the citizens of the county that this matter does not again reach the proportions that it did last summer. The failure to recognize that the problem existed at the time it arose and the resulting inaction is a matter for your conscience and not mine. I attempted to solve and bring about a peaceful solution to the St. Augustine racial problems at the request of the governor. . . . Whether I succeeded or failed is not important. . . . What is important is that I tried to do something about it. I am willing to rest my clear conscience for the actions that I did take in the hands of the concerned people of the Seventh Judicial District.[4]

Hardgrove Norris, a member of the John Birch Society and a lay leader in Trinity Episcopal Church in St. Augustine who opposed integrating his church, spoke before the Daytona Beach Kiwanis Club on March 24. Most of his speech was devoted to the claim that Martin Luther King Jr. and the "Negro" civil rights movement were part of a "Communist plot," and King's endorsement of the practices of the late Mahatma Gandhi were wrong, because Gandhi was no saint. Norris accused me of failing to "oust" Lynch and Stoner from St. Augustine, and quoted me, incorrectly, as testifying before Judge Simpson that the two were not doing anything in violation of the law.[5]

St. Augustine was crowded with tourists during the quadricentennial celebration of 1965 but racial tension was still apparent. Hotels and motels, as well as tourist attractions throughout the city, were jammed. The economy was on the rebound, but the wounds inflicted during the racial strife continued to smart. James Brock of the Monson Motor Lodge announced on May 2, 1965, that he was broke. Banks refused to give him loans to cover debts incurred during the integration drive as long as he remained the principal stockholder. "I'd hoped right along that something good would happen that would enable me to continue in St. Augustine," he said, "but since June 11, the day I put Martin Luther King in jail, there's been some kind of a stigma I haven't been able to shake. . . . I'd always been a moderate on the racial issue, and we always said we'd integrate if the [civil rights] bill was passed. Months before the bill came up, I had reason to feel that it would pass and the public accommodations action would be included. I tried my best to arrange quiet talks in our community."[6]

A Florida legislative investigating committee, called for by the mayor, issued a report on May 21. In a remarkable lack of understanding, the committee said the racial problems in St. Augustine "could have been solved amicably by Negro and White citizens last summer had they been free from outside agitation." In the report, the committee blamed St. Augustine's troubles on Martin Luther King, the Ku Klux Klan, television, and newspapers, deploring the racial disorder that had cost St. Augustine an estimated $5 million, "which means that all citizens of Florida indirectly paid for Martin Luther King's visit." The committee interviewed thirty or more "knowledgeable individuals" over several weeks.[7] They didn't interview me but I had not expected they would.

Ben Funk, an Associated Press writer who had been on hand during the troubles the previous year, revisited St. Augustine in the summer of 1965. He posed the question of what happens to a city when it becomes a focus of the fight for equality. He interviewed a number of local residents in an attempt to get an answer and his article was published on June 6 in the *Daytona Beach News-Journal*. Of the blacks interviewed, most agreed that the demonstrations created "a new type of Negro, one now determined to break out of the caste system in which he has lived all his life."[8]

Rosalie Gordon, widow of R. N. Gordon, the dentist whose practice Hayling had assumed in 1960, said in an interview that "there had to come a time when attention had to be called to the situation. The demonstrations did this. Little people who could never before make a contribution to society will rise now and will have a voice. I have been shocked by the reaction of some whites I had thought were fine people. A hostile element was brought out that we didn't realize existed." When Rosalie Gordon ran for the city commission she stated that "the Negro is not qualified to hold many jobs to which he aspires for lack of educational opportunities."[9] She won the primary, but not the election, thus losing her bid to become the first black elected to office in the nation's oldest city.

Funk also interviewed Mayor Shelley. He said, "I met with leaders of the Southern Christian Leadership Conference and I pointed out to them that there was less discrimination here than in most cities. I asked if there was anything we could do to prevent trouble. They said there was nothing."[10]

In 1965, Hayling moved his practice from St. Augustine to Cocoa Beach; he practiced there until 1972 when he moved to Ft. Lauderdale. The terms "radical" and "militant" were applied to his attempts to end segregation in St. Augustine. The radical and militant action by the founders of this country to rid the colonies of the tax policies of George III provoked a revolution, and they were called patriots. Hayling would have been right at home with the likes of Patrick Henry. In every sense of the word, Hayling was a patriot, one armed with a passion for justice and equality. His sacrifices paved the way for others to enjoy life free from segregation. He is a hero in my book.

Racial unrest continued in St. Augustine, and in a talk in Miami on Saturday, June 26, 1965, King threatened to return "if conditions do not change." He did not return. On July 6, 1965, the home of a civil rights activist was set ablaze after a white student moved in for the summer. Witnesses saw three white men drive off in a green pickup truck shortly after the house was set on fire. Meanwhile, in Daytona Beach, I remember Horace Reed, president of the local NAACP chapter, saying that everything was "going remarkably well. We're both surprised and pleased."

The civil rights movement of the 1950s and 1960s forced the entire nation to recognize that blacks have the same inviolate claims to basic human rights guaranteed under the Constitution as whites do. Passage of civil rights laws in 1964, 1965, and 1968 finally cast those rights in formal terms and established the legal means to enforce them.

In the larger context, the struggle over civil rights and Martin Luther King's dream of a race-neutral society did not end with St. Augustine or with passage of the 1964 Civil Rights Act. But passage of the bill was certainly part of King's legacy, one shared by thousands who followed his lead. King, with the help of his army of followers and buttressed by the growing outrage of the nation over the brutal enforcement of segregation, forced the South to abandon the Jim Crow laws that had repressed 17 million citizens for more than a hundred years.

In 1967 I resigned as state attorney and gave up my plans to run for Congress, but St. Augustine remained in my mind. As the years passed, I often thought of that time in America when the promise of equality for all its citizens was just that—a promise. Now the promise has become reality.

I have come to view the violence that occurred in St. Augustine as but a microcosm of the evil that occurs when good people fail to act when conscience demands action. Segregation was maintained in the South by political leaders, acting on the will of the majority, who misused the doctrine of states' rights by consecrating it through custom and were buttressed by decisions of the Supreme Court. It prevailed because of a lack of moral leadership within communities, because of a desire to maintain mores and customs rather than fundamental human rights.

King warned me that there were those in the civil rights movement who "don't think America is worth saving" and who "want to burn it down." His victories bought us precious time to build a society in which practices such as segregation will not find fertile ground in which to grow and destroy America.

I know my responses to the St. Augustine crisis were true to the values instilled in me by my mother and father. Even so, I initially viewed the moral issue in a rather parochial way. I should have moved forcefully against the Klan sooner than I did. Of all the decisions I made during the eight weeks I was in St. Augustine, I regret this failure more than any other misstep I made.

As I write this, more than forty years have passed since those terrible dark days and nights when the flames of prejudice were allowed to burn out of control. The civil rights movement of the 1950s and 1960s brought great change to the social contract made in 1776. The men who affixed their names to the Declaration of Independence pledged to one another "our lives, our fortunes, and our sacred honor." It took nearly two hundred years for blacks to obtain the same rights the original patriots enjoyed. Now we, too, must be willing to put our lives, our fortunes, and our sacred honor at risk to sustain the fundamental right of equality.

If we are to continue to enjoy the basic human rights expressed in the Declaration of Independence, we must recognize the evil that exists in our society, evil that is rarely manifest in stark and unmistakable forms. It is more often clouded by symbols and ideals shrouded in the mythology of the past. The evil of prejudice, the heart of segregation, begins in small places, so too do the means to combat it. As Eleanor Roosevelt observed:

> Where after all, do universal human rights begin? In small places, close to home—so close and so small that they cannot be seen on any maps of the world. Yet they are the world of the individual person; the neighborhood he lives in; the school or college he attends; the factory, farm or office where he works. Such are the places where every man, woman and child seeks equal justice, equal opportunity, equal dignity without discrimination.
>
> Unless these rights have meaning there, they have little meaning anywhere. Without concerted citizen action to uphold them close to home, we shall look in vain for progress in the larger world.[11]

The 1964 Civil Rights Act would be tested across the South as resisters contested the constitutionality of the new law and attempted to avoid its effects. Nonetheless it was a milestone, as President Johnson said, "in America's progress toward full justice for all citizens." Yet despite passage of the Civil Rights Act and the Voting Rights Act of 1965, our country still suffers from the evils of racism. There seems to be a strain of racism, of bias and prejudice, that surfaces now and again in America. It was apparent in the resurgence of the KKK during the Great Depression; it was evident in Japanese internment camps after Pearl Harbor; it appeared during the McCarthy era when the nation was swept up in an unrealistic fear of Communism. And so it was with the civil rights movement in the 1950s and 1960s. It is apparent now in the nation's ill-advised war on drugs, which unfairly targets minorities, and in racial profiling.

In each fearful season, the nation seems to suffer a psychic fit of anxiety, one that suspends common sense while elected leaders blindly lash out to fight some perceived enemy. In each troubled time the nation seems to unite in turning a blind eye to human dignity guaranteed by the Bill of Rights, apparently content to bend or suspend these rights in an effort to overcome the perceived threat to its collective security.

Did the legal end of segregation bring equality of opportunity to the generation of blacks it affected? The answer seems to be, not yet. King's dream of a color-blind America with equal opportunity for all was not realized during his lifetime, and the movement lost cohesion after his death. No comparable leader with the depth of his convictions or the eloquence of his appeal has appeared on the scene to complete his goals. It will take several generations to overcome the terrible wounds inflicted by segregation and the prejudice it fostered.

In retelling the story of the St. Augustine racial crisis, I have cast King as first among equals in challenging the evil of segregation that engendered so much hate and prejudice in a nation founded on the principles of equality and justice for all. It is to Martin Luther King's courage and his devotion to the cause of equality that much of the credit for passage of the Civil Rights Act of 1964 must be given. There were many others who suffered and died along the way, just as he did, but in the long struggle for human rights, while others achieved greatness, King's determination was historic and heroic.

Martin Luther King came along at exactly the right moment in history to bring about radical change. A new breed of blacks were ready to risk all for equality. The nation as a whole was beginning to recognize the shameful truth of segregation. The right person was in the White House. And when King chose St. Augustine as his venue for continuing the struggle for human rights, a meaningful civil rights bill was working its way through the Senate. His timing was perfect.

He joins other great leaders who in times of extreme danger have held to a noble ideal and persevered against all odds. It was not just the soul of America for which he fought, but the soul of mankind. And he knew, as Elie Wiesel has said, "The opposite of love is not hate, it's indifference. . . . The opposite of faith is not heresy, it's indifference. And the opposite of life is not death, it's indifference."

That is, perhaps, the most important lesson to be learned from the events that transpired in St. Augustine during the civil rights movement. It was indifference—on the part of politicians, community leaders, churchmen, ordinary men and women—that allowed the Klan to step into the limelight and carry out its agenda of hate and brutality.

The only thing necessary for the triumph of evil is for good men to do nothing.

—Edmund Burke

Notes

Introduction

1. *Encyclopedia Britannica,* 15th ed., vol. 10 (Chicago: University of Chicago Press), 310.

2. Dumas Malone, *Jefferson and His Time: The Sage of Monticello,* vol. 6 (Boston: Little, Brown, 1981), 335–36.

3. Carl Sandburg, *Abraham Lincoln: The War Years,* vol. 11 (New York: Harcourt, Brace, 1939), 469.

Chapter 1

1. "Restoration Dedication to Be Given Wide Coverage," *St. Augustine Record,* Mar. 7, 1963.

2. "Congress Asked to Appropriate $350,000 to Help Finance 400th Anniversary," *St. Augustine Record,* May 1, 1963.

3. "Negro Group Asks President to Block 400th Anniversary Funds," *St. Augustine Record,* May 7, 1963.

4. David R. Colburn, *Racial Change and Community Crisis: St. Augustine, Florida, 1877–1980* (New York: Columbia University Press, 1985), 29.

5. Ibid., 33.

6. Ibid.

7. "City Commission Issues Statement," *St. Augustine Record,* June 16, 1963; Mabel Norris Chesley, "Nine Fined on St. Augustine Sit-in Charge," *Daytona Beach News-Journal,* Aug. 2, 1963.

8. Mabel Norris Chesley, "Nine Fined on St. Augustine Sit-in Charge," *Daytona Beach News-Journal*, Aug. 2, 1963.

9. "Negro Leaders Here Say They Are Arming in the Event of Race Trouble," *St. Augustine Record*, June 20, 1963.

10. Ibid. See also "City Commission Issues Statement," in n7 above.

11. "Legal Action Taken on Demonstrations," *Daytona Beach News-Journal*, July 30, 1963.

12. Mabel Norris Chesley, "Nine Fined on St. Augustine Sit-in Charge," *Daytona Beach News-Journal*, Aug. 2, 1963.

13. "Legal Action Taken on Demonstrations," *Daytona Beach News-Journal*, July 30, 1963.

14. Mabel Norris Chesley, "We Are Not Immune," editorial, *Daytona Beach News-Journal*, May 14, 1963.

15. Mark K. Bauman and Berkley Kalin, eds., *The Quiet Voices: Southern Rabbis and Black Civil Rights, 1880s to 1990s* (Tuscaloosa: University of Alabama Press, 1997).

16. "Group to Press for Race Relations," *Daytona Beach News-Journal*, June 11, 1963.

17. Ibid.

18. "Rights Issue Discussed at Convention," *Daytona Beach News-Journal*, July 25, 1963.

19. "A Real Civic Enterprise," editorial, *Daytona Beach News-Journal*, July 9, 1963.

20. "Smyrna Integrates Facilities," *Daytona Beach News-Journal*, July 10, 1963.

21. "Titusville Integrates," Brevard Section, *Daytona Beach News-Journal*, July 11, 1963; "Integration in St. Pete," *Daytona Beach News-Journal*, July 12, 1963; Mabel Norris Chesley, "Some Progress Made, More Sought [in Jacksonville]," *Daytona Beach News-Journal*, July 24, 1963.

22. "Negro Group in Request," *Daytona Beach News-Journal*, Aug. 7, 1963.

23. "Ancient City Teems with Unrest," *Daytona Beach News-Journal*, Aug. 17, 1963.

24. Mabel Norris Chesley, "Report Raps Government," *Daytona Beach News-Journal*, Sept. 8, 1963.

25. "Civil Rights Advisors Ask [for] Klan-WCC Probe," *Daytona Beach News-Journal*, Oct. 20, 1963.

26. Ibid.

27. "Mayor Denies Race Charge," *Daytona Beach News-Journal*, Aug. 18, 1963.

28. Ibid.

29. J. Allen Broyles, *The John Birch Society: Anatomy of a Protest* (Boston: Beacon Press, 1964), 6.

30. Colburn, *Racial Change and Community Crisis*, 142.

31. Ibid., 8, 44.

32. A. J. Heinsohn Jr., "St Augustine: Rape of the Ancient City," reprinted in *American Opinion* (Oct. 1964).

33. Merrill D. Peterson, *The Great Triumvirate: Webster, Clay, and Calhoun* (New York: Oxford University Press, 1987), 196.

34. *Peterson v. Greenville, U.S. Supreme Court Reports,* 10 Law Ed 2d 326, May 20, 1963, 327.

35. "Dr. Shelley to Retire to End 42-Year Practice," *St. Augustine Record,* Mar. 30, 1985.

36. Broyles, *The John Birch Society.*

37. Mabel Norris Chesley, "Report Raps Government," *Daytona Beach News-Journal,* Sept. 8, 1963.

38. "The Issue Is Where It Belongs," *Daytona Beach News-Journal,* June 20, 1963.

39. Mabel Norris Chesley, "Judge Fines 19 Demonstrators," *Daytona Beach News-Journal,* Sept. 11, 1963.

40. James Houser, "And Finally Attackers Dropped Their Mask," *Daytona Beach News-Journal,* Sept. 19, 1963.

41. "Injunction Asked by Negroes," *Daytona Beach News-Journal,* Sept. 27, 1963

42. "Negro Dentist Convicted of Assault on Klansmen," *Daytona Beach News-Journal,* Oct. 17, 1963.

43. Colburn, *Racial Change and Community Crisis,* 8.

44. "Three Charged in Murder," *Daytona Beach News-Journal,* Nov. 6, 1963.

45. "NAACP Pledges Support for Negroes Charged in Slaying," *Daytona Beach News-Journal,* Nov. 9, 1963.

46. "Negro Claim Rejected," *Daytona Beach News-Journal,* Nov. 15, 1963;

47. "Federal Judge Critical of Negro Leaders While Handing Down Decision," *St. Augustine Record,* Nov. 13, 1963.

48. Ibid.

49. "Negro Has Right to Demonstrate," *Daytona Beach News-Journal,* June 9, 1963.

50. Niebuhr cited in David L. Chappell, *A Stone of Hope: Prophetic Religion and the Death of Jim Crow* (Chapel Hill: University of North Carolina Press, 2004), 41.

51. "Demonstrations Will Resume, King Says after Meeting Johnson," *St. Augustine Record,* Dec. 3, 1963.

52. "Jury Issues Report on Racial Situation," *St. Augustine Record,* Dec. 17, 1963.

53. Ibid.

Chapter 2

1. "Klan Leader Convinced He 'Done Right,'" *Key West Citizen,* June 15, 1977.

2. Mabel Norris Chesley, "Nine Fined on St. Augustine Sit-in Charge," *Daytona Beach News-Journal,* Aug. 2, 1963.

3. "Civil Rights Advisers Ask [for] Klan-WCC Probe," *Daytona Beach News-Journal,* Oct. 20, 1963.

4. Fred J. Cook, *The Ku Klux Klan: America's Recurring Nightmare* (New York: J. Messner, 1980), 77.

5. Biographical information about Stoner is from Michael Newton and Judy Ann Newton, *The Ku Klux Klan: An Encyclopedia* (New York, Garland, 1991), 543–44.

6. David R. Colburn, *Racial Change and Community Crisis: St. Augustine, Florida, 1877–1980* (New York: Columbia University Press, 1985), 6.

7. "Manucy Says Checks [Club's] Only Record," *Daytona Beach News-Journal,* Aug. 18, 1964.

8. "Bryant's Help Asked by Group," *Daytona Beach News-Journal,* Mar. 4, 1964.

9. "Governors Ignore State Rights," *St. Augustine Record,* Oct. 3, 1962.

10. "Rights Leader Predicts 'Miracles' from the President," *St. Augustine Record,* Apr. 12, 1964.

11. Colburn, *Racial Change and Community Crisis,* 61.

Chapter 3

1. Ethel Stephens Arnett, written under the direction of Walter Clinton Jackson, *Greensboro, North Carolina: The County Seat of Guilford* (Chapel Hill: University of North Carolina Press, 1955), 91.

2. James Patterson, *Brown v. Board of Education: A Civil Rights Milestone and Its Troubled Legacy* (New York: Oxford University Press, 2001), xxii.

3. Liston Pope, *Millhands and Preachers* (New Haven: Yale University Press, 1942), 72.

4. Ibid.

5. Ibid, 189.

6. David R. Colburn, *Racial Change and Community Crisis: St. Augustine, Florida, 1877–1980* (New York: Columbia University Press, 1985), 27.

Chapter 4

1. "Arrests Here Mount as Demonstrations Continue in City," *St. Augustine Record,* Mar. 30, 1964.

2. "Mrs. Peabody Also Jailed; More Negroes Are Arrested Following New Demonstrations," *St. Augustine Record,* Mar. 31, 1964.

3. "Dogs, Yes; People, No—Simpson," *Daytona Beach News-Journal,* Apr. 2, 1964.

4. Ibid.

5. "Picked Up, Released Again," *Daytona Beach News-Journal,* May 12, 1964.

6. Simon would later represent me when I was held in contempt of court by a federal judge in Miami.

7. Mabel Norris Chesley, "Rev. King Tells of Death Threat in St. Augustine," *Daytona Beach News-Journal,* June 5, 1964.

8. "More Arrested in St. Augustine," *Daytona Beach News-Journal,* Apr. 1, 1964.

9. "Boston Pastor Says Demonstrations by Northerners Harmful, Not Good," *St. Augustine Record,* Apr. 2, 1964.

10. "New England Pastor Rejects NAACP Chapter," *St. Augustine Record,* Apr. 13, 1964; "President Is Critical of Demonstrations," *St. Augustine Record,* Apr. 17, 1964.

11. "This City Shall Survive," *St. Augustine Record,* Sunday Apr. 5, 1964.

12. Ibid.

13. David R. Colburn, *Racial Change and Community Crisis: St. Augustine, Florida, 1877–1980* (New York: Columbia University Press, 1985), 66–67.

14. "King Starts Crusade against FBI," *St. Augustine Record,* Apr. 26, 1964.

15. "Negroes Attend Services at Church," *St. Augustine Record,* Apr. 13, 1964.

16. Colburn, *Racial Change and Community Crisis,* 167.

17. Ibid, 168.

18. "City Asks Time to Answer Statements on TV Program," *St. Augustine Record,* Apr. 17, 1964

19. "Mayor Tells Television Audience Mrs. Peabody Harmed Race Relations," *St. Augustine Record,* May 10, 1964.

20. Colburn, *Racial Change and Community Crisis,* 127.

21. "Demonstrations by Juveniles Prohibited Here," *St. Augustine Record,* July 23, 1963.

Chapter 5

1. "King Jailed in St. Augustine," *Daytona Beach News-Journal,* June 11, 1964.

2. "Cloture Invoked by 71–29 Vote," *Daytona Beach News-Journal,* June 10, 1964.

3. Mabel Norris Chesley, "Police Dogs, Assaults, Silence," *Daytona Beach News-Journal,* May 29, 1964.

4. Mabel Norris Chesley, "Negroes Barred from Entering Church," *Daytona Beach News-Journal,* June 1, 1964.

5. "Sheriff Denies Being in Klan," *Daytona Beach News-Journal,* June 3, 1964.

6. "Regulations on Parking Changed," *Daytona Beach News-Journal,* June 2, 1964.

7. "King May 'Call Army' to Fight Segregation," *Daytona Beach News-Journal,* June 6, 1964.

8. Jack W. Gore, "St. Augustine Events Show How Civil Rights Leaders Think They're above Law," *Fort Lauderdale News,* reprinted in *St. Augustine Record,* June 1, 1964.

9. "It's Time for Bryant to Act," *Daytona Beach News-Journal,* June 5, 1964.

10. David R. Colburn, *Racial Change and Community Crisis: St. Augustine, Florida, 1877–1980* (New York: Columbia University Press, 1985), 162.

11. Mabel Norris Chesley, "What Manner of Man Is Leading America's Negro?" *Daytona Beach News-Journal,* June 7, 1964.

12. "Judge Simpson Rules on Demonstration Ban," *Daytona Beach News-Journal,* June 10, 1964.

13. Ibid.

14. George Allen, "Dr. King Arraigned on Three Charges; Bond Placed at $900," *Daytona Beach News-Journal,* June 12, 1964.

15. "Grand Jury Moves to Ease Growing Racial Unrest Here," *St. Augustine Record,* June 12, 1964.

Chapter 6

1. "Court OK's Demonstrations: Whites March Once Again," *Daytona Beach News-Journal,* June 14, 1964.

2. Ibid.

3. Ibid.

4. "King Gets Degree," *Daytona Beach News-Journal,* June 16, 1964.

5. "Gov. Bryant Organizes Police," *Daytona Beach News-Journal,* June 16, 1964.

6. "Local Business Leaders Adopt Resolution on Racial Situation Here," *St. Augustine Record,* June 17, 1964.

7. "Tell Tourists to Come to St. Augustine," *St. Augustine Record,* June 12, 1964.

8. "Jackie Robinson Urges Action," *Daytona Beach News-Journal,* June 16, 1964.

9. Virginia Delavan, "St. Augustine Park Cleared during March," *Daytona Beach News-Journal,* June 16, 1964.

10. "White Marches Newest Weapons in Nerve War," *Daytona Beach News-Journal,* June 14, 1964.

11. Mark K. Bauman and Berkley Kalin, eds., *The Quiet Voices: Southern Rabbis and Black Civil Rights, 1880s to 1990s* (Tuscaloosa: University of Alabama Press, 1997). Because their own historical experience included intense discrimination, Jews in local communities often supported the civil rights movement.

12. "New Tactics in Demonstrations," *Daytona Beach News-Journal,* June 18, 1964.

13. "Two Sides to the Coin," *St. Augustine Record,* June 18, 1964.

14. "Jury Wants Truce in Racial Crisis—Proposes Biracial Body after Month; King Says He Won't Go Along," *Daytona Beach News-Journal,* June 19, 1964.

15. George Allen, WNDB news director, "King Says He'd Appear before Grand Jury," *Daytona Beach News-Journal,* June 12, 1964.

16. "Bulletin," *Daytona Beach News-Journal,* [June 19,] 1964.

17. "Rights Issue Discussed at Convention," *Daytona Beach News-Journal,* July 25, 1963.

18. Robert Dallek, *Flawed Giant: Lyndon Johnson and His Times, 1961–1973* (New York: Oxford University Press, 1998).

19. "Action Hailed by LBJ: Major Step," *Daytona Beach News-Journal,* June 20, 1964.

20. "State Officials, Leaders in Integration, Comment on Civil Rights Bill," *Daytona Beach News-Journal,* June 21, 1964.

Chapter 7

1. "Bryant Puts Ban on Night Marches in St. Augustine," *Daytona Beach News-Journal,* June 21, 1964.

2. "Text of Governor's Executive Order," *St. Augustine Record,* June 21, 1964.

3. "Governor Bans Night Demonstrations," *St. Augustine Record,* June 21, 1964.

4. Ibid.

5. "A Clear and Present Danger?" editorial, *St. Augustine Record,* June 21, 1964.

6. "Beach Clash in St. Augustine," *Daytona Beach News-Journal,* June 22, 1964.

7. "The Time and Place to Stand," *St. Augustine Record,* June 23, 1964.

8. "No Incidents Reported as Two Races March," *Daytona Beach News-Journal,* June 25, 1964.

9. "More Than a Score Hurt in Racial Disorders," *St. Augustine Record,* June 26, 1964.

10. "More Cops Ordered in by Bryant," *Daytona Beach News-Journal,* June 27, 1964.

11. Mabel Norris Chesley, "Governor Bryant to St. Augustine—Hearings on Ban Begin," *Daytona Beach News-Journal,* June 26, 1964.

12. "Rodriguez Blasts King's Policies," *Daytona Beach News-Journal,* June 28, 1964.

13. "Governor: Local Officials Show Courage Not Brawn," *St. Augustine Record,* June 18, 1964.

Chapter 8

1. "St. Augustine Truce Called—Demonstrations Off for Two Weeks," *Daytona Beach News-Journal,* July 1, 1964.

2. Ibid.; other quotes in the paragraph are from David R. Colburn, *Racial Change and Community Crisis: St. Augustine, Florida, 1877–1980* (New York: Columbia University Press, 1985), 11. According to Colburn, "King, sensing an opportunity to leave St. Augustine gracefully, called off further demonstrations, praising Bryant and white leaders for taking 'a first important step' toward peace" (11).

3. "[King's Attorney] Withdraws Petition," *Daytona Beach News-Journal,* July 2, 1964.

4. "St. Augustine Group in Civil Rights Pledge," *Daytona Beach News-Journal*, July 2, 1964.

5. Ibid.

6. George Allen, WNDB news director, wrote three articles for the *Daytona Beach News-Journal:* "7 Men in Key Roles in Crisis," July 1; "King, Manucy Brought Clash," July 2; and "Middle Ground Disappeared," July 3, 1964.

7. Allen, "King, Manucy Brought Clash," July 2; "Middle Ground Disappeared," July 3, 1964, both in *Daytona Beach News-Journal*.

8. "Bryant Won't Enforce New Federal Civil Rights Law," *Daytona Beach News-Journal*, July 12, 1964.

9. "Bryant Asks [for] Peaceful Response to New Act," *Daytona Beach News-Journal*, July 14, 1964.

10. Paul Willis, "Warren's Role as Peace Seeker in St. Augustine Strife Reviewed," *Daytona Beach News-Journal*, July 5, 1964.

11. "White Youths Attack Negroes," *Daytona Beach News-Journal*, July 6, 1964.

12. "Warrants Issued in Beating," *Daytona Beach News-Journal*, July 7, 1964.

13. Mabel Norris Chesley, "We're Proud of Dan Warren," editorial, *Daytona Beach News-Journal*, July 8, 1964.

14. "More Picketing at St. Augustine, *Daytona Beach News-Journal*, July 15, 1964.

15. "Integration Gains Are Undone," *Daytona Beach News-Journal*, July 16, 1964.

16. W. R. Weaver, "Truce in St. Augustine—Racial Peace Helped by Greensboro Native," *Greensboro Daily News*, July 18, 1964.

17. "King Pledges Negro Fight," *Daytona Beach News-Journal*, July 17, 1964.

18. Mabel Norris Chesley, "King Discusses His St. Augustine Dilemma," *Daytona Beach News-Journal*, July 18, 1964.

19. "Rights Leader Appeals for Volunteers," *Daytona Beach News-Journal*, July 9, 1964.

20. "Ku Klux Klan Rallies at St. Augustine," *Daytona Beach News-Journal*, July 20, 1964.

21. "St. Augustine Motel Hit by Predawn Fire Bomb," *Daytona Beach News-Journal*, July 24, 1964.

22. "Warrants Out for Klansmen," *Daytona Beach News-Journal*, July 25, 1964.

23. " Two Charged in Threat Tossing," *Daytona Beach News-Journal*, July 28, 1964.

24. "Obedience to Rights Law Asked by Bryant," *Daytona Beach News-Journal*, July 20, 1964.

25. Mabel Norris Chesley, "King Discusses His St. Augustine Dilemma," *Daytona Beach News-Journal*, July 18, 1964.

26. "No Rights Lull in St. Augustine," *Daytona Beach News-Journal*, July 31, 1964.

27. Austin Scott, "Rights Leaders Give Reasons for Opposing Moratorium," *Daytona Beach News-Journal*, Aug. 3, 1964.

28. "Protection from Klan Sought," *Daytona Beach News-Journal*, July 21, 1964.

29. "Judge Throws Out Action on Bryant," *Daytona Beach News-Journal*, July 22, 1964.

30. "We Were Scared, Two Men Testify," *Daytona Beach News-Journal*, July 23, 1964.

31. "Manucy Won't Talk as Rights Witnesses," *Daytona Beach News-Journal*, July 28, 1964.

32. "St. Augustine Motel Man Points Finger at Hoss," *Daytona Beach News-Journal*, July 29, 1964.

33. "Two Tell Court Manucy Denied Any Influence," *Daytona Beach News-Journal*, July 30, 1964.

34. Mabel Norris Chesley, "King Claims Victory for Civil Rights in Old City," *Daytona Beach News-Journal*, Aug. 6, 1864.

35. "8 Rights Cases Go Undecided," *Daytona Beach News-Journal*, Jan. 18, 1965.

Chapter 9

1. "Threatening Letter Received," *St. Augustine Record*, Feb. 21, 1965. All quotes from the SCLC's letter are from this article.

2. "State Attorney Speaks at Boston U—Radical Control of St. Augustine Last Summer Still Puzzles Dan Warren," *Daytona Beach News-Journal*, February 21, 1965. All quotes from the speech are from this article.

3. "St. Augustine Mayor Answers Warren Boston Speech on City's Racial Trouble," *Daytona Beach News-Journal*, Mar. 24, 1965. All quotes by Mayor Shelley in this section are from this article.

4. Ibid.

5. "Bircher Sees Demonstrations [as] Threat," *Daytona Beach News-Journal*, Mar. 25, 1965.

6. "Brock Says He's Broke," *Daytona Beach News-Journal*, May 2, 1965.

7. "Agitation Blamed in Rioting," *Daytona Beach News-Journal*, May 21, 1965.

8. Ben Funk, "Tourists Return to St. Augustine Streets, but Wounded Feelings Still Fester," *Daytona Beach News-Journal*, June 6, 1965.

9. Ibid.

10. Ibid.

11. Eleanor Roosevelt, Chairman of the United Nations Human Rights Commission, 1948.

Index